Microsoft

MCSE

Exam
70-220

Designing Microsoft® Windows® 2000 Network Security

Readiness Review

Jeff Durham and
MeasureUp, Inc.

PUBLISHED BY
Microsoft Press
A Division of Microsoft Corporation
One Microsoft Way
Redmond, Washington 98052-6399

Library of Congress Cataloging-in-Publication Data
Durham, Jeff.
    MCSE Designing Microsoft Windows 2000 Network Security Readiness Review : Exam
70-220 / Jeff Durham and MeasureUp, Inc.
        p. cm.
    Includes index.
    ISBN 0-7356-1365-6
    1. Computer networks--Security measures--Examinations--Study guides. 2. Microsoft
Windows NT--Examinations--Study guides. I. MeasureUp, Inc. II. Title.

TK5105.59 .D87 2001
005.8--dc21   2001034569

Printed and bound in the United States of America.

1 2 3 4 5 6 7 8 9   QWE   6 5 4 3 2 1

Distributed in Canada by Penguin Books Canada Limited.

A CIP catalogue record for this book is available from the British Library.

Microsoft Press books are available through booksellers and distributors worldwide. For further information about international editions, contact your local Microsoft Corporation office or contact Microsoft Press International directly at fax (425) 936-7329. Visit our Web site at www.microsoft.com/mspress. Send comments to *mspinput@microsoft.com*.

Microsoft Press
Acquisitions Editor: Thomas Pohlmann
Project Editor: Kurt Stephan

Body Part No. X08-22402

nSight, Inc.
Project Manager: Kristen Ford
Technical Editor: Toby Andrews
Manuscript Editor: Joe Gustaitis
Desktop Publisher: Patty Fagan
Indexer: Rebecca Plunkett

Contents

Welcome to Designing Security for a Microsoft Windows 2000 Network................. vii
    Before You Begin.. viii
    Using the MCSE Readiness Review x
    Exam Objectives Summary... xvi
    Getting More Help xviii

Objective Domain 1: Analyzing Business Requirements........................ 1

    Tested Skills and Suggested Practices..1
    Further Reading...3

    Objective 1.1: Analyze the existing and planned business models..........................5
        Questions..6
        Answers..9

    Objective 1.2: Analyze the existing and planned organizational structures................13
        Questions..14
        Answers..16

    Objective 1.3: Analyze factors that influence company strategies. 19
        Questions..20
        Answers..22

    Objective 1.4: Analyze business and security requirements for the end user. 25
        Questions..26
        Answers..28

    Objective 1.5: Analyze the structure of IT management. 31
        Questions..32
        Answers..34

    Objective 1.6: Analyze the current physical model and information
    security model. 37
        Questions..38
        Answers..40

Objective Domain 2: Analyzing Technical Requirements 43

    Tested Skills and Suggested Practices..43
    Further Reading...44

Objective 2.1: Evaluate the company's existing and planned
technical environment. 45
    Questions 47
    Answers 51

Objective 2.2: Analyze the impact of the security design on the existing
and planned technical environment. 55
    Questions 56
    Answers 58

Objective Domain 3: Analyzing Security Requirements. 61

    Tested Skills and Suggested Practices 61
    Further Reading 63

Objective 3.1: Design a security baseline for a Windows 2000 network. 65
    Questions 66
    Answers 68

Objective 3.2: Identify the required level of security for each resource. 71
    Questions 72
    Answers 74

Objective Domain 4: Designing a Windows 2000 Security Solution. 77

    Tested Skills and Suggested Practices 78
    Further Reading 79

Objective 4.1: Design an audit policy. 83
    Questions 84
    Answers 85

Objective 4.2: Design a delegation of authority strategy. 89
    Questions 90
    Answers 93

Objective 4.3: Design the placement and inheritance of security policies for sites,
domains, and organizational units. 97
    Questions 98
    Answers 100

Objective 4.4: Design an Encrypting File System strategy. 103
    Questions 104
    Answers 106

Objective 4.5: Design an authentication strategy..109
    Questions..110
    Answers..111

Objective 4.6: Design a security group strategy...113
    Questions..114
    Answers..116

Objective 4.7: Design a Public Key Infrastructure..119
    Questions..120
    Answers..121

Objective 4.8: Design Windows 2000 network services security. 123
    Questions..124
    Answers..126

Objective Domain 5: Designing a Security Solution for Access Between Networks 129

Tested Skills and Suggested Practices...130
Further Reading..131

Objective 5.1: Provide secure access to public networks from a private network. 133
    Questions..134
    Answers..136

Objective 5.2: Provide external users with secure access to
private network resources..139
    Questions..140
    Answers..141

Objective 5.3: Provide secure access between private networks. 143
    Questions..144
    Answers..145

Objective 5.4: Design Windows 2000 security for remote access users....................147
    Questions..148
    Answers..149

Objective Domain 6: Designing Security for Communication Channels 153

Tested Skills and Suggested Practices...154
Further Reading..154

Objective 6.1: Design an SMB-signing solution...157
    Questions..158
    Answers..160

Objective 6.2: Design an IPSec solution. 163
    Questions 164
    Answers 165

Case Study 1: Blue Yonder Airlines.. 167

    Questions 172
    Answers 177

Case Study 2: Adventure Works. 189

    Questions 193
    Answers 198

Case Study 3: Fabrikam, Inc. 209

    Questions 212
    Answers 217

Case Study 4: Trey Research. 227

    Questions 230
    Answers 235

Case Study 5: Contoso, Ltd. 245

    Questions 248
    Answers 253

    Glossary **261**

    Index.. **277**

Welcome to Designing Security for a Microsoft Windows 2000 Network

Welcome to *MCSE Readiness Review—Exam 70-220: Designing Security for a Microsoft Windows 2000 Network*. The Readiness Review series gives you a focused, timesaving way to identify the information you need to know to pass the Microsoft Certified Professional (MCP) exams. The series combines a realistic electronic assessment with a review book to help you become familiar with the types of questions that you will encounter on the MCP exam. By reviewing the objectives and sample questions, you can focus on the specific skills that you need to improve before taking the exam.

This book helps you evaluate your readiness for the MCP Exam 70-220: Designing Security for a Microsoft Windows 2000 Network. When you pass this exam, you earn core or elective credit toward Microsoft Certified Systems Engineer (MCSE) certification. In addition, when you pass this exam you achieve Microsoft Certified Professional status.

Note You can find a complete list of MCP exams and their related objectives on the Microsoft Certified Professional Web site at *http://www.microsoft.com/mcp*.

The MCP Exam 70-220 uses case study–based questions. The case study model is used to simulate an on-the-job environment. Using the case studies, you have an opportunity to make decisions based on your analysis of the information.

The case studies do not correspond to any particular objective, but the questions map to all of the objectives. In addition, you should download the case study demo to familiarize yourself with the exam environment. Download the demo from *http:// www.microsoft.com/trainingandservices/exams/examasearch.asp?PageURL=/ TrainingAndServices/content/exams/70-220.txt*.

The Readiness Review series lets you identify any areas in which you may need additional training. To help you get the training you need to successfully pass the certification exams, Microsoft Press publishes a complete line of self-paced training kits and other study materials. For comprehensive information about the topics covered in the Designing Security for a Microsoft Windows 2000 Network exam, see the corresponding MCSE training kit—*Designing Microsoft Windows 2000 Network Security*.

Before You Begin

This MCSE Readiness Review consists of two main parts: the Readiness Review electronic assessment program on the accompanying compact disc and this Readiness Review book.

The Readiness Review Components

The electronic assessment is a practice certification test that helps you evaluate your skills. It provides instant scoring feedback, so you can determine areas in which additional study may be helpful before you take the certification exam. Although your score on the electronic assessment does not necessarily indicate what your score will be on the certification exam, it does give you the opportunity to answer questions that are similar to those on the actual certification exam.

The Readiness Review book is organized according to the exam's objectives. Each chapter pertains to one of the six primary groups of objectives on the actual exam, called the *Objective Domains*. Each Objective Domain lists the tested skills you need to master to adequately answer the exam questions. Because the certification exams focus on real-world skills, the Tested Skills and Suggested Practices lists provide practices that emphasize the practical application of the exam objectives. Each Objective Domain also provides suggestions for further reading or additional resources to help you understand the objectives and increase your ability to perform the task or skills specified by the objectives.

Within each Objective Domain, you will find the related objectives that are covered on the exam. Each objective provides you with the following:

- **Key terms** you must know to understand the objective. Knowing these terms can help you answer the objective's questions correctly.

- Several sample exam questions with the correct answers. The answers are accompanied by explanations of each correct and incorrect answer. (These questions match the questions on the electronic assessment.)

The Readiness Review book also includes five Case Studies, each of which presents a real-world scenario with questions very much like the ones on the actual exam. Each Case Study details an on-the-job scenario at a fictitious company and then is followed by a number of sample exam questions based on the scenario.

You use the electronic assessment to determine the exam objectives that you need to study and then use the Readiness Review book to learn more about those particular objectives and discover additional study materials to supplement your knowledge. You can also use the Readiness Review book to research the answers to specific sample test questions. Keep in mind that to pass the exam you should understand not only the answer to the question, but also the concepts on which the correct answer is based.

MCP Exam Prerequisites

No exams or classes are required before you take the Designing Security for a Microsoft Windows 2000 Network exam. However, in addition to the skills tested by the exam, you should have a working knowledge of the operation and support of hardware and software on Windows 2000 Server networks. This knowledge should include:

- Analyzing Business Requirements

- Analyzing Technical Requirements

- Analyzing Security Requirements

- Designing a Windows 2000 Security Solution

- Designing a Security Solution for Access Between Networks

- Designing Security for Communication Channels

Note After you have used the Readiness Review and determined that you are ready for the exam, use the Get More MCP Information link provided on the home page of the electronic assessment tool for information on scheduling for the exam. You can schedule exams up to six weeks in advance or as late as one working day before the exam date.

Know the Products

Microsoft's certification program relies on exams that measure your ability to perform a specific job function or set of tasks. Microsoft develops the exams by analyzing the tasks performed by people who are working in the field. Therefore, the specific knowledge, skills, and abilities relating to the job are reflected in the certification exam.

Because the certification exams are based on real-world tasks, you need to gain hands-on experience with the applicable technology in order to master the exam. In a sense, you might consider hands-on experience in an organizational environment to be a prerequisite for passing an MCP exam. Many of the questions relate directly to Microsoft products or technology, so use opportunities at your organization or at home to practice using the relevant tools.

Using the MCSE Readiness Review

Although you can use the Readiness Review in a number of ways, you might start your studies by taking the electronic assessment as a pretest. After completing the exam, review your results for each Objective Domain and focus your studies first on the Objective Domains for which you received the lowest scores. The electronic assessment allows you to print your results, and a printed report of how you fared can be useful when reviewing the exam material in this book.

After you have taken the Readiness Review electronic assessment, use the Readiness Review book to learn more about the Objective Domains that you find difficult and to find listings of appropriate study materials that may supplement your knowledge. By reviewing why the answers are correct or incorrect, you can determine if you need to study the objective topics more.

You can also use the Readiness Review book to focus on the exact objectives that you need to master. Each objective in the book contains several questions that help you determine if you understand the information related to that particular skill. The book is also designed for you to answer each question before turning the page to review the correct answer.

The best method to prepare for the MCP exam is to use the Readiness Review book in conjunction with the electronic assessment and other study material. Thoroughly studying and practicing the material combined with substantial real-world experience can help you fully prepare for the MCP exam.

Understanding the Readiness Review Conventions

Before you start using the Readiness Review, it's important that you understand the terms and conventions used in the electronic assessment and book.

Question Numbering System

The Readiness Review electronic assessment and book contain reference numbers for each question. Understanding the numbering format will help you use the Readiness Review more effectively. When Microsoft creates the exams, the questions are grouped by job skills called *Objectives*. These Objectives are then organized by sections known as *Objective Domains*. Each question can be identified by the Objective Domain and the Objective it covers. The question numbers follow this format:

Test Number.Objective Domain.Objective.Question Number

For example, question number 70-220.02.01.003 means this is question three (003) for the first Objective (01) in the second Objective Domain (02) of the Designing Security for a Microsoft Windows 2000 Network exam (70-220). Refer to the "Exam Objectives

Summary" section later in this introduction to locate the numbers associated with particular objectives. Each question is numbered based on its presentation in the printed book. You can use this numbering system to reference questions on the electronic assessment or in the Readiness Review book. Even though the questions in the book are organized by objective, questions in the electronic assessment and actual certification exam are presented in random order.

The case studies do not correspond to any particular objective, but the questions map to all of the objectives. Case Study questions are numbered similarly to Objective Domain questions; however, the objective number is replaced by the Case Study number. For example, question number 70-220.CS1.003 indicates this is question three (003) of the first Case Study (CS1).

Notational Conventions

- Characters or commands that you type appear in **bold lowercase** type.

- Variable information and URLs are *italicized*. *Italic* is also used for book titles.

- Acronyms, filenames, and utilities appear in FULL CAPITALS.

Notes

Notes appear throughout the book.

- Notes marked *Caution* contain information you'll want to know before continuing with the book's material.

- Notes marked *Note* contain supplemental information.

- Notes marked *Tip* contain helpful process hints.

Using the Readiness Review Electronic Assessment

The Readiness Review electronic assessment simulates the actual MCP exam. Each iteration of the electronic assessment consists of 50 questions covering all the objectives for the Designing Security for a Microsoft Windows 2000 Network exam. (MCP certification exams consist of approximately 50 questions.) Questions in the electronic assessment are drawn from both the Objective Domains and Case Studies. Just like a real certification exam, you see questions from the objectives in random order during the practice test. Similar to the certification exam, the electronic assessment allows you to mark questions and review them after you finish the test.

To increase its value as a study aid, you can take the electronic assessment several times. Each time you're presented with a different set of questions in a revised order; however, some questions may be repeated.

If you've used one of the certification exam preparation tests available from Microsoft, the Readiness Review electronic assessment should look familiar. The difference is that this electronic assessment gives you the opportunity to learn as you take the exam.

Installing and Running the Electronic Assessment Software

Before you begin using the electronic assessment, you need to install the software. You need a computer with the following minimum configuration:

- Multimedia PC with a 75 MHz Pentium or higher processor

- 16 MB RAM for Windows 95 or Windows 98, or

- 32 MB RAM for Windows NT, or

- 64 MB RAM for Windows 2000

- Internet Explorer 5.01 or 5.5

- 17 MB of available hard disk space (additional 70 MB minimum of hard disk space to install Internet Explorer 5.5 from this CD-ROM)

- A double-speed CD-ROM drive or better

- Super VGA display with at least 256 colors

▶ **To install the electronic assessment**

1. Insert the Readiness Review companion CD-ROM into your CD-ROM drive.

   A starting menu will display automatically, with links to the resources included on the CD.

Note If your system does not have Microsoft Internet Explorer 5.01 or later, you can install Internet 5.5 now by selecting the appropriate option on the menu.

---

2. Click Install Readiness Review.

   A dialog box appears, indicating that you will install the MCSE Readiness Review to your computer.

3. Click Next.

   The License Agreement dialog box appears.

4. To continue with the installation of the electronic assessment engine, you must accept the License Agreement by clicking Yes.

5. The Choose Destination Location dialog box appears showing a default installation directory. Either accept the default or change the installation directory if needed. Click Next to copy the files to your hard disk.

6. A Question dialog box appears asking whether you would like Setup to create a desktop shortcut for this program. If you click Yes, an icon will be placed on your desktop.

7. The Setup Complete dialog box appears. Select whether you want to view the README.TXT file after closing the Setup program, and then click Finish.

   The electronic assessment software is completely installed. If you chose to view the README.TXT file, it will launch in a new window. For optimal viewing, enable word wrap.

▶ **To start the electronic assessment**

1. From the Start menu, point to Programs, point to MCSE Readiness Review, and then click MCSE RR Exam 70-220.

   The electronic assessment program starts.

2. Click Start Test.

   Information about the electronic assessment program appears.

3. Click OK.

Taking the Electronic Assessment

The Readiness Review electronic assessment consists of 50 multiple-choice questions, and as in the certification exam, you can skip questions or mark them for later review. Each exam question contains a question number that you can use to refer back to the Readiness Review book.

Before you end the electronic assessment, you should make sure to answer all the questions. When the exam is graded, unanswered questions are counted as incorrect and will lower your score. Similarly, on the actual certification exam you should complete all questions or they will be counted as incorrect. No trick questions appear on the exam. The correct answer will always be among the list of choices. Some questions might have more than one correct answer, and this will be indicated in the question. A good strategy is to eliminate the most obvious incorrect answers first to make it easier for you to select the correct answer.

You have 75 minutes to complete the electronic assessment. During the exam you will see a timer indicating the amount of time you have remaining. This will help you to gauge the amount of time you should use to answer each question and to complete the exam. The amount of time you are given on the actual certification exam varies with each exam. Generally, certification exams take approximately 100 minutes to complete.

Ending and Grading the Electronic Assessment

When you click the Score Test button, you have the opportunity to review the questions you marked or left incomplete. (This format is not similar to the one used on the actual certification exam, in which you can verify whether you are satisfied with your answers and then click the Grade Test button.) The electronic assessment is graded when you click the Score Test button, and the software presents your section scores and your total score.

Note You can always end a test without grading your electronic assessment by clicking the Home button.

After your electronic assessment is graded, you can view the correct and incorrect answers by clicking the Review Questions button.

Interpreting the Electronic Assessment Results

The Score screen shows you the number of questions in each Objective Domain section, the number of questions you answered correctly, and a percentage grade for each section. You can use the Score screen to determine where to spend additional time studying. On the actual certification exam, the number of questions and passing score will depend on the exam you are taking. The electronic assessment records your score each time you grade an exam so that you can track your progress over time.

▶ **To view your progress and exam records**

1. From the electronic assessment Main menu, click View History. Each test attempt score appears.

2. Click on a test attempt date/time to view your score for each objective domain.

   Review these scores to determine which Objective Domains you should study further. You can also use the scores to determine your progress.

Ordering More Questions

MeasureUp, Inc., offers practice tests to help you prepare for a variety of MCP certification exams. These practice tests contain hundreds of additional questions and are similar to the Readiness Review electronic assessment. For a fee, you can order exam practice tests for this exam and other Microsoft certification exams. Click on the Order More Questions link on the electronic assessment home page for more information.

Using the Readiness Review Book

You can use the Readiness Review book as a supplement to the Readiness Review electronic assessment or as a stand-alone study aid. If you decide to use the book as a stand-alone study aid, review the Table of Contents or the list of objectives to find topics of interest or an appropriate starting point for you. To get the greatest benefit from the book, use the electronic assessment as a pretest to determine the Objective Domains on which you should spend the most study time. Or if you would like to research specific questions while taking the electronic assessment, you can use the question number located on the question screen to reference the question number in the Readiness Review book.

One way to determine areas in which additional study may be helpful is to carefully review your individual section scores from the electronic assessment and note objective areas where your score could be improved. The section scores correlate to the Objective Domains listed in the Readiness Review book.

Reviewing the Objectives

Each Objective Domain in the book contains an introduction and a list of practice skills. Each list of practice skills describes suggested tasks you can perform to help you understand the objectives. Some of the tasks suggest reading additional material, while others are hands-on practices with software or hardware. You should pay particular attention to the hands-on practices, as the certification exam reflects real-world knowledge you can gain only by working with the software or technology. Increasing your real-world experience with the relevant products and technologies will improve your performance on the exam.

Once you have chosen the objectives you would like to study, turn to the Table of Contents to locate the objectives in the Readiness Review book. You can study each objective separately, but you may need to understand the concepts explained in other objectives.

Make sure you understand the key terms for each objective. You will need a thorough understanding of these terms to answer the objective's questions correctly. Key term definitions are located in the Glossary of this book.

Reviewing the Questions

Each objective includes questions followed by the possible answers. After you review the question and select a probable answer, turn to the Answer section to determine if you answered the question correctly. (For information about the question numbering format, see "Question Numbering System," earlier in this introduction.)

The Readiness Review briefly discusses each possible answer and explains why each answer is correct or incorrect. After reviewing each explanation, if you feel you need more information about a topic, question, or answer, refer to the Further Readings section for that domain for more information.

The answers to the questions in the Readiness Review are based on current industry specifications and standards. However, the information provided by the answers is subject to change as technology improves and changes.

Exam Objectives Summary

The Designing Security for a Microsoft Windows 2000 Network (70-220) exam measures your ability to implement, administer, and troubleshoot Windows 2000 Server networks. Before taking the exam, you should be proficient with the job skills presented in the following sections. The sections provide the exam objectives and the corresponding objective numbers (which you can use to reference the questions in the Readiness Review electronic assessment and book) grouped by Objective Domains.

Objective Domain 1: Analyzing Business Requirements

The objectives in Objective Domain 1 are as follows:

- Objective 1.1 (70-220.01.01)—Analyze the existing and planned business models.

- Objective 1.2 (70-220.01.02)—Analyze the existing and planned organizational structures.

- Objective 1.3 (70-220.01.03)—Analyze factors that influence company strategies.

- Objective 1.4 (70-220.01.04)—Analyze business and security requirements for the end user.

- Objective 1.5 (70-220.01.05)—Analyze the structure of IT management.

- Objective 1.6 (70-220.01.06)—Analyze the current physical model and information security model.

Objective Domain 2: Analyzing Technical Requirements

The objectives in Objective Domain 2 are as follows:

- Objective 2.1 (70-220.02.01)—Evaluate the company's existing and planned technical environment.

- Objective 2.2 (70-220.02.02)—Analyze the impact of the security design on the existing and planned technical environment.

Objective Domain 3: Analyzing Security Requirements

The objectives in Objective Domain 3 are as follows:

- Objective 3.1 (70-220.03.01)—Design a security baseline for a Windows 2000 network.

- Objective 3.2 (70-220.03.02)—Identify the required level of security for each resource.

Objective Domain 4: Designing a Windows 2000 Security Solution

The objectives in Objective Domain 4 are as follows:

- Objective 4.1 (70-220.04.01)—Design an audit policy.

- Objective 4.2 (70-220.04.02)—Design a delegation of authority strategy.

- Objective 4.3 (70-220.04.03)—Design the placement and inheritance of security policies for sites, domains, and organizational units.

- Objective 4.4 (70-220.04.04)—Design an Encrypting File System strategy.

- Objective 4.5 (70-220.04.05)—Design an authentication strategy.

- Objective 4.6 (70-220.04.06)—Design a security group strategy.

- Objective 4.7 (70-220.04.07)—Design a Public Key Infrastructure.

- Objective 4.8 (70-220.04.08)—Design Windows 2000 network services security.

Objective Domain 5: Designing a Security Solution for Access Between Networks

The objectives in Objective Domain 5 are as follows:

- Objective 5.1 (70-220.05.01)—Provide secure access to public networks from a private network.

- Objective 5.2 (70-220.05.02)—Provide external users with secure access to private network resources.

- Objective 5.3 (70-220.05.03)—Provide secure access between private networks.

- Objective 5.4 (70-220.05.04)—Design Windows 2000 security for remote access users.

Objective Domain 6: Designing Security for Communication Channels

The objectives in Objective Domain 6 are as follows:

- Objective 6.1 (70-220.06.01)—Design an SMB-signing solution.

- Objective 6.2 (70-220.06.02)—Design an IPSec solution.

Case Studies

The five Case Studies are as follows:

- Case Study 1—Blue Yonder Airlines.

- Case Study 2—Adventure Works.

- Case Study 3—Fabrikam, Inc.

- Case Study 4—Trey Research.

- Case Study 5—Contoso, Ltd.

Getting More Help

A variety of resources are available to help you study for the exam. Your options include instructor-led classes, seminars, self-paced kits, or other learning materials. The materials described here are created to prepare you for MCP exams. Each training resource fits a different type of learning style and budget.

Microsoft Official Curriculum (MOC)

Microsoft Official Curriculum (MOC) courses are technical training courses developed by Microsoft product groups to educate computer professionals who use Microsoft technology. The courses are developed with the same objectives used for Microsoft certification, and MOC courses are available to support most exams for the MCSE certification. The courses are available in instructor-led, online, or self-paced formats to fit your preferred learning style.

Self-Paced Training

Microsoft Press self-paced training kits cover a variety of Microsoft technical products. The self-paced kits are based on MOC courses and feature lessons, hands-on practices, multimedia presentations, practice files, and demonstration software. They can help you understand the concepts and get the experience you need to take the corresponding MCP exam.

To help you prepare for the Designing Security for a Microsoft Windows 2000 Network 70-220 MCP exam, Microsoft has written the *Designing Microsoft Windows 2000 Network Security* training kit. With this official self-paced training kit, you can learn the fundamentals of designing Windows 2000 network security. This kit gives you training for the real world by offering hands-on training through CD-ROM–based exercises.

MCP Approved Study Guides

MCP Approved Study Guides, available through several organizations, are learning tools that help you prepare for MCP exams. The study guides are available in a variety of formats to match your learning style, including books, compact discs, online content, and videos. These guides come in a wide range of prices to fit your budget.

Microsoft Seminar Series

Microsoft Solution Providers and other organizations are often a source of information to help you prepare for an MCP exam. For example, many solution providers present seminars to help industry professionals understand a particular product technology, such as networking. For information on all Microsoft-sponsored events, visit *http://www.microsoft.com/usa/events/default.asp.*

Analyzing Business Requirements

The first course of action you should undertake when preparing to implement a new system is the analysis process. Because migrating to a new version of Windows 2000 is such a large procedure, you need to look at how it will affect the company at the organizational level. To understand which features of Windows 2000 a business needs to employ, you should be prepared to answer certain questions about the organization itself: How does communication flow through the company? How does information flow through the company? You should analyze the products or services the company offers and determine the life cycles of those products or services. You should also try to understand how decisions are made and carried out within the structure of the business. These components will help you enormously when you move into the implementation stage. By understanding how a company operates, you'll be better suited to configure Windows 2000 to meet its needs.

Tested Skills and Suggested Practices

The skills that you need to successfully master the Analyzing Business Requirements objective domain on the *Designing Security for a Microsoft Windows 2000 Network* exam include:

- **Analyzing the existing and planned business models.**

    - Practice 1: Write out all the proposed changes that will take place in the company. Rank them according to which changes will have the greatest effect on the network security design.

    - Practice 2: Find a colleague to play devil's advocate to your design. After illustrating the layout, have your colleague ask you tough questions about its structure that you might not think of on your own.

■ **Analyzing the existing and planned organizational structures.**

  ▪ Practice 1: Create a chart of the company's organizational structure. Use the pyramid approach so that you can see how the company is laid out.

  ▪ Practice 2: Write out and catalog the company's vendors, partners, and customers. From there you can assign a value to the level of security that would be needed if each were allowed some form of network access.

■ **Analyzing the factors that influence the company's strategies.**

  ▪ Practice 1: Try to get a concrete understanding of the company's specific priorities. If they have a mission statement, find out how well they're following it. If they don't seem to be in line with it, think about options that might help them follow it more closely.

  ▪ Practice 2: Using the mission statement, develop a prioritized list of Windows 2000 features that can help achieve the mission. Correlate this list with the security requirements of the proposed network.

■ **Analyzing the business and security requirements for the end user.**

  ▪ Practice 1: Basically, there are five types of end users: external authenticated users, Internet users, regular users, roaming users, and traveling users. Review all the personnel in the company and decide which type of user each person is and how the users are grouped.

  ▪ Practice 2: Once you have this list and the corresponding designations assigned, try to ascertain who needs what level of security according to what they access and what types of information they have access to.

■ **Analyzing the structure of IT management.**

  ▪ Practice 1: Determine whether the company uses a centralized or decentralized company structure.

  ▪ Practice 2: Examine the company structure to decide if there are any resources that should be outsourced, as opposed to doing everything in-house.

■ **Analyzing the current physical model and information security model.**

  ▪ Practice 1: Identify the different types of security risks that are common within an organization and that might hinder your network design or disable your proposed network outline.

  ▪ Practice 2: Spend some time reviewing the current security standards before presenting any new network design. One way of doing this is to have a third party perform a formal risk assessment.

Further Reading

This section lists supplemental readings by objective. We recommend that you study these sources thoroughly before taking exam 70-220.

Objective 1.1

Microsoft Corporation. *Windows 2000 Server Resource Kit*. Volume: *Microsoft Windows 2000 Server Deployment Planning Guide*. Redmond, Washington: Microsoft Press, 2000. Review Chapter 1, "Introducing Windows 2000 Deployment Planning," which gives you information about how to analyze and begin planning for network OS installation.

Microsoft Corporation. "Site Analysis Worksheet." (This worksheet can be downloaded for free at *http://msdn.microsoft.com/library/winresource/ssreskit/ rk_siteanalysisworksheet_bvfi.htm*.) Although it was developed for Microsoft Site Server, you can use this worksheet to gather and record information about a network site for your Windows 2000 deployment. This will take you step-by-step through the business analysis components.

Objective 1.2

Microsoft Corporation. *Windows 2000 Server Resource Kit*. Volume: *Microsoft Windows 2000 Server Deployment Planning Guide*. Redmond, Washington: Microsoft Press, 2000. Review Case Study 3, "Multinational Financial Services Corporation," and Case Study 4, "International Software Development Company," in Chapter 1. Both of these give detailed descriptions of the existing IT environment as well as the deployment goals for Windows 2000.

Microsoft Corporation. "After Major Merger, BP chooses Windows 2000 as Common Operating Environment." (This case study can be downloaded for free at the Windows 2000 Product Guide at *http://www.microsoft.com/windows2000/guide/server/profiles/ bp.asp*.) This case study covers the issues involved with both international deployment and multiple business integration.

Objective 1.3

Microsoft Corporation. "Honeywell Europe S. A." (This case study can be downloaded for free at the MSDN Online Library at *http://msdn.microsoft.com/library/ default.asp?URL=/library/books/thin/honeywelleuropesa.htm*.) Although not completely parallel with a standard Windows 2000 deployment, this case study offers some notable insights into analyzing company factors and strategies.

Microsoft Corporation. *MCSE Training Kit: Designing Microsoft Windows 2000 Network Security*. Redmond, Washington: Microsoft Press, 2001. Review Chapter 1, "Introduction to Microsoft Windows 2000 Security," Lesson 2, "Determining Security Business Requirements." This lesson identifies some of the business factors that will influence your network security design.

Objective 1.4

Microsoft Corporation. *Windows 2000 Server Resource Kit*. Volume: *Microsoft Windows 2000 Server Deployment Planning Guide*. Redmond, Washington: Microsoft Press, 2000. Review the section in Chapter 1 titled "Mapping Windows 2000 Features to Your Business Needs," which will aid you in analyzing business requirements. Also pay close attention to the section titled "Security Features" in order to review analyzing security requirements.

Microsoft Corporation. *Windows 2000 Server Resource Kit*. Volume: *Microsoft Windows 2000 Server TCP/IP Core Networking Guide*. Redmond, Washington: Microsoft Press, 2000. Review the "IPSec Planning" section of Chapter 8, "Internet Protocol Security." This section covers best practices and considerations for establishing a security plan based on IPSec.

Objective 1.5

Microsoft Corporation. *Windows 2000 Server Resource Kit*. Volume: *Microsoft Windows 2000 Server Deployment Planning Guide*. Redmond, Washington: Microsoft Press, 2000. Review the section titled "Mapping Windows 2000 Features to Your Business Needs," which reviews how to determine which Windows 2000 technologies are applicable to your proposed IT management structure.

Microsoft Corporation. *MCSE Training Kit: Designing Microsoft Windows 2000 Network Security*. Redmond, Washington: Microsoft Press, 2001. Review Chapter 2, "Designing Active Directory for Security." This chapter contains lessons that cover designing a forest structure and a domain and their relationship with your business.

Objective 1.6

Microsoft Corporation. *Windows 2000 Server Resource Kit*. Volume: *Microsoft Windows 2000 Server Deployment Planning Guide*. Redmond, Washington: Microsoft Press, 2000. Review Case Study 3, "Multinational Financial Services Corporation" and Case Study 4, "International Software Development Company" in Chapter 1.

The Coriolis Group. *Windows 2000 System Administrator's Black Book*. Scottsdale, Arizona: Coriolis, 2000. Chapter 2, "Comparing Windows 2000 to Windows NT," highlights new features in Windows 2000. Chapter 4, "Windows NT 4.0 to Windows 2000 Migration," covers the migration from an existing Windows NT 4 network.

OBJECTIVE 1.1

Analyze the existing and planned business models.

Almost nothing is more important than understanding the degree and scope of the network you're about to design and implement. The company's size and its particular model greatly influence how security becomes a part of the network. When dealing with an international business model, for example, you might have security circumstances that are standard in one country/region but not accepted in another. You also might run into problems regarding encryption, which, because of economic agreements or treaties, may not be legal to use in all places. Also, language barriers and other cultural factors pose a certain degree of security risk.

In dealing with a national model, you might tend to run into security considerations because of growth rate. Although a company would be secure if its Web page took only a certain number of hits each day, the chances for a security breach increase as the company grows and more people visit the site—especially if you haven't taken precautions to deal with the added risk the increased traffic generates.

Regional offices pose unique security and design considerations because the infrastructure in each location might differ in availability and equipment. For example, you might have a branch office located in a major metropolitan area with a corresponding warehouse in a rural area in which digital telephone technology hasn't become a reality, making certain dial-up options risky, if not altogether infeasible.

Still, a branch-office model poses unique circumstances, risks, and situations. In this scenario data would probably move from the branch offices to and through regional offices and into corporate headquarters. In this circumstance, certain choices come into play—such as whether information comes directly from the branches or is stored locally in a centralized database. Having centralized storage makes it easier for the IT personnel to manage data and keep track of interrelated security issues. Such a centralized model may not always be possible, however.

As shown from these few but somewhat wide-ranging examples, understanding the organization's unique business model is the first key step to effectively planning adequate security.

Objective 1.1 Questions

70-220.01.01.001

While preparing to migrate from a Windows NT 4 network to a Windows 2000 network, Eva spent several weeks analyzing key processes, including the communication flow, information flow, and the decision-making infrastructure. Currently, a Headquarters domain contains the user accounts for the New York office. There also are two Resource domains, located in White Plains and Hackensack, that contain mostly file and print services in support of the New York staff. The Sales domain, located in Philadelphia, contains user accounts in support of the company's nationwide network of retail stores. Each retail location is set up as a separate Resource domain containing the file and print services needed by the users who work in a given store.

Trust relationships enable members of the Sales domain to access resources in the Headquarters domain. Any two domains that have established a trust relationship have a shared password, also known as an interdomain password. The users in Headquarters don't need access to the resources in the Sales domain, nor do they need access to the resources in the retail locations. Administrators in both master user domains need full administrative control over their own resources.

Communications between Headquarters and Sales take place over a virtual private network (VPN) over the Internet. These communications are encrypted and encapsulated for confidentiality.

How should Eva design her Windows 2000 domain and organizational unit (OU) structure to best accommodate the information flow requirements?

A. Create one account domain and migrate the resource domains into OUs under the Headquarters domain.

B. Create two account domains and migrate the resource domains into OUs under the Sales domain.

C. Create two account domains, migrate the existing retail stores resource domains into OUs under Sales, and migrate White Plains and Hackensack into OUs under Headquarters.

D. Create two account domains, migrate the existing retail stores' resource domains into OUs under Headquarters, and migrate White Plains and Hackensack into OUs under Headquarters.

70-220.01.01.002

Proseware, Inc., started out manufacturing a single item in a single manufacturing facility in Atlanta. Proseware's computer network infrastructure was limited to a couple of isolated file-and-print networks. All employees maintained individual Internet-based e-mail accounts. Virtually all company business was handled by means of department meetings and paper memos.

This year Proseware acquired a manufacturing facility in San Jose, California, for the purpose of expanding Proseware's product line. With planned expansion to include an additional facility in Colorado within six months, the company recognized the need for an integrated computer network.

The budget for network infrastructure was limited, but the growing company decided to focus on four core goals:

- Standardize on Microsoft Windows 2000

- Maintain centralized IT administration from Atlanta

- Implement a company-wide e-mail system

- Ensure secure, encrypted communication between facilities

You've been hired as the chief information officer (CIO) of Proseware. Which of the following proposals best meets the company's goals at minimum cost?

A. Create a single Active Directory directory service domain with an OU hierarchy. Establish a site plan based on physical geography/network infrastructure. Install a Microsoft Exchange 5.5 server in Atlanta. Hire an IT staff in Atlanta and hire IT support personnel for the other facilities. Establish VPN connections over the Internet between sites.

B. Create an Active Directory forest structure with a separate tree for each facility. Within each tree, create departmental domains. Establish a site plan based on the logical network layout. Install a Microsoft Exchange 5.5 server in Atlanta. Hire an IT staff in Atlanta. Provide Atlanta-based IT support personnel at the other facilities on an as-needed basis. Establish VPN connections across dedicated wide area network (WAN) links between sites.

C. Create a single Active Directory domain with an OU hierarchy. Establish a site plan based on physical geography/network infrastructure. Install Microsoft Outlook on each desktop. Hire an IT staff in Atlanta, San Jose, and each newly acquired facility. Connect the facilities with dedicated WAN links.

D. Create a single master domain in Atlanta, and resource domains for each manufacturing facility. Install a Microsoft Exchange 5.5 server in Atlanta. Hire an IT staff in Atlanta and hire IT support personnel for the other facilities. Establish VPN connections over the Internet between sites.

70-220.01.01.003

Your company manufactures products for the aerospace industry. Traditionally, products in your industry have followed an 18-month development cycle from planning to full-scale distribution. Recently, following extensive modeling of emerging industry trends, you've discovered that competitive pressures, coupled with improved manufacturing methods, have compressed this cycle to 12 months or less.

Through a series of ongoing initiatives, every facet of your company's operations is being reevaluated and overhauled to place your company at a competitive advantage. You're the chief information officer (CIO). Among the initiatives you're responsible for is information security. Many projects involve the cooperative efforts of multiple specialized facilities, in both the United States and abroad. For the last 50 years, most confidential data was transferred from facility to facility by courier, and later, by commercial delivery services such as Federal Express and United Parcel Service.

Your company is currently upgrading to a native-mode Windows 2000 Active Directory network worldwide. Most company facilities are connected with T1 backbone connections, with some facilities connected using slower Frame Relay leased connections. The entire network infrastructure is considered reliable. Because of regulatory and accountability issues, couriers and delivery services will never become completely extinct. What recommendation should you make concerning the supplemental information flow of confidential data within the company?

A. Transfer data across the existing infrastructure using IPSec with Encapsulating Security Payload (ESP).

B. Transfer data across the existing infrastructure using Layer Two Tunneling Protocol (L2TP) over IPSec.

C. Transfer data across the high-speed portion of the existing infrastructure using IPSec with ESP and over the slow-speed portion using VPN technology.

D. Transfer data across the high-speed portion of the existing infrastructure using IPSec with ESP, and over the slow-speed portion using IPSec with Authentication Header (AH).

Objective 1.1 Answers

70-220.01.01.001

▶ **Correct Answers: C**

A. **Incorrect:** Creating a single account domain would be incorrect for this situation. Migrating the resource domains into OUs under the Headquarters domain is an inefficient design. This is appropriate for the White Plains and Hackensack resource domains but not for the retail resource domains. The administration of the retail OUs should fall under Sales, where the resources are managed and controlled.

B. **Incorrect:** A similar argument exists against migrating all resource domains into OUs under the Sales domain.

C. **Correct:** The basic design process for Windows 2000 domains differs from the design process for Windows NT domains. In Windows NT networks, the domain structure is guided by the relationship between master user domains and resource domains. The existing Windows NT domain model shouldn't be the basis for the Windows 2000 domains. Instead, you should consider your company's physical and operational structure, as well as your network administrators' requirements. A major reason to use multiple Windows 2000 domains is to support decentralized administration. Through decentralization, IT structures can utilize smaller data sites in regional areas. Your company's administrative units may not accept a domain design that gives them limited administrative control over their own resources. This is the case in our scenario, where the resource access limitations are clearly defined. Creating two account domains is the right choice for Eva.

After you establish the number of domains that's appropriate for your company, you must consider how to organize them into a useful hierarchy. As one of your essential Windows 2000 design tasks, you need to decide whether to arrange your company's domains into a tree or a forest. Groups of domains that exist within the forest with contiguous Domain Name System (DNS) domain names are known as domain trees. Some companies, such as the one in this question, need a single tree to support their enterprise. All domains forming a tree or forest can share their resources globally.

After determining your domain design strategy, you must decide how your company will arrange its OUs. Your company can use OUs to organize its resources into a more meaningful hierarchy. OUs form a meaningful structure for the various objects in a domain. Your primary goal in forming this structure is to make the OUs useful for users and administrators. In our scenario it makes sense to migrate the retail resource domains into OUs under the Sales domain.

This allows for efficient administration and ease of use. Migrating the New York resource domains into OUs under Headquarters would serve the same purpose.

D. **Incorrect:** Migrating the existing retail stores' resource domains into OUs is correct, but placing them under the Headquarters domain is not.

70-220.01.01.002

▶ **Correct Answers: A**

A. **Correct:** Given the scenario's constraints, the correct choice would be to first create a single Active Directory domain with an OU hierarchy. With this model, the IT administrators can easily be granted permissions at the domain root, thus allowing simplified administration throughout the domain. Next, establish a site plan based on physical geography/network infrastructure. Creating separate sites for areas of common networking infrastructure is a well-accepted practice. This allows you to analyze the relationship between logon traffic and domain controller replication traffic and to place network assets where they will operate most efficiently. It might also be helpful to consider implementing Internet Authentication Services (IAS) in this scenario.

Once this is completed, you'll need to install a Microsoft Exchange 5.5 server in Atlanta. A single, centrally located e-mail server is a common deployment practice for enterprise networks. Administration is simplified and network traffic is reduced. As the company expands to thousands of users, it might make sense to add additional e-mail servers to the network, but there is no compelling reason to do that now.

The next step in the process is to hire an IT staff in Atlanta and IT personnel for the other facilities. The majority of the IT staff should be in Atlanta, where the network is centrally managed. The other facilities, however, would need on-site personnel to handle the day-to-day issues of maintaining a network. Through delegation of authority, these local personnel could be given the appropriate level of authority over local matters without having their authority extend to other facilities.

Finally, you'll need to establish VPN demand-dial connections over the Internet. In order to establish demand-dial connection, the answering router will need to establish a connection through the demand-dial router. Using this technology, the Internet can function as an extension of your internal network at minimum cost, while you still achieve your goals of security and confidentiality. Dedicated connections would yield additional benefits, but they aren't specifically required by the scenario.

B. **Incorrect:** Creating an Active Directory forest structure with separate trees for each facility would be incorrect. The scenario doesn't require it, and such a structure would make centralized network administration by the Atlanta IT staff very difficult because each domain represents a security boundary requiring multiple redundant assignments of access permissions. In addition, a site plan should be based on the physical network infrastructure, not the logical structure. Finally, supplying IT personnel from Atlanta to the separate facilities on an ad hoc basis would likely result in excessive travel costs.

C. **Incorrect:** Microsoft Outlook is the client interface to the e-mail system. It doesn't provide the actual e-mail services that a service such as Microsoft Exchange 5.5 does. Concerning the staffing issue, because IT administration is to be handled centrally, there's no reason to duplicate the staff functions at each facility. Support personnel are all that should be required outside of Atlanta. Finally, dedicated WAN links are a good idea, but they don't by themselves address the issue of secure, confidential communications. You should establish additional implementation steps, such as an IP Security (IPSec) policy.

D. **Incorrect:** The concept of master domains and resource domains isn't necessary or desirable with Windows 2000. Widely used in prior Windows operating systems, the master/resource domain model has been effectively replaced in Windows 2000 by the OU hierarchical structure. This allows you to more efficiently handle the same issues within a single domain environment.

70-220.01.01.003

▶ **Correct Answers: A**

A. **Correct:** The correct choice would be IPSec with ESP. IPSec enables encrypted network communication. IPSec uses cryptography-based protection services, security protocols, dynamic key management, access control, and integrity to accomplish two goals: protect IP packets and provide a defense against network attacks. IPSec is based on an end-to-end security model, which means that the sending computer encrypts the packet before it's ever placed on the wire and the receiving computer decrypts the packet only after it has been received. The underlying assumption is that the communication media are inherently insecure. Since T1 and Frame Relay connections use public media for transmission, you must assume that they fit this description. IPSec comes in two types—with or without payload encryption. For IPSec with encryption, as specified by the particulars of the scenario, the encryption is handled by ESP. IPSec with ESP provides confidentiality, authentication, integrity, and antireplay. ESP functions by inserting the ESP header between the IP header and the TCP/UDP header. It also will include ESP trailers in this process.

B. **Incorrect:** There are two ways to securely transfer data between geographically isolated sites: IPSec and VPN. VPN technology has two primary manifestations—Point-to-Point Tunneling Protocol (PPTP) and L2TP. Because both types of VPNs are associated with dial-up connections, this isn't the appropriate choice for this scenario.

C. **Incorrect:** This answer is incorrect for the reasons stated in B.

D. **Incorrect:** AH is essentially the same as ESP, only without the actual data being encrypted. ESP will, under standard conditions, sign the complete packet. AH will not. You use IPSec with AH if you require authentication, integrity, and antireplay, but not data encryption. This wouldn't be an appropriate choice for our scenario.

Analyze the existing and planned organizational structures.

The most fundamental element in creating a secure network is understanding the company's organizational structure. The keystone of this organizational structure is creating an **organizational chart** for the company for which you're planning the network design. In addition to an organizational chart, you'll need to create several documents that illustrate the physical placement of sites, administrative duties and tasks, as well as technical information about network speed and other factors. Once you create an organizational chart, it will help to guide your security design. Once you achieve a thorough understanding of the network, implementing security becomes a logical placement of policies and domain structures to form the basis of the security infrastructure.

In order to achieve this, you need to have certain information about the management and overall organization. You should formulate a list of questions that allow you to understand how information flows and how you should secure it. Some of these questions are:

- Who is in charge of administration and support of the existing network?

- Who is in charge of data management or resource management or both?

- What types of categories does the existing data fall into, such as Secret, Public, or Internally Confidential?

- Which types of users are granted access to information and resources?

Objective 1.2 Questions

70-220.01.02.001

Adventure Works is a manufacturing company. It assembles products at several locations in the southeast United States but has business offices all over the country. Many product teams require varying levels of access to internal documents and customer records. Additionally, multiple vendors and subcontractors require network access—some access inside the firewall, some external. Network administrators need to apply security constraints based on each team's unique requirements.

Currently, Adventure Works supports a mixed Windows NT Server 4 Service Pack (SP) 4 and UNIX network operating system environment and a mixed Windows 95 and 98, Windows NT Workstation 4, and UNIX client environment. IT is centrally managed with control of applications and resources distributed to lower-level IT managers. An upgrade/migration to Windows 2000 is planned for this year. While the move has many goals, some of the primary goals include:

- Install and support a single client operating system for ease of maintenance and rapid deployment

- Reduce deployment and management costs by using a single server image

- Create a centralized IT administrative model, allowing for distributed control to lower levels

- Provide interoperability with existing UNIX servers and use a common security protocol

Windows 2000 Professional provides the client operating system they need. Also, creating a single Windows 2000 Server image for rapid deployment will address that issue. What Windows 2000 features should be incorporated into the design to address the remaining goals?

A. Active Directory, DNS dynamic update, Kerberos

B. IntelliMirror, Remote Install Services, Systems Management Server

C. Active Directory, DNS, NT LAN Manager (NTLM)

D. Active Directory, IPSec, Kerberos

70-220.01.02.002

You're the network administrator for Trey Research, a subsidiary of Northwind Traders. You're in a partner relationship with Fabrikam, Inc., another subsidiary. This partnership will last between 18 and 36 months. During that time, designated Fabrikam employees must have limited access to Trey Research's Project X resources, and your Project X people must have limited access to Fabrikam's Project X resources.

With the above exception, Fabrikam and Trey Research have no shared administrative needs and don't need to access each other's resources.

All of Northwind Traders' companies are currently configured as Windows NT 4 domains. Northwind is planning an upgrade to Windows 2000 with Active Directory. You're on the Northwind Active Directory steering committee. The Northwind IT staff will be responsible for infrastructure issues, and each individual company's IT staff will be responsible for autonomous company administration.

What basic plan should you propose to facilitate the required partnership arrangements with the least amount of administrative effort?

A. Create a multidomain, single-tree forest structure with *northwindtraders.com* as the root domain. Create a Project X OU under both *treyresearch.northwindtraders.com* and *fabrikam.northwindtraders.com*. Create global groups in *treyresearch.northwindtraders.com* and *fabrikam.northwindtraders.com*, and populate the groups with the appropriate personnel. Create a universal group and populate it with the two global groups created earlier. Assign access permissions at the Project X OU level for both OUs to the universal group.

B. Create a multidomain, multiple-tree forest structure. Within the Northwind tree, create the domain structure for Northwind Traders headquarters. Within the Fabrikam tree, create the domain structure for Fabrikam, Inc. Repeat this process for each subsidiary. Create a Project X domain in both the Fabrikam and Trey Research trees. Create global groups in the Project X domains and populate the groups with the appropriate personnel. Assign access permissions at the Project X domain level for both domains to the global groups.

C. Create a single-domain, single-tree forest structure with an OU for each subsidiary. Create an additional OU under both Fabrikam and Trey Research named Project X. Create a global group containing the appropriate personnel from Fabrikam and Trey Research. Assign access permissions for the Project X OUs to the global group.

D. Create a master account domain for Northwind Traders and resource domains for the subsidiaries. Create two additional resource domains, Project X Fabrikam and Project X Trey Research. Create a global group in the Northwind Traders master account domain containing appropriate user accounts from Fabrikam and Trey Research. Assign access permissions for the Project X resource domains to the global group.

70-220.01.02.003

You're the network administrator for Wingtip Toys. Your Windows 2000 Active Directory structure is configured as a multiple-domain, single-tree model with *wingtiptoys.com* designated as the root domain. Your child domains consist of semiautonomous Wingtip Toys subsidiaries that share resources with one another but retain administrative control. You control overall network infrastructure and Active Directory maintenance issues.

Wingtip Toys has entered into a multiyear partnership with Tailspin Toys. It's rumored that merger talks are being held. You and your counterpart at Tailspin understand the need to facilitate, but tightly control, resource access between the two companies. Tailspin Toys is planning a Windows 2000 migration, and you're on the steering committee. Which Active Directory structure should you propose for the Wingtip/Tailspin relationship?

A. A multiple-tree forest. Create *tailspintoys.com* in the same forest as *wingtiptoys.com* and establish a two-way transitive trust relationship between the root domains.

B. A multiple-domain tree. Create a new root domain and establish both Wingtip Toys and Tailspin Toys as child domains. Trust relationships are automatic.

C. A multiple-domain tree. Create *wingtiptoys.tailspintoys.com* as a child domain under *wingtip.com*. Further create an OU hierarchy within *wingtiptoys.tailspintoys.com* to facilitate resource access.

D. Multiple forests. Create one-way explicit trusts between the appropriate domains of the different Active Directory directories.

Objective 1.2 Answers

70-220.01.02.001

▶ **Correct Answers: A**

A. **Correct:** Active Directory allows administrators to delegate control for specific elements within Active Directory to individuals or groups. This eliminates the need for multiple administrators to have authority over an entire domain.

DNS dynamic update protocol provides interoperability with existing UNIX servers. Dynamic update enables DNS client computers to register and dynamically update their resource records with a DNS server whenever changes occur. This reduces the need for manual administration of zone records, especially for clients who frequently move or change locations and use Dynamic Host Configuration Protocol (DHCP) to obtain an IP address.

Kerberos security, the default Windows 2000 authentication mechanism, works on both platforms. Kerberos is a multivendor standard, so it allows secure interoperability and the potential for single sign-in between Microsoft implementations and other vendor environments.

B. **Incorrect:** IntelliMirror, Remote Install Services, and Systems Management Server are client management features and automated client install and upgrade technologies. They don't address the scenario's requirements.

C. **Incorrect:** The Windows NTLM protocol is the default for authentication in Windows NT 4. It's retained in Windows 2000 for compatibility with clients and servers that are running Windows NT version 4 and earlier. It's also used to authenticate logons to stand-alone computers that are running Windows 2000. Windows 3.11, 95, 98, or Windows NT 4 must use the NTLM protocol for network authentication in Windows 2000 domains. Computers with Windows 2000 use NTLM when they are authenticating to servers that are running Windows NT 4 and when they are requesting access to resources in Windows NT 4 domains. NTLM isn't UNIX-compatible. Also, DNS by itself doesn't provide interoperability with existing UNIX servers. The dynamic update protocol is required.

D. **Incorrect:** IPSec is a Windows 2000 implementation allowing secure network communications. There is no UNIX interoperability with IPSec.

70-220.01.02.002

▶ **Correct Answers: A**

A. **Correct:** The key to this scenario is that the Northwind Traders administrators have some influence throughout the organizational structure. The proper way to design the Active Directory structure for the Northwind administrators' role is to create a multiple domain tree with Northwind as the root domain. By configuring the subsidiaries as child domains of Northwind, you eliminate the problem of inappropriate administrative access between child domains, like Fabrikam and Trey Research, while allowing the Northwind Traders administrators to have access throughout the organization. A major benefit of a Windows 2000 Active Directory structure is the ability to construct an OU hierarchy to facilitate delegation of control. In this manner, computers and services can be trusted for delegation. This means that services can make other network connections on the user's behalf without knowing the user's password. When you create two separate OUs to house the resources for the joint project, you simplify access. The universal group is designed with this in mind—when users or groups from different domains in the same forest have similar access needs.

B. **Incorrect:** Setting up a structure with multiple trees would require additional administrative effort for the Northwind Traders administrators to have administrative control over network resources. Multiple trees are only indicated in situations where no centralized control is required. This answer also suggests that access permissions be assigned to the global groups. You should never do this. You should use global groups solely to organize user accounts or to combine users who share a similar resource access profile based either on their roles in the company or on their job functions. Universal groups and domain local groups are used to assign access permissions.

C. **Incorrect:** A single domain structure isn't correct. It would require tremendous administrative effort to ensure that one group of administrators doesn't have control over inappropriate parts of the OU hierarchy. If you desire autonomous administrative control, you should use a multiple-domain architecture. This answer also incorrectly suggests assigning access permissions to global groups.

D. **Incorrect:** A master/resource domain model is a Windows NT 4 model and is replaced in Windows 2000 by the OU hierarchy concept. You might choose to structure your Windows 2000 network this way if there were some overriding need to maintain the existing Windows NT infrastructure, but this isn't indicated in our scenario. This answer also contains the global group access permission error.

70-220.01.02.003

▶ **Correct Answers: A**

A. **Correct:** A properly planned Active Directory structure can facilitate resource access while ensuring that security and administration needs are met. Active Directory accomplishes this through storing information by means of the access control. Of the several possible structures you could have chosen, the most appropriate would be a multiple-tree forest. You can make the other proposals work, but the multiple-tree forest is the solution you should recommend. Trees in a forest share a common directory schema, configuration information, and Global Catalog, which would be a collection of forest-wide data. Although the roots of the separate trees in the forest have noncontiguous DNS names, the fact that they are a part of a unified overall hierarchy enables Active Directory to resolve the names of every object in the forest efficiently. Large organizations involved in partnering relationships often use this structure to facilitate, but tightly control, partner resource access.

B. **Incorrect:** Creating a new root domain would add undesirable complexity to Wingtip's hierarchy and place Wingtip and Tailspin Toys in an administrative relationship that doesn't reflect the independent nature of the two companies. Even though merger talks are underway, it's possible that the two companies may terminate their relationship, which would render the single-tree solution unworkable. Likewise, establishing Tailspin Toys as a child domain subordinate to Wingtip doesn't reflect the relationship and would be equally inappropriate should the two companies terminate the business relationship.

C. **Incorrect:** Creating a new child domain under the Wingtip Toys root domain is incorrect for the reasons stated in B.

D. **Incorrect:** Multiple forests would impose an unnecessary administrative burden on the two companies. To allow any access between forests, explicit one-way trusts must be established. These can be difficult to establish and actively manage. Additionally, should the two companies eventually merge, a complete Active Directory restructuring would be required to allow for effective, efficient network administration.

O B J E C T I V E   1 . 3

Analyze factors that influence company strategies.

In order to analyze the factors that influence how a company does business, the first thing you must look at are the company priorities, or what the company thinks is most important to the long life of the firm. You must conduct research to ascertain exactly what a company's priorities are.

You must also get a feel for the company's projected growth and its growth strategy. In order to do this, you must look at the company's track record and compare it to its projections. This will enable you to get a handle on any new trends and practices that will affect your network design in the future.

While factoring relevant laws and regulations into your network design, the most important area in regard to security is **encryption**. Current U.S. regulations prohibit the export of 128-bit encryption. Windows 2000 supports a 128-bit encryption standard. Because of its strength, you aren't allowed to use it outside the United States without a license. Such a situation is extremely important if your network design spans countries/ regions outside the United States.

You also need to analyze and project the company's tolerance for risks and the associated costs with any security breach that might happen. This will largely depend on the type of business for which you're designing the network. For example, the security risk might be different for a small company that operates in a rural area than it would be for a large financial lender headquartered in a major metropolitan area.

Lastly, **total cost of operations (TCO)** is an important factor in putting together a network system. You need to understand the complete cost for the network startup, as well as its projected life cycle. This cost isn't just the associated cost of the software but should include hardware costs, extra labor needed for installation, user training, and other expenses.

Objective 1.3 Questions

70-220.01.03.001

Heather is configuring laptop computers for use by the sales force. The company sells proprietary products and services to a niche audience in a very competitive market. Heather's sales representatives need access to up-to-date company databases while on sales calls, and they need to be able to communicate securely with the home office. The company is extremely sensitive to the risk of having laptop computers stolen, giving proprietary company information to thieves. Also, Heather wants to ensure that any data that's transmitted is absolutely secure from network hacker attacks. How can Heather allay management concerns about risk of loss and exposure while maximizing productivity and security for her deployed sales force?

A. Configure Routing and Remote Access Service (RRAS) on a remote access server at the home office. Configure RRAS callback to use a predefined number. Use Kerberos V5 authentication. Configure Encrypting File System (EFS), providing a unique recovery key to each laptop user.

B. Configure a VPN server at the home office. Create a VPN tunnel using encryption features. Configure Distributed File System (DFS) on all laptop computers and servers.

C. Configure a VPN server at the home office. Create a VPN tunnel using encryption features. Configure EFS on all laptop computers.

D. Configure RRAS on a remote access server at the home office. Configure RRAS callback to use a specified number. Use Kerberos V5 authentication. Configure DFS, don't specify a recovery agent.

70-220.01.03.002

The marketing manager wants to expand the company's Web site to include real-time inventory data from a production database server to select customers. The operations manager is concerned with the possibility of database access from unauthorized individuals. The marketing manager comes up with the following plan:

- Employ certificate-based authentication through setting up a public key infrastructure (PKI)

- Expose the database data using Secured Sockets Layer (SSL)

- Create SQL Server logon credentials for each designated customer

As security manager, how would you rate this proposal?

A. It's an excellent proposal. Identity of the user is assured and data integrity is enforced.

B. It's a good proposal. The user's identity is assured and data integrity is enforced, but the user is limited to Microsoft browsers.

C. It's a marginal proposal. Only the server is authenticated and the logon credentials must be passed in the clear, inviting compromise.

D. It's a poor proposal. SQL Server security isn't compatible with certificate-based authentication. The proposal will not work.

70-220.01.03.003

Your company maintains a significant online presence. Your Web server has recently surpassed a utilization rate of over one million hits per day. Your company is expanding rapidly through acquisitions and mergers, and this activity is causing steady growth of Web traffic. You project that within three months the current hardware will be unable to cope with the increased traffic. Extrapolation from the marketing department indicates the current level of Web traffic should increase by a factor of at least 25 within two years.

It's imperative that current and future Web traffic be handled efficiently with minimal downtime. What strategy should you employ to handle the rapid growth?

A. Network Load Balancing

B. Windows 2000 Server Clustering

C. Multiprocessor Scaling

D. DNS Round-Robin Distribution

Objective 1.3 Answers

70-220.01.03.001

▶ **Correct Answers: C**

A. **Incorrect:** Configuring RRAS with callback security allows the administrator to regulate access to the dial-in server. This is a good thing to do, but it doesn't address the issues of securing the communication channel the way a VPN does.

B. **Incorrect:** To address the issue of secure data transmission, Heather should use VPN features. By encrypting the payload, she ensures that even if a malicious network user intercepts the transmission, the data integrity and confidentiality are assured. Creating a VPN tunnel indicates that data encryption features are enabled.

DFS is a technology that takes parts of multiple file systems and integrates them into a single hierarchical structure. This is primarily an ease of use issue and doesn't provide encryption services as dictated by our scenario.

C. **Correct:** To address the issue of secure data transmission, Heather should use VPN features. By encrypting the payload, she ensures that, even if a malicious network user intercepts the transmission, the data integrity and confidentiality are assured. Creating a VPN tunnel indicates that data encryption features are enabled.

For the laptop theft issue, Heather should use EFS features on the laptop computers. This is a technology that encrypts data on computers configured with Windows 2000 NT file system (NTFS). Now, even if a laptop does get stolen, the data on that laptop will remain confidential. For safety, EFS won't function if a recovery agent isn't designated. This protects the administrator from the disgruntled sales representative who decides to encrypt files before exiting the building.

D. **Incorrect:** Configuring RRAS with callback security allows the administrator to regulate access to the dial-in server. This is a good thing to do, but it doesn't address the issues of securing the communication channel the way a VPN does.

DFS is a technology that takes parts of multiple file systems, and integrates them into a single hierarchical structure. This is primarily an ease of use issue and doesn't provide encryption services as dictated by our scenario.

70-220.01.03.002

▶ **Correct Answers: A**

A. **Correct:** This is an excellent proposal. Certificate-based authentication enables you to have a secure Web site with the capability of certificate mapping to a specific user account on the network. You can accomplish PKI either by using Microsoft Certificate Services or by using a third-party certificate authority. You can then use SQL Server security to regulate access to the database using logon credentials supplied on the secure Web site. Then SSL can provide confidential communication between server and client.

B. **Incorrect:** All of the proposal's elements are browser-neutral. There is wide-ranging support for SSL and certificate-based authentication. SQL Server is a server-side technology that doesn't communicate directly with the browser.

C. **Incorrect:** With certificate-based authentication, both the client and server can be authenticated. From a secure site, the SQL Server logon credentials are encrypted when transmitted.

D. **Incorrect:** Barring unforeseen difficulties, the basic proposal should work well.

70-220.01.03.003

▶ **Correct Answers: A**

A. **Correct:** Of all the choices available, the best choice is Network Load Balancing. The Network Load Balancing feature of Windows 2000 Advanced Server allows you to create server clusters containing up to 32 machines. Network Load Balancing can enhance both the availability and scalability of programs used in conjunction with an Internet server. Network Load Balancing is a distributed solution that is entirely software-based, requiring no specialized hardware. It functions solely by loading the WLBS.SYS driver, which is loaded into each host in the cluster. This feature transparently distributes client requests among the hosts in the cluster, using virtual Internet Protocol (IP) addresses. You must run IIS 5.0 or another Transmission Control Protocol/Internet Protocol (TCP/IP) service on each host, and the hosts must serve the same content so that any of them can handle any request. If the content is sent via a streaming media application, then both TCP and User Datagram Protocol (UDP) must be enabled.

B. **Incorrect:** Windows 2000 Server Clustering allows you to set up applications, such as a Web server, on two servers (nodes) in a cluster. This cluster maintains its own IP address and appears to be a single device to clients. If one server should fail, the other server will transparently take over in a process known as failover. A Windows 2000 server cluster is most useful in a situation where you must ensure the reliability of one or more mission-critical applications. A Windows 2000 server cluster wouldn't meet our scenario's growth needs.

C. **Incorrect:** Multiprocessor scaling can improve throughput and performance by increasing the number of processors per computer. However, this technique alone can't hope to meet our performance and reliability requirements in the future.

D. **Incorrect:** DNS round-robin distribution is an older, less sophisticated technique for allocating requests among a group of servers. It's a good, low-cost technique for distributing requests to a small group of servers, but it wouldn't meet our scenario's needs.

O B J E C T I V E   1 . 4

Analyze business and security requirements for the end user.

In order to understand the security requirements for the end user, you must first know who that end user is. Within Windows 2000, end users are categorized into five types: regular user, roaming user, traveling user, external authenticated user, and Internet user.

Regular users are the most standard form of user. They're the ones who have specific job functions, stay at one machine throughout the day, and require access to network objects, such as printers, and application services, such as e-mail clients. The most important issue for security with regular users is what they might be accessing on the Internet and, therefore, what unwanted problems they might be bringing to the network. Another concern for regular users is how they are grouped and which group has access to which network components.

A roaming user is someone who doesn't stay at one machine but needs access to the same resources regardless of where the user is. An example would be some sort of troubleshooting team that moves from location to location and works with various other groups within the organizational network.

A traveling user might be someone who works in the field, such as a sales representative, and who needs access to certain company resources as well as the ability to update databases and file reports within the company. The security risk here is the possibility of someone introducing an unwanted component into the system, such as a virus, or the possibility that the person accessing the network isn't who that person claims to be and is possibly stealing confidential information.

An external authenticated user might be someone, such as a contract employee, who requires network access. It might also be someone who is a part of a company subsidiary, a vendor, or someone from another company with which the primary company has a temporary partnership.

An Internet user is someone who will be accessing your site on the Internet, such as a customer. You might be providing that person everything from cursory information to the ability to download software and fill out forms. The types of services that you provide for such people will greatly affect the degree of security you should assign to this group.

Objective 1.4 Questions

70-220.01.04.001

Marta is the network administrator. She has a small group of managers who often work from home and need access to the corporate intranet. Marta has installed and configured a remote access server for this purpose.

Marta needs to allow her designated users to dial in to the network, but she also needs to put a mechanism in place to ensure that *only* those users can dial in. How should she configure her network?

A. Set up proxy server on the private side of the remote access server. Configure proxy server to accept appropriate IP addresses.

B. Set up proxy server on the public side of the remote access server. Configure proxy server to accept appropriate IP addresses.

C. Configure RRAS on the remote access server to use callback. Configure callback to dial a predefined number.

D. Configure RRAS on the remote access server to use callback. Configure callback to dial the specified number.

70-220.01.04.002

You're the network administrator for Wide World Importers. Several users access the company intranet remotely through VPN connections. To thwart dictionary attacks, remote access account lockout has been enabled. After three unsuccessful connection attempts, the user can't gain access remotely for 15 minutes.

One of your users calls your office to report that she is unable to connect remotely and asks if you can solve the problem. You go to the General tab for her user account, view the Account Locked Out check box, and observe it to be cleared. The user tries again but gets the same result.

What could be the problem?

A. You must manually remove the following registry subkey on the RRAS server:

    HKEY_LOCAL_MACHINE\SYSTEM\CurrentControlSet\Services\RemoteAccess\
    Parameters\AccountLockout\domain name:<user name>.

B. The user is affected by a Windows 2000 Group Policy concerning administration of account lockout policies.

C. The replication latency interval is greater than 15 minutes.

D. From the Account tab, you must manually select Account Locked Out and then click Apply or OK. Then manually clear the Account Locked Out check box and click Apply or OK.

70-220.01.04.003

You manage several mobile sales representatives. These sales representatives carry laptop computers that contain confidential pricing schedules and proprietary information concerning company products. Whether on-site at customer locations or off-site at their hotel, the sales representatives need to establish secure communication channels with their respective regional sales offices. In order to check inventory status and place orders, they need real-time access to secure company database files. Some client locations provide analog phone lines for external access, and others allow direct access to the Internet through the company network.

Any information that is received across the communication channel and is to be stored on the laptop computers must be encrypted. Once a week, each sales representative must back up laptop data using the onboard CD-RW drive each laptop contains. Since the sales representative maintains the burned CD locally, the encryption requirement extends to the CD.

Your company doesn't maintain a server configured for dial-up access. To the maximum extent possible, you want to configure each laptop to meet these minimum requirements using software provided with the operating system to minimize support costs.

How should you configure the laptop computers to meet the requirements?

A. Install Microsoft Windows 2000 Professional. Create two dial-up networking entries: one to connect to a local Internet Service Provider (ISP) and the other to your company's VPN server. Use EFS for all local data. Use Microsoft Windows 2000 Backup and EFS to back up to the CD-RW drive.

B. Install Microsoft Windows 98, Windows ME, or Windows 2000 Professional. Create two dial-up networking entries: one to connect to a local ISP and the other to your company's VPN server. Use EFS for all local data. Use a third-party utility to perform encrypted backup to the CD-RW drive.

C. Install Microsoft Windows 98, Windows ME, or Windows 2000 Professional. Create one dial-up networking entry to connect to your company's VPN server. Use EFS for all local data. Use a third-party utility to perform encrypted backup to the CD-RW drive.

D. Install Microsoft Windows 2000 Professional. Create two dial-up networking entries: one to connect to a local ISP and the other to your company's VPN server. Use EFS for all local data. Use a third-party utility to perform encrypted backup to the CD-RW drive.

Objective 1.4 Answers

70-220.01.04.001

▶ **Correct Answers: C**

A. **Incorrect:** A proxy server acts as an intermediary between your computer and the Internet. It's most frequently used when there is a corporate intranet and users are connected to a local area network (LAN). It can also work with a firewall to provide a security barrier between your internal network and the Internet. Neither proxy server solution would work in Marta's situation. Once the user authenticates with the remote access server, the proxy server isn't necessary. If the user is unable to authenticate with the remote access server, the proxy server isn't necessary again! Besides, a proxy server would filter by IP addresses but, in all likelihood, the IP address of the client machine is going to be dynamically assigned by a DHCP server anyway.

B. **Incorrect:** This answer is incorrect for the reasons stated in A.

C. **Correct:** Marta should configure her remote access server to use callback. When you use the callback feature, the user initiates a call and connects with the remote access server. After authentication and authorization, the remote access server then drops the call and calls back a moment later to a negotiated or preassigned callback number. You can use this configuration when you have traveling users in order to cut down on long distance charges. You have three callback options to choose from: No Callback (the default), Set By Caller (specified by caller), and Always Call Back To (predefined by the administrator).

For additional security, select the Always Call Back To option and type another phone number, such as the one at the user's home. Also, make sure that callback is always configured to call back a single number for secure callback to be in place. When the user's call reaches the remote access server, the server sends a message announcing that the user will be called back. The server then disconnects and calls the user back at the preset number. Once connected, the client and server continue the connection negotiation.

You should set this option for stationary remote computers, such as those used by the managers in our scenario.

D. **Incorrect:** The Set By Caller option isn't really a security feature, because the caller can specify any number. For the callback to be secure, you need to make sure that callback is always configured to call back a single number. This increases your exposure to a malicious user who has appropriated the identity of an authorized user. So, for the sake of security, you would want to use the Always Call Back To option.

70-220.01.04.002

▶ **Correct Answers: A**

A. **Correct:** You may elect to enable remote access account lockout if there is a real or perceived threat of unauthorized remote access, especially when using VPN connections. To do this, you change certain settings in the Windows 2000 registry on the computer that provides the authentication. These two settings are MaxDenials and ResetTime. Our scenario states that these were configured for 3 attempts and 15 minutes, respectively. To unlock the account before the ResetTime has elapsed, you must manually remove the following registry entry:

```
HKEY_LOCAL_MACHINE\SYSTEM\CurrentControlSet\Services\RemoteAccess\Paramters\
AccountLockout\domain name:<user name>.
```

B. **Incorrect:** The remote access account lockout feature isn't related to the Account Locked Out check box on the Account tab on the properties of a user account or the administration of account lockout policies using Windows 2000 Group Policies.

C. **Incorrect:** Replication latency is the time in which domain controllers are unsynchronized between replication events. This isn't the correct answer because the problem isn't associated with a user account setting. Also, it's highly unlikely that the RRAS server is a domain controller.

D. **Incorrect:** This answer is incorrect for the reasons stated in B.

70-220.01.04.003

▶ **Correct Answers: A**

A. **Correct:** To meet the requirements of the scenario, install Windows 2000 Professional on all laptops. There are two scenario-driven reasons to do this. First, EFS is available only with the Windows 2000 operating system. This ensures that all local data is encrypted. Even if someone steals a laptop, the information is useless without a decryption key. Second, the Windows 2000 Backup utility (which supports CD-RW drives) allows you to retain the files in their encrypted state. No third-party utility is required.

Additionally, you should create two dial-up networking entries. One dial-up connection allows you to connect to a local ISP (remember, your company doesn't have a dial-up server). Once you've established this connection, the second dial-up entry, the VPN entry, creates a secure tunnel to your company's VPN server using the dial-up connection previously established with the ISP. This will work on-site with a phone line or off-site from the hotel. In the event you can access the Internet directly from the network, you need only use the VPN dial-up connection. Because that connection is configured with an IP address and not a phone number, secure communications are enabled without the need to dial a phone number. Note: if the network is protected by a firewall, the company your sales representative is visiting may have to create a packet filter specifically allowing VPN traffic to pass through.

B. **Incorrect:** This choice is incorrect because Windows 98 and Windows ME don't support EFS.

Once you've established a dial-up connection to a local ISP, the second dial-up entry, the VPN entry, creates a secure tunnel to your company's VPN server using the connection previously established with the ISP. This will work on-site with a phone line or off-site from the hotel. In the event you can access the Internet directly from the network, you need only use the VPN dial-up connection. Because that connection is configured with an IP address and not a phone number, secure communications are enabled without the need to dial a phone number. Note: if the network is protected by a firewall, the company your sales representative is visiting may have to create a packet filter specifically allowing VPN traffic to pass through.

C. **Incorrect:** This answer is incorrect for the reasons stated in B.

D. **Incorrect:** Once you've established a dial-up connection to a local ISP, the second dial-up entry, the VPN entry, creates a secure tunnel to your company's VPN server using the connection previously established with the ISP. This will work on-site with a phone line or off-site from the hotel. In the event you can access the Internet directly from the network, you need only use the VPN dial-up connection. Because that connection is configured with an IP address and not a phone number, secure communications are enabled without the need to dial a phone number. Note: if the network is protected by a firewall, the company your sales representative is visiting may have to create a packet filter specifically allowing VPN traffic to pass through. A third-party solution isn't necessary in this context. Use Microsoft Windows 2000 Backup and EFS to back up to the CD-RW drive.

Analyze the structure of IT management.

Within the Windows model, you have two basic types of administration, a **centralized model** and a **decentralized model**. Within the centralized model, you have the domain as the starting point for the Windows 2000 network. The Windows 2000 domain can support up to 10 million objects, such as people, hardware, or peripherals. With this object capacity, it's highly unlikely that any company will need additional domains.

With the decentralized model, administration is conducted locally. This gives each individual site more control over the daily production and policies of its network. The downside to the decentralized model is possible problems with communication, data transfer, logon difficulties, and other related problems. Whether centralized or decentralized, it's important to have a standard set of security protocols in place throughout the organization.

Outsourcing is another consideration that has both advantages and drawbacks. When you outsource certain IT tasks, you (hopefully) leave the more specific jobs to experts and let your own personnel stay on task with their IT job functions. The drawback to outsourcing is that having some people in-house and others off-site might present its own management difficulties. It also creates a potential security risk because you're exposing the network to individuals outside the company framework.

You should understand the decision-making process in an organization so you can prepare for changes. These changes can be driven by such things as corporation growth, IT and World Wide Web advances, downsizing, and other factors.

You should also understand change-management strategies so you can make any change process run as smoothly as possible.

Objective 1.5 Questions

70-220.01.05.001

Coho Winery is headquartered in New York City with four regional distribution centers located throughout the United States. Currently, all processing tasks take place on the mainframe computer in New York. This location has about 250 terminals scattered throughout the facility for access to all data and applications. The regional distribution centers each have 10 terminals connected through dedicated circuits to the mainframe for the purpose of entering sales data and accessing applications.

To improve efficiency, Coho is planning a Windows 2000 rollout throughout the company. All mainframe data will be placed on Windows 2000 servers, and existing applications will be upgraded as necessary to operate in a Windows 2000 environment. Active Directory will be used. Each regional distribution center will become an OU under the Headquarters domain. Through delegation, administration of each distribution center will be handled locally. Four administrative groups will be added to the Headquarters domain. Administrators in each region will be added to the appropriate group and those groups will be assigned appropriate permissions over the respective OUs. Each distribution center will perform all functions associated with supporting its networks of retail outlets, including inventory control, sales, and marketing. Headquarters will support and coordinate these efforts.

As Coho Winery moves to a Windows 2000 infrastructure, how would you describe the existing and envisioned IT administrative models?

A. Existing—Centralized / Envisioned—Decentralized

B. Existing—Decentralized / Envisioned—Decentralized

C. Existing—Decentralized / Envisioned—Centralized

D. Existing—Centralized / Envisioned—Centralized

70-220.01.05.002

Consolidated Messenger is a large manufacturing conglomerate consisting of five independently operating companies. Currently, the Consolidated IT staff maintains six Windows NT master account domains and six resource domains. Trust relationships are set up between the appropriate account domain and its associated resource domain. Each account domain is managed by the IT staff of that company. Consolidated IT exists primarily to provide support services to the other IT organizations.

To benefit from increased standardization and economies of scale, Consolidated has launched a Windows 2000 migration initiative. Despite large up-front costs, Consolidated believes an Active Directory migration will pay off in a more efficient administrative function with better control and increased standardization.

Consolidated Messenger wants to have more centralized control of user accounts and leave control of resources to local personnel. Consolidated will take over infrastructure and support issues and handle all personnel issues related to benefits. The local IT staff will maintain on-site assets and handle all local personnel issues, including staffing responsibilities.

How would you characterize the existing and envisioned IT structure at Consolidated Messenger?

A. Existing—Decentralized / Envisioned—Centralized

B. Existing—Decentralized / Envisioned—Decentralized

C. Existing—Centralized / Envisioned—Centralized

D. Existing—Centralized / Envisioned—Decentralized

70-220.01.05.003

In the 15 years Contoso, Ltd., has been in business, it has grown from a single manufacturing facility to 14 separate facilities located in 4 countries/regions. During this period of growth and expansion, Contoso hasn't kept pace with technological advances in the field of computer networking infrastructure. Network operations are highly fragmented, with network configurations evolving spontaneously at each location with little regard to standardization or interoperability. Contoso has grown from a single production line manufacturing company to a conglomerate encompassing manufacturing, insurance, financial services, and consulting. In an effort to control costs and increase productivity, Contoso is embarking on a project to incorporate Microsoft Windows 2000 company-wide within 18 months. You're heading up the task force. After six weeks of committee meetings and executive-level directives, you've distilled the following pertinent facts:

■ Company headquarters in Atlanta will coordinate and install network infrastructure elements. The IT staff in Atlanta will control infrastructure issues in the future.

■ Local network administrators will have no administrative control over networks from other locations.

■ The Contoso network administrator will gain administrative access to all network resources, but local administration will be handled through delegation of authority.

■ Contoso's legal department must ensure compliance with all regulatory requirements imposed on Contoso's insurance and financial services components, particularly as they relate to international business.

It's now your job to recommend an appropriate Active Directory architecture that takes these factors into account. Base your recommendation on security requirements, administrative control, and access control issues. Which of the following is the most simplified model that effectively addresses your requirements?

A. Multiple-domain tree in a single forest with multiple OU hierarchies

B. Single-domain tree in a single forest with an OU hierarchy

C. Multiple-tree forest

D. Master-user domain/multiple-resource domain

Objective 1.5 Answers

70-220.01.05.001

▶ **Correct Answers: D**

A. **Incorrect:** Neither of the IT environments is an example of a decentralized model. There is no departmental server structure specific to each business area. The existing mainframe processing structure doesn't support a decentralized model, and the envisioned Windows 2000 model would have to be structured in such a way as to have separate IT departments in the different regions, which isn't the case here.

B. **Incorrect:** This answer is incorrect for the reasons stated in A.

C. **Incorrect:** This answer is incorrect for the reasons stated in A.

D. **Correct:** Any time a mainframe computer provides all processing power, you're constrained to operate within a centralized model. In our scenario, all processing and administration takes place in New York, with the distribution centers doing little more than providing input. This is a classic centralized IT model.

With the envisioned model, Active Directory provides the ability for higher-level administrators to delegate control for specific elements within Active Directory to individuals, groups, computers, and other OUs. This eliminates the need for multiple administrators to have authority over an entire domain. Don't be fooled by the relative autonomy afforded the distribution centers. IT functions can remain centralized when administrative authority is delegated from the central unit to the local level.

70-220.01.05.002

▶ **Correct Answers: A**

A. **Correct:** The current structure would suggest a decentralized environment. Consolidated Messenger has no control over the day-to-day issues at the subsidiary companies, a condition resulting from the domain structure. It appears that the IT staff exists solely to support Consolidated's headquarters and to provide limited support services to the subsidiary companies. Following the migration, the structure takes a definite shift toward centralization. Even though a high degree of autonomy continues to exist at the subsidiary companies, Consolidated IT has assumed a controlling role, allowing authority to be delegated to the subsidiary companies.

B. **Incorrect:** The existing structure has no discernable elements of centralized control. Likewise, the envisioned structure has all the elements of a centralized IT structure, with appropriate delegation of control elements. It isn't correct to characterize the envisioned structure as decentralized even though the subsidiaries maintain control over day-to-day matters.

C. **Incorrect:** This answer is incorrect for the reasons stated in A.

D. **Incorrect:** This answer is incorrect for the reasons stated in A.

70-220.01.05.003

▶ **Correct Answers: A**

A. **Correct:** Since we haven't established a compelling reason to use a multiple-tree structure, the best fit for our scenario is a multiple-domain single-tree structure. By using a single tree, we've made it a simple matter to delegate administration of resources to local administrators. An OU hierarchy simplifies resource access and allows for effective delegation of control. For example, you can assign security duties for an OU to a departmental administrator. This will give the person who's most responsible for allocating network resources the most power in making those decisions. By incorporating multiple domains, you can comply with certain locations' regulatory requirements without imposing unnecessarily strict guidelines on the rest of your network population.

B. **Incorrect:** The existing fragmented network structure follows a decentralized model. Little, if any, control is exercised from corporate headquarters over the different network environments. The proposed structure will have a much higher level of centralized control, with elements of decentralization propagating downward through the hierarchy. Different countries/regions impose different regulatory requirements, specifically in the financial services areas. In a Windows 2000 Active Directory environment, the domain serves as the primary security boundary. It's highly likely that different locations will have different security requirements (such as password requirements and access control requirements), so we know that a single domain environment isn't appropriate.

C. **Incorrect:** The primary reason to incorporate a multiple-tree structure is to accommodate distinct DNS names. The security risk associated with DNS is that it serves as a prominent target for hackers. This is because DNS would make available the IP address of every host on the network. This was never alluded to as part of our scenario. It may also be appropriate to incorporate multiple trees if you're involved in partnering relationships where you must tightly control resource access. Clearly, the multiple-tree model isn't the most simplified model that meets your requirements.

D. **Incorrect:** The master-user domain/multiple-resource domain model is an outmoded structure that was widely used in network configurations prior to Windows 2000. Unless you have an existing Windows NT 4 structure that you want to retain, this model is effectively obsolete.

OBJECTIVE 1.6

Analyze the current physical model and information security model.

To be prepared to thwart unwanted attack, you must first understand the scope of security risks and then decide what products or strategies will work best for your needs. To make the right choices, you must first understand the two most basic types of security risks: internal and external.

Internal risks probably comprise the greatest risk and are the most common type of risk to the network. Employees who have limited computing capacities but insist on having their machines "their way" are a significant threat because they may compromise your security just by trying to set things up the way they like them. Disgruntled employees seeking to sabotage resources are always a threat, as well as employees who are just "messing around."

External risks are anything from one person who accesses your network once to hackers who are specifically trying to gain access to remove confidential information or cause some type of data destruction. Understanding what kind of external access is available is the first step to protecting your network from a potential threat.

In addition to categorizing risks, you should always take your analysis one step further and identify risks. The best time for this is always before an attack takes place. Having formalized discussions with colleagues is the best step toward preventative maintenance. Once your network has been compromised, recognizing what type of attack you encountered is of little help.

Objective 1.6 Questions

70-220.01.06.001

Loren is analyzing potential security risks to her network. Her mobile users have Windows 2000 Professional installed on their laptops. These users need access to sensitive client and company information while they're at client sites making sales and support calls. These users dial in to a remote access server twice a day in order to access public and private data on the company intranet.

Her remote access server is also the company Web server, the sole connection point to the Internet. The intranet uses a proxy server to regulate access to the Internet, and there is a firewall in place on the private side of the proxy.

What is Loren's primary threat and what are some strategies to counter it?

A. The primary threat is external. Authenticate laptop users with Remote Authentication Dial-In User Service (RADIUS). Establish callback security with RRAS.

B. The primary threat is internal. Secure server-to-server communications with IPSec policies. Authenticate all users with Kerberos.

C. The primary threat is a combination of internal and external factors. Secure laptop data with NTFS permissions. Secure external communications with Secure/Multipurpose Internet Mail Extensions (S/MIME). Authenticate external users with database verification. Authenticate internal users with Kerberos. Secure internal communications with SSL.

D. The primary threat is external. Secure laptop data with EFS, and secure laptop communications with a VPN.

70-220.01.06.002

You're the senior network administrator at Graphic Design Institute. You're in charge of a classified, high-visibility project. Because the nature of your industry is highly competitive, any leakage of information could doom the project and cost the company millions of dollars in lost revenue.

You've conducted a risk assessment of the project and have determined that you can delegate responsibility for five major subareas to trusted personnel in five geographically separate remote sites. Your objective is to deal one-on-one with each of these five project leaders. To minimize the potential for information compromise, you've decided that each project leader should be concerned only with that person's direct area of responsibility. You'll collate relevant information from the five key personnel and give sanitized summaries to each, briefing them on overall project status but withholding "unnecessary" details. The overriding principle for this project is "need to know," and nobody but you has a "need to know."

Given the need to maintain a high level of secrecy, how would you rate your approach to risk management?

A. This is a poor approach. The loss of one or more key personnel at a critical point in the process could result in failure.

B. This is a poor approach. Without a well-conceived "risk-driven" schedule, you reduce the time available to resolve complex problems.

C. This is a good approach. By proceeding based on your risk assessment, you maximize your chances for a successful deployment.

D. This is an excellent approach. By maintaining centralized control, you can more readily influence the factors affecting the project without exposing the decision-making process.

70-220.01.06.003

Users have been reporting a variety of computer problems, and you suspect some sort of virus or other external phenomenon. After troubleshooting, you believe the problem to be isolated to users who have accessed a particular Web site on the Internet. In addition, it appears to affect only users of Microsoft browsers.

What is the most likely category of threat this problem represents?

A. Malicious mobile code

B. Trojan horse

C. Macro virus

D. Denial of service

Objective 1.6 Answers

70-220.01.06.001

▶ **Correct Answers: D**

A. **Incorrect:** This answer suggesting RADIUS authentication and callback security is only partially viable. RRAS supports RADIUS, which makes it possible to manage remote user authentication through a variety of authentication protocols. Callback security ensures that you can control the phone number the server is instructed to call, which reduces the threat of an identity thief compromising a valid user account. However, both these techniques address only the issue of authentication. The encryption requirement for hard disk data isn't addressed, nor is the necessity for confidential communications.

B. **Incorrect:** In the absence of any amplifying data, you can't safely assume that any threat to the internal network is primary. Securing server-to-server communications with IPSec policies and using Kerberos to authenticate users is probably a good idea, but our scenario does not warrant it.

C. **Incorrect:** The answer suggesting a combination of factors is likewise incorrect. NTFS permissions don't go far enough in securing physical data. There are ways a malicious user can bypass NTFS to get at the underlying (unencrypted) text. The S/MIME protocol ensures the integrity, origin, and confidentiality of e-mail messages. Other communications are unaffected.

SSL is normally associated with providing secure access to a Web site, because it provides message integrity, data encryption, and server authentication. It's also utilized for credit card transaction over the Internet. Applications must be SSL-enabled to benefit from SSL.

Kerberos is the Windows 2000 standard user authentication mechanism. This can be used for both internal and external authentication purposes.

D. **Correct:** Security risks manifest themselves in a variety of forms, but a thorough understanding of the different types of network attacks that may be attempted should assist the administrator in minimizing these risks. Any security plan is, by necessity, a compromise between flexibility and security. Prioritizing any perceived threats would help in determining the levels of risk and those areas that require special attention.

In Loren's situation the primary threat is external. Sensitive material resides on laptop computers, and sensitive communications originate from those computers. To combat attacks against our mobile workforce, we must perform a number of tasks. We must protect the data residing on the laptop's disk structure, ensure that we know the identities of the laptop users, and be able to transmit secure data over an unsecured channel. Doing this requires the use of a couple of technologies.

EFS provides confidentiality for the sensitive client and company data on the laptop computers. Using public key technology, we can be assured that only the owner of a file has access to it. Unauthorized access attempts result in an Access Denied message. For safety, recovery agents are specified in case the authorized user has technical problems that make the user unable to open a protected file. With Windows 2000, the default recovery agent is the Administrator account.

A VPN provides a simple answer to the problem of data integrity and confidentiality. A VPN is the extension of a private network that encompasses links over public networks like the Internet. A VPN enables you to send data between two computers in a way that appears to be a point-to-point private link. To emulate a point-to-point link, data is encapsulated, or wrapped, with routing information allowing it to cross the public network to reach its endpoint. The data being sent is encrypted for confidentiality. Packets that are intercepted are unreadable without the encryption keys. The link in which the private data is encapsulated and encrypted is known as a VPN connection.

70-220.01.06.002

▶ **Correct Answers: A**

A. **Correct:** Many factors play a part in a successful project. Critical to any project is a thorough risk-assessment analysis. A risk-management plan helps you identify potential problem areas and provides a plan of action should a problem occur. In order to assess risk correctly, you need to determine your network's assets, assign a value to each, determine all possible security threats, and then ascertain the risk probability.

A risk-management plan can do many things, including reduce the likelihood that a risk factor will actually occur, reduce the magnitude of the loss if a risk does occur, change the consequences of a risk, and prepare the administrator to migrate risk during deployment.

In our scenario, only a single key player knows all the factors affecting the project. If this player (you) leaves during a critical time in the deployment, the project's failure is almost guaranteed. This factor alone makes your approach to risk management a poor one.

B. **Incorrect:** Although it's true that a well-conceived schedule is critical to the success of any complex project, our scenario doesn't provide us with any indication that such a schedule is missing.

C. **Incorrect:** A risk assessment helps you plan for potential risks before they occur. Since the loss of yourself would seriously jeopardize the project, your risk assessment is faulty and won't maximize your chances of a successful deployment. This isn't a good approach.

D. **Incorrect:** This isn't an excellent approach. Even though your approach has merit, it could be made much more viable by training a backup for each key expert and keeping documentation up-to-date and accessible.

70-220.01.06.003

▶ **Correct Answers: A**

A. **Correct:** IT managers today face a variety of network security problems. These problems range from intruders invading computer systems with stolen passwords or spoofed IP addresses to malicious code and destructive programs. The threat scenario represents such an occurrence. In this case the evidence leads us to believe that the problem is of the malicious mobile code variety. This threat is defined as code running as an autoexecuted ActiveX control downloaded from a Web page. Since the damage appears limited to Microsoft browsers, the problem is most likely a rogue ActiveX control.

B. **Incorrect:** A Trojan horse is a malicious utility masquerading as a harmless and desirable utility. These programs often come with an extension of .exe. Unlike an ActiveX control, which can download from a Web page automatically, depending on your browser's security settings, a Trojan horse is specifically activated—the most common scenario being receiving one as an e-mail attachment.

C. **Incorrect:** A macro virus is one that exploits the built-in programming interface (macro language) of a sophisticated application, such as Microsoft Word or Microsoft Excel. An infected document or spreadsheet can activate a chunk of code (often written in Visual Basic Scripting Edition, the macro language of the Microsoft Office suite of products) with potentially damaging results. Your best defense is to disable macros on a suspect application file. It's worth noting, though, that macro viruses could be written for browsers as well, therefore disabling any browser application once it comes into contact with the problem site.

D. **Incorrect:** A denial of service attack is different from the other three. In this case the intruder floods a server with requests, consuming excess system resources. This type of attack can bring down the server or make its performance so sluggish that you can't do any useful work. In some cases a server crash leaves a system vulnerable to further penetration. Every once in a while you hear about a problem with a major site in which it goes down for hours or, sometimes, days. This is often the result of a denial of service attack.

Analyzing Technical Requirements

Although any network design should begin with a discussion of business requirements, the core of realizing your design and implementation needs is the analysis of your situation's technical requirements.

One component you'll need to consider is a hardware and software inventory of your organization. The hardware inventory consists of documenting all your peripherals, such as modems, printers, routers, scanners, and any other hardware pieces. As part of this inventory, you should take note of any and all drivers and their version numbers, basic input/output system (BIOS) settings, and any configuration-related information. For the software inventory, you need to record all applications, their version numbers, and any dynamic link libraries (DLLs) that are associated with these applications. A host of third-party applications will provide this information for you. You might consider using one of these applications when undertaking this task.

Other specifics will be covered later in this chapter.

Tested Skills and Suggested Practices

The skills that you need to successfully master the Analyzing Technical Requirements objective domain on the *Designing Security for a Microsoft Windows 2000 Network* exam include:

- **Evaluating the company's existing and planned technical environment.**

    - Practice 1: Create a physical network diagram of the existing network. Also, create a physical network diagram that illustrates remote locations if they exist for your particular network structure.

    - Practice 2: Create a logical network diagram of the existing network. With this diagram you can look at the configuration and management components of what you have to work with.

- **Analyzing the impact of the security design on the existing and planned technical environment.**

  - Practice 1: Use the Windows 2000 Security, Configuration, and Analysis Tool to check configuration settings with the standard security template that you're using. After doing that, use the tool to import a security template into a Group Policy object (GPO) and apply the security profile to more than one machine on the network.

  - Practice 2: Develop a network plan in relation to your organization's perceived growth model. Begin by asking the following questions: What will be the amount of new sites for the following year, as well as the following two years? What are the size and capacity of each network at each site? How many users will need network access in the following year and in the following two years? How many new servers are required?

Further Reading

This section lists supplemental readings by objective. We recommend that you study these sources thoroughly before taking exam 70-220.

Objective 2.1

Microsoft Corporation. *Windows 2000 Server Resource Kit*. Volume: *Microsoft Windows 2000 Server Deployment Planning Guide*. Redmond, Washington: Microsoft Press, 2000. Review the "Creating a Project Plan" section in Chapter 2, "Creating a Deployment Roadmap." This section covers the steps you should take to form your Windows 2000 deployment project plan.

Microsoft Corporation. *Windows 2000 Server Resource Kit*. Volume: *Microsoft Windows 2000 Server Deployment Planning Guide*. Redmond, Washington: Microsoft Press, 2000. Review the "Determining Goals and Objectives" section in Chapter 2, "Creating a Deployment Roadmap." This section raises some of the questions you should answer in your Windows 2000 deployment plan.

Objective 2.2

Microsoft Corporation. *Windows 2000 Server Resource Kit*. Volume: *Microsoft Windows 2000 Server Deployment Planning Guide*. Redmond, Washington: Microsoft Press, 2000. Review the "Risk Assessment" section in Chapter 3, "Planning for Deployment." This section details some areas of risk that a risk management plan in conjunction with your deployment plan can mitigate.

Microsoft Corporation. *Windows 2000 Server Resource Kit*. Volume: *Microsoft Windows 2000 Server Deployment Planning Guide*. Redmond, Washington: Microsoft Press, 2000. Review the "Using the Lab for Risk Management" section in Chapter 4, "Building a Windows 2000 Test Lab." This section covers how you can utilize your Windows 2000 test lab to control and mitigate risks in your production environment.

OBJECTIVE 2.1

Evaluate the company's existing and planned technical environment.

Before you begin analyzing the technical environment, you might want to consider obtaining and using a few tools that will help you do it. One of these tools is **Systems Management Server (SMS)**. You can use SMS to produce detailed analyses of hardware and software configurations and placement, as well as the applications that are currently being used in the infrastructure.

As long as you have Windows Management Instrumentation (WMI) in place on an existing Windows NT network, you can obtain a variety of third-party applications that can help you in your network analysis as well.

One component of this task will be creating a physical network diagram. Items that you need to include in this diagram are as follows:

- All the servers that are currently included in the network: their type, name, and role in the network

- The location of all peripherals and devices, such as switches, hubs, routers, bridges, and modems (be explicit about location, such as "in the back closet")

- All the physical communication links and their configurations

- The number of users and mobile users at each site

- WAN Communication links

In addition to the physical network diagram, you should have a logical network diagram. A logical network diagram illustrates the following:

- Details of trust relationships

- All operating systems used, such as UNIX, NetWare, Windows NT, Windows 2000, and Mac OS

- The role that each server plays

- The domain architecture

These two diagrams will allow you to form the basis of your technical analysis. From here you can begin to decide what should go where and how your overall design will work out based on the organization's requirements.

In addition to looking at the physical and logical structure, you also need to ascertain bandwidth capacities and restrictions. Upgrading to Windows 2000 will certainly affect your bandwidth usage. Having some of the following information will prepare you for this:

- Link speed in regard to remote sites

- Amount of external link traffic

- Amount of internal traffic

- Type of network wiring being used

- Hub and cabling speed and throughput data

It's also important to understand how data and systems will be accessed. In regard to security, Windows 2000 supports **Public Key Infrastructure (PKI)**. PKI forms the backbone of the Windows 2000 distributed security services.

Remember that the backward compatibility of Windows NT to Windows 2000 makes authentication requests easier and also facilitates moving from a Windows NT domain controller to a Windows 2000 domain controller in a mixed OS environment.

Additionally, it will be important to identify administrative roles within the structure you're creating. Make sure that all personnel fit into one of the five following types: administrative, user, service, resource ownership, and application.

Objective 2.1 Questions

70-220.02.01.001

Amy is supervising a migration from Windows NT Server 4 to Windows 2000. The company headquarters is in Denver, with nine regional distribution centers located throughout North America and Europe. All user accounts are maintained centrally, and various security mechanisms have been employed to ensure that users with access rights to resources in one region don't obtain rights to resources in another region. Servers in the distribution centers need to communicate securely with their outlet locations and with headquarters. Also, each region maintains a Web presence, handling a high volume of Web-based SSL-enabled transactions, which is used to authenticate clients.

Amy has analyzed these and other factors and must create an efficient, effective forest design. Which security requirement will affect the design of the forest plan?

A. Kerberos V5 authentication services

B. Secure Web transactions

C. Secure communication between servers

D. Organization of user accounts

70-220.02.01.002

Rob is the network administrator for a toy manufacturer based in Atlanta. His company, Wingtip Toys, has three manufacturing facilities located in geographically dispersed regions throughout the southeastern United States. These facilities are connected to the home office by 256 kilobits per second (Kbps) dedicated WAN links. Wingtip Toys has recently entered into a partnership agreement with Tailspin Toys in Vienna in order to expand internationally. Tailspin Toys has several manufacturing plants located throughout Europe, all connected to the main office in Vienna by an X.25 network. Both companies have standardized on Windows 2000.

Wingtip Toys and Tailspin Toys each have a handful of designated users who require access to both networks. Most of these users are traveling sales representatives who require dial-up access. Rob's strategy is to set up a VPN server at each location. Each VPN server will have three interfaces—one connected to the internal network, one set up as an on-demand router-to-router VPN connection (to handle home office to corporate office traffic), and one exposed to the Internet (to handle dial-up traffic).

How should Rob protect the Internet interface of the VPN servers from unauthorized users?

A. Ensure that a routing protocol is bound to the interface. Regulate access to the Internet through static routing. Use IPSec filtering to set input and output permit filters for L2TP and Internet Key Exchange (IKE). Configure packet filtering in the remote access policy profile for user groups, permitting or denying certain types of IP traffic.

B. Ensure that no routing protocol is bound to the interface. Regulate access to the corporate network through static routing. Use RRAS filters to set input and output permit filters for L2TP and IKE. Configure packet filtering in the remote access policy profile for user groups, permitting or denying certain types of IP traffic.

C. Ensure that no routing protocol is bound to the interface. Regulate access to the corporate network through static routing. Use dynamic DNS updates to ensure that dial-up clients are properly registered. Configure packet filtering in the remote access policy profile for user groups, permitting or denying certain types of IP traffic.

D. Ensure that no routing protocol is bound to the interface. Regulate access to the Internet through static routing. Use IPSec filtering to set input and output permit filters for L2TP and PPTP. Configure packet filtering in the remote access policy profile for user groups, permitting or denying certain types of IP traffic.

70-220.02.01.003

Charlie is the network administrator for Contoso, Ltd., a rapidly expanding financial services company. Contoso is headquartered in Muskogee, Oklahoma, and has 58,000 users there. It has three regional offices: Bend, Oregon, with 37,000 users; Skeeter Flats, Louisiana, with 8,500 users; and Tundra, Maine, with 14,500 users. Each of these offices is connected to Muskogee by a T1 connection. Bandwidth utilization on all three lines is heavy to very heavy, with the Bend connection consistently running above 90 percent of capacity.

Contoso operates a single Active Directory tree, with Muskogee on top and the three regional offices configured as OUs under that. Each satellite office is organized as an OU under the appropriate regional office. Many dynamic events take place at Contoso throughout the day, and replication traffic is a significant percentage of the total traffic.

Some administrative control is delegated to the regional offices, but Charlie maintains centralized control from Muskogee. He makes extensive use of Group Policies to help him conform to the many requirements that govern Contoso's business. All domain controllers are 500 MHz quad-processor Pentium III computers with 512 MB of RAM.

As more users and services are added, the bandwidth problem is exacerbated. The entire network is affected, but the Bend office feels the symptoms first. The Bend office services approximately 350 satellite offices with 15–25 users per satellite. All computers in the satellite offices are equipped with Windows 2000 Professional. The satellites are connected to the regional offices by 256 Kbps WAN links. Users in the satellite offices are starting to complain about long delays during logon. The Bend office has a Windows 2000 server configured as a domain controller.

Charlie must maintain an acceptable level of network performance that continues to provide the necessary security level. What strategy should Charlie employ to meet his goal?

A. Add domain controllers to the satellite offices to facilitate logging on locally. Adjust the Group Policy slow link detection setting to set Administrative Templates to Off.

B. Add an additional domain controller to the Bend office.

C. Adjust the Group Policy slow link settings to set Administrative Templates, Folder Redirection, and Internet Explorer Maintenance to Off.

D. Disable background refresh of Group Policy.

70-220.02.01.004

Clair administers a Windows NT 4 network. She is preparing for a Windows 2000 migration and needs to assess security requirements for application access. Her new domain controllers will receive clean installs, but all other servers will be upgraded to Windows 2000 Server and all workstations will be upgraded to Windows 2000 Professional.

Clair needs to maintain several mission-critical legacy desktop applications that aren't Windows 2000 certified. What actions can Clair take to enable existing users to run these legacy applications? (Choose all that apply.)

A. Apply the compatibility security template from the command line as follows:

```
secedit /configure /DB compatws.sdb /CFG compatws.inf
```

B. Register the legacy applications at *www.microsoft.com/windows2000/upgrade/compat/search/ software.asp* to enable the applications to run under the User context.

C. Instruct the users to run the application as a service under the Local System context.

D. Modify the security context on the upgraded workstations to default Windows 2000 security settings from a command prompt as follows:

```
secedit /configure /DB basicwk.sdb /CFG basicwk.inf /log basicwk.log/verbose
```

E. Modify the security context on the upgraded servers to default Windows 2000 security settings from a command prompt as follows:

```
secedit /configure /DB basicsv.sdb /CFG basicsv.inf /log basicsv.log/verbose
```

F. Add the affected users to the Power Users group.

Objective 2.1 Answers

70-220.02.01.001

▶ **Correct Answers: C**

A. **Incorrect:** Kerberos is the default Windows 2000 authentication mechanism. It will adapt to whatever forest structure you design.

B. **Incorrect:** Secure Web transactions involve SSL technology and aren't really dependent on placement within the forest. Typically, they can be plugged into the Active Directory directory service structure where they are most convenient.

C. **Correct:** Two areas to keep in mind when you're creating forests and domains in a Windows 2000 environment are replication traffic and resource access. In our scenario server security requirements have the most direct impact on our forest design. If you have servers that must communicate securely, it's generally advised to place them into their own OU, allowing you to apply the appropriate security policies at the OU level. The typical OU-level security settings that you should keep in mind in this situation are: User Rights, File/Registry discretionary access control lists (DACLs), Audit/Event Logs, Local Policy, and EFS Policy.

D. **Incorrect:** User accounts are very flexible. You can put users where you want them for administrative purposes. You can further accomplish delegation of control with users by delegating administration for a domain within the forest. For resource access considerations, use security groups to regulate access. It doesn't matter where in the forest you place the security groups, and they can contain users from anywhere in the forest.

70-220.02.01.002

▶ **Correct Answers: B**

A. **Incorrect:** Don't bind a routing protocol to the Internet interface because this will potentially allow access to internal routers that shouldn't be visible from the Internet.

Static routing wouldn't be appropriate for Internet access. A routing protocol is required.

You would use RRAS filters (which consist of IP and Internet Packet Exchange [IPX] packet filtering), not IPSec filtering, to secure the interface. Also, you wouldn't use both L2TP and PPTP. These are different tunneling protocols. Instead, you would most likely use L2TP over IPSec (L2TP/IPSec) for router-to-router VPN connections. L2TP provides higher security and is the standard for Windows 2000 installations.

B. **Correct:** Rob can protect the Internet-exposed interface on the VPN server from unauthorized users by first ensuring that no routing protocol is bound to the interface. The corporate network needs to be accessed through static routes. In addition to utilizing static routes, you should also implement packet filters to control where traffic goes throughout the network. Use Active Directory to manage access controls to the services being used. Do this by applying centrally managed access control and authentication policies. Next, you'll need to have a routing protocol running on the corporate network interface. Finally, use RRAS filters (not IPSec filtering) on the Internet interface to set input and output permit filters for L2TP and the IKE protocol, prohibiting everything but L2TP over IPSec (L2TP/IPSec) traffic. Then, configure packet filtering in the remote access policy profile for user groups, permitting or denying certain types of IP traffic. These filters are configured when you use the RRAS setup wizard. No configuration by the user is required.

C. **Incorrect:** Don't bind a routing protocol to the Internet interface because this will potentially allow access to internal routers that shouldn't be visible from the Internet.

Dynamic DNS updates allow for your DNS zone records to be updated dynamically, freeing the administrator from the overhead of trying to manually update DNS records when clients are dynamically assigned IP addresses. The issue here is that IP addresses are automatically entered. Therefore, there's no control over how IP addresses are being entered, modified, or both, in the DNS zone. Overall, this doesn't protect an Internet-exposed VPN server interface.

D. **Incorrect:** This answer is incorrect for the reasons stated in A.

70-220.02.01.003

▶ **Correct Answers: B**

A. **Incorrect:** Given the large number of satellite offices (and the associated administrative overhead) it wouldn't be prudent to place domain controllers in each satellite. The increase in replication traffic would more than offset any benefit.

B. **Correct:** Charlie's biggest problem is an inadequate number of domain controllers available to facilitate logons. Based on testing, domain controllers configured as in our scenario should be able to handle up to 17,000 interactive user logons within a 10-minute period. In fact, Contoso should only need eight domain controllers in the entire organization. For our scenario, adding an additional domain controller to the Bend office ensures high availability and fault tolerance. The Group Policy setting Group Policy Refresh Interval For Domain Controllers should also be enabled in this context.

C. **Incorrect:** Adjusting the Group Policy slow link detection setting would be ineffective. The bottleneck in the system is a shortage of domain controllers. Besides, you aren't able to set the Administrative Templates setting to Off.

D. **Incorrect:** Unless purposely misconfigured, background refresh of Group Policy shouldn't significantly affect network traffic. By default, this is done every 90 minutes with a randomized offset of up to 30 minutes, or when the user logs off.

70-220.02.01.004

▶ **Correct Answers: A and F**

A. **Correct:** Legacy desktop applications that ran under a User context on Windows NT 4 will probably have to run under a Power User context on a Windows 2000-based system. In practice, members of the Users group won't be able to run most legacy applications because most legacy applications weren't designed with operating system security in mind. Power Users are ranked between Administrators and Users in terms of system access. The default Windows 2000 security settings for Power Users are backward compatible with the default security settings for Users in Windows NT 4.

However, the Power Users group gives users more access than they had under Windows NT 4. Specifically, members of this group can install and remove applications that don't install system services on their computers and customize system-wide resources (for example, System Time, Display Settings, Shares, Power Configuration, and Printers). They can also have Modify access to %windir% and %windir%\system32.

If you don't want your users to have this additional power, you can apply a security template that exists for just this purpose. In addition, you can have the administrator assign any specific privilege that the user might require.

You can apply the template to a system with the Security Configuration Toolset using the following syntax:

```
secedit /configure /cfg compatws.inf /db compatws.sdb
```

This has the effect of reducing the system's security level somewhat in order to allow the access required by some legacy applications.

B. **Incorrect:** You can check to see if your applications meet the Windows 2000 criteria, and even find out what you need to do to have your application tested by going to the Web site in one of the answers, but you can't register your legacy applications there.

C. **Incorrect:** Running the application as a service is incorrect. Not all applications are designed to run as a service, and members of the Users or Power Users groups can't install services. If users install programs that don't install system services, access to those programs can only be obtained through whichever user installed the program.

D. **Incorrect:** Default Windows 2000 security settings aren't applied on machines that are upgraded from a previous operating system version. The administrator can run the secedit executable to apply the Windows 2000 default security settings after the upgrade has been completed. However, this procedure doesn't provide the capability required by our scenario.

E. **Incorrect:** This answer is incorrect for the reasons given in D.

F. **Correct:** This answer is correct for the reasons stated in A.

OBJECTIVE 2.2

Analyze the impact of the security design on the existing and planned technical environment.

To understand how the new network design will integrate into the existing one, you'll need to assess the existing systems and their subsequent applications.

One type of application you need to assess to ensure security is virus detection software. You need to see what the organization has in place and whether it's currently updated to thwart any of the latest viruses and bugs.

Another application you need to assess is the current use of firewalls. You should use whatever strategies you deem necessary to screen the existing firewall setup for its reliability. One way is to screen requests to make sure they're originating from the appropriate sender, with all packet header information enclosed.

You also need to look at how the organization currently handles planned upgrades and rollouts. Every new introduction of an application or a piece of hardware has security implications. The best thing to do is to decide on a set series of applications to use and then to stick with it. Before any new application is introduced, you should scrutinize it to make sure no security risks might result from its use. You can always use a variety of channels such as the Microsoft Web site or magazines and newsletters to alert you of potential problems with existing applications.

You'll also need to take a look at how the current support structure is organized. Different sets of users have different support requirements. While some users may be advanced in terms of using their applications and equipment, others may not be. You also need to ascertain the degree to which your support structure both improves network security and creates a network security risk.

You also need to consider the systems management and planning model in both the existing structure and the planned structure. Make sure you're aware of the potential downside of increased security components and precautions. For instance, you may implement passwords and smart cards, which can be forgotten, lost, or used by another party to compromise your network structure.

Objective 2.2 Questions

70-220.02.02.001

Paul is the network administrator for the computer learning center at a college. He's responsible for maintaining the network lab reserved for student use as well as the college administrative network. The lab consists of a mix of computers running Windows NT 4 Server and Workstation. Every five weeks, Paul must reconfigure the lab for the next crop of students, and every day Paul must ensure the computers are configured properly for that day's events.

The students store their lab files on floppy disks, and each student has a personal home folder on an NTFS partition on the lab server. The students run a variety of applications, both server-based and desktop. Lab computers have Internet access. Access to resources is controlled through the Users group, to which all students belong. This has proven to be a suitable arrangement from a security standpoint, even though the occasional overzealous student might tamper with and sometimes delete critical files on lab workstations. This isn't a major problem because the damage is limited to the workstation, and Paul can easily rebuild a lab workstation from a server-based image.

Paul has been charged with upgrading the lab to Windows 2000. He plans to perform fresh installs on all machines. Most applications aren't Windows 2000 certified. Paul knows he will need to make some changes to the existing security level to allow the students to have sufficient access to run legacy applications. He has identified four courses of action, each one allowing the students to function in the proposed lab environment. Which choice gives the students the most freedom with the least likelihood of getting Paul into trouble?

A. Put the students into the Power Users group.

B. Leave the students in the Users group. Use only Windows 2000 certified applications, even if this means that there's no direct replacement for some programs currently in use.

C. Leave the students in the Users group. Use the Security Configuration Toolset to apply the compatibility security template.

D. Ensure that the lab is physically isolated from the college administrative network. Add the Users group to the Administrators group.

70-220.02.02.002

Mike is the network administrator for Litware, Inc., an independent software vendor with a facility in Atlanta. Mike also provides tech support for about 50 computers at the facility and answers technical support calls from customers. Mike is very busy.

Mike's network consists of a Windows 2000 Active Directory tree with a single domain. Recently, Litware purchased Proseware, Inc. Mike created an OU under Litware for Proseware. Proseware has a setup similar to Litware, with about 50 users to manage, support calls, and so on.

Mike doesn't want to drive to Skeeter Flats, Louisiana, every time a user there has a technical support issue. Angela, the local administrator in Skeeter Flats, has many of the same job responsibilities that Mike has. Mike wants Angela to handle day-to-day administrative issues for Proseware, but Mike needs to retain centralized control. Because of the competitive job market in the greater Skeeter Flats area, turnover in the IT field is quite high. It's unknown how long Angela will remain in her current job.

What is the appropriate strategy for Mike?

A. Create the Proseware-admins group. Put Angela in the group. Modify the access control list (ACL) for the Proseware OU to include Allow Proseware-admins Full Control Of User Objects, Allow Proseware-admins Full Control Of Group Objects, and Allow Proseware-admins Full Control Of Computer Objects.

B. Add Angela to the Power Users group for the Proseware OU. Modify the ACL for the Proseware OU to include Allow Power Users Full Control Of This Object And All Child Objects.

C. Create the Proseware-admins group. Put Angela in the group. Modify the ACL for the Proseware OU to include Allow Proseware-admins Full Control Of This Object And All Child Objects.

D. Modify the ACL for the Proseware OU to include Allow Angela Full Control Of User Objects, Allow Angela Full Control Of Group Objects, and Allow Angela Full Control Of Computer Objects.

70-220.02.02.003

You're migrating your network to Windows 2000. You promote a domain controller and select Permissions Compatible Only With Windows 2000 Server from the Active Directory Installation Wizard. You discover that some of the applications that previously ran on that server no longer function correctly.

What is the recommended procedure for resolving this problem?

A. Add the special group Everyone to the Pre–Windows 2000 Compatible Access security group and reboot the domain controllers.

B. Rerun the Active Directory Installation Wizard, selecting Permissions Compatible With Pre–Windows 2000 Servers.

C. Add the special group Everyone to the Power Users built-in group and reboot the domain controllers.

D. Add the special group Authenticated Users to the Pre–Windows 2000 Compatible Access security group and reboot the domain controllers.

Objective 2.2 Answers

70-220.02.02.001

▶ **Correct Answers: A**

A. **Correct:** The correct answer for our scenario is to put the students into the Power Users group. This is generally required to allow legacy applications to run. For a moment, let's consider the downside of this choice—Power Users have far more capabilities than Users, making them potentially far more dangerous. In addition to the capabilities of the Users group, Power Users can create local users and groups; modify users and groups that they've created; create and delete nonadmin file shares; create, manage, delete, and share local printers; install software; change the system Date and Time settings; and configure power settings.

In a production environment, these may be more capabilities than you want to grant. However, even if a student with these rights failed to exercise prudence and good judgment, any damage would be limited to the local machine. Paul already contends with this issue. One other worthwhile aspect of the Power Users setting is that Power Users can't access other users' data on NTFS volumes, so one student can't access another student's home folder.

B. **Incorrect:** Choosing not to use legacy applications would technically be perfect, but this option isn't fully supported by the facts of our scenario. It would be wrong to assume that replacements are readily available or that you could simply eliminate a given application from the curriculum.

C. **Incorrect:** If you didn't want the students to have Power User rights, the next step would be to use the Security Configuration Manager (which is the Security Settings extension of the Group Policy console) to apply the compatibility security template. In effect, this technique "dumbs down" Windows 2000 security to the equivalent level of a Windows NT 4 system. What makes this an incorrect choice is that, although it keeps Paul out of trouble, it's more restrictive for the students than our correct answer.

D. **Incorrect:** Putting the users into the Administrators group gives the students virtually unlimited access within the lab network. If one student changed the administrator's password, Paul would be effectively locked out.

70-220.02.02.002

▶ **Correct Answers: A**

A. **Correct:** In Windows 2000 a common technique for the delegation of control is to create an OU and assign the appropriate permissions to create or modify objects or attributes of objects. In our scenario, by giving Angela (by way of her group membership) Full Control access to User, Group, and Computer objects, she can perform day-to-day administration for her OU, but at the same time she's prohibited from performing other administrative tasks such as creating OUs. You can also perform all of these functions by using the Delegation of Control Wizard from the Active Directory Users and Computers console.

B. **Incorrect:** The Power Users group doesn't appear by default in the ACL for the Proseware OU. The Power Users group is associated with member servers and workstations and doesn't even appear in the list of available groups at the domain level.

C. **Incorrect:** Giving Angela Full Control to the OU and all child objects would create the exact situation we are trying to avoid. Angela would become master of her OU, violating the concept of centralized control. We could give Angela the ability to create additional OUs under her own OU, but that doesn't rectify the problem of keeping centralized control in the main Litware facility.

D. **Incorrect:** It would be incorrect to assign access directly to Angela's user object. From our scenario, we know that her tenure at Proseware may soon be cut short. This would require Mike to explicitly remove access from Angela and add access to her replacement. To avoid this, use security groups to provide access control.

70-220.02.02.003

▶ **Correct Answers: A**

A. **Correct:** For security reasons, Windows 2000 Active Directory doesn't allow accounts logged on anonymously the ability to view group memberships and other user and group information. Windows NT 4, on the other hand, does provide this ability. Several existing applications, including Microsoft BackOffice applications like SQL Server as well as some third-party applications, depend on this type of access to function properly. Windows 2000 includes the built-in local security group Pre–Windows 2000 Compatible Access. Adding or removing the special group Everyone as a member of this group and then rebooting the domain controllers in that domain allows you to operate your network either with pre–Windows 2000 security levels or with the greater security provided by Windows 2000. You can then use this group to assign access to files, folders, and registry keys that previous security setting defaults would deny.

B. **Incorrect:** Running the wizard again, this time selecting Permissions Compatible With Pre–Windows 2000 Servers, would achieve the desired result, but it isn't the recommended procedure. This procedure simply adds the group Everyone to the Pre–Windows 2000 Compatible Access group, something that you could have achieved with much less administrative overhead by following the recommended procedure.

C. **Incorrect:** When a legacy application designed to run under the Users context doesn't function properly following an upgrade, one technique for solving the problem is to add the users to the Power Users group. This provides the proper security context for running the application. This may not be desirable in normal circumstances because of the extra capabilities afforded users by virtue of membership in the Power Users group. In any case, this isn't the recommended procedure for our scenario.

D. **Incorrect:** The Authenticated Users group wouldn't function the same as the Everyone group in the stated context. The Everyone group has special meaning and can't be substituted with the Authenticated Users group.

Analyzing Security Requirements

As the exam's focus turns to the material specific to Windows 2000 security, so, too, does your need to analyze specific security requirements. Now that you've studied both the business and technical requirements, you're ready to move on to understanding the current security framework.

It's crucial that you understand the level of security for the various resources within the domain. This includes both network elements, such as files and shares, and hardware, such as printers.

You must also be able to examine the required level of security for accessing resources from the Internet or from direct dial-up access. In Domains 1 and 2, we explore situations in which companies forge temporary partnerships, and we analyze the technical impact of temporarily merging systems. Now, in this domain, we pay close attention to issues such as the use of proxy servers, possible firewall solutions, network address translation, and the pervasive use of VPNs to establish secure and encrypted network links through the Internet.

On the component side of things, this domain tests your knowledge of security implementations for such network aspects as dial-up access, Remote Access Service (RAS) servers, and laptop security through EFS.

Tested Skills and Suggested Practices

The skills that you need to successfully master the Analyzing Security Requirements objective domain on the *Designing Security for a Microsoft Windows 2000 Network* exam include:

- **Designing a security baseline for a Windows 2000 network.**

    - Practice 1: Use the Active Directory Installation Wizard to create a new forest and domain using a Windows 2000 server as the first domain controller. Write out the steps of this process according to what you'll require to make this work.

▪ Practice 2: You have branches in three different states: Indiana, Ohio, and Illinois. The users are experiencing slow WAN speed between branches. List the network factors that impact WAN communication. Design a network structure that will minimize latency on the WAN links.

▪ Practice 3: Within one branch of your multistate company, one domain group does the printer management for the entire organization. As a result, print times are drastically slowed. Brainstorm what you can do to fix this problem. List the Windows 2000 features that are most applicable.

▪ **Identifying the required level of security for each resource.**

▪ Practice 1: All network components, such as files, printers, shares, and Internet and dial-up access, are security risks. Common security attacks include: manipulation, relay attack, social engineering, and denial of service. With each of these components, identify the specific network element exposed, the degree of security risk, and the solution, based on a Windows 2000 model.

▪ Practice 2: Here is a list of primary security strategies that Microsoft mandates you pursue when securing your enterprise network: apply appropriate access control, set uniform security policies, deploy only secure applications, authenticate all user access to system resources, establish correct and appropriate trust relationships, and enable data protection. Using a network system that you're most familiar with, rate each of these factors from one to five in terms of how complete your current network makeup is. Write out what it would take to bring each of these components up to speed in your current network system layout.

Further Reading

This section lists supplemental readings by objective. We recommend that you study these sources thoroughly before taking exam 70-220.

Objective 3.1

Microsoft Corporation. *Windows 2000 Server Resource Kit*. Volume: *Microsoft Windows 2000 Server Deployment Planning Guide*. Redmond, Washington: Microsoft Press, 2000. Review the section titled "Developing a Network Security Plan" in Chapter 11, "Planning Distributed Security." This section details the many factors and choices involved in planning security for a Windows 2000 network.

Microsoft Corporation. *Windows 2000 Server Resource Kit*. Volume: *Microsoft Windows 2000 Server Deployment Planning Guide*. Redmond, Washington: Microsoft Press, 2000. Review the section titled "Planning Task List for Distributed Security" in Chapter 11, "Planning Distributed Security." This section contains a detailed task list that can help when planning security for your Windows 2000 network.

Objective 3.2

Microsoft Corporation. *Windows 2000 Server Resource Kit*. Volume: *Microsoft Windows 2000 Server Deployment Planning Guide*. Redmond, Washington: Microsoft Press, 2000. Review the sections titled "Authenticating All User Access" and "Applying Access Control" in Chapter 11, "Planning Distributed Security." This section details the planning considerations and options for users authentication.

Microsoft Corporation. *Windows 2000 Server Resource Kit*. Volume: *Microsoft Windows 2000 Server Deployment Planning Guide*. Redmond, Washington: Microsoft Press, 2000. Review the section titled "Enabling Data Protection" in Chapter 11, "Planning Distributed Security." This section covers how EFS and IPSec work to protect data on a Windows 2000 network.

O B J E C T I V E   3 . 1

Design a security baseline for a Windows 2000 network.

A **security baseline** is the standard by which you can judge the completeness of your security choices. It's the combination of your settings and configurations that are in place before you introduce them into your system. Think of your security baseline as the equipment an astronaut might need before stepping into the vacuum of space. Certain settings, such as oxygen mixture and suit temperature, must be correct in order for the astronaut to function and interact in the "system" of outer space.

A security baseline affects all network parameters and subsystems, such as file and print servers, domain controllers, operations masters, and application servers, as well as other components. You should keep in mind in real situations, just as in the test environment, that even though several answers may be correct, choosing the solution that's most appropriate for the given situation is what's most important. Because each networking scenario is unique, there will never be one absolute way of doing things in every situation. Basically, establishing a security baseline means making use of the available tools and components to protect your system under a variety of circumstances. The degree of risk, exposure, and necessities for each component depends solely on how each machine and network subsystem is used.

The most important thing to consider both in the real world and while taking the test is that no perfect security solution exists. The best solution lies with the administrator making the best choices according to particular needs and circumstances. Also, when it comes to vulnerability, always remember that the largest security gap is the one between the administrator and the keyboard. If something isn't implemented correctly (or at all) because of human error, the system can do nothing to stop the potential vulnerability.

Objective 3.1 Questions

70-220.03.01.001

Robert is running a Windows 2000 test lab in order to determine appropriate security baseline settings. He's currently testing his IPSec policies to determine which policies and policy structures are necessary. Robert is running normal workloads on applications to gain realistic feedback. During testing, he wants to view the packet contents with Network Monitor. What can Robert do to accomplish this? (Choose all that apply.)

A. Create a custom IPSec policy by selecting High (ESP) from the Security Method tab.

B. Use the Server (Request Security) template to implement the IPSec policy.

C. Create a custom IPSec policy by selecting Medium (AH) from the Security Method tab.

D. Set the security zone level for the intranet zone to Medium.

E. Use the Secure Server (Require Security) template to implement the IPSec policy.

70-220.03.01.002

Patricia is the network administrator for her company. A Windows 2000 Professional workstation is located in the lobby and not connected to the company LAN. This computer kiosk allows users to access a company directory and limited information about the company. This kiosk isn't Internet-active, nor can it be used to check e-mail.

Patricia wants to modify some of the settings to the Local Group Policy object. When she attempts to make the change, however, she's unable to access the Group Policy object. Patricia is in the local Administrators group, and she can also log on as Administrator. She notices that the local Group Policy applies to her when she is logged on as a member of the local Administrators group, even though it isn't supposed to. What's the likely cause of Patricia's problem?

A. The Administrators group has Read access to the %SystemRoot%\System32\GroupPolicy folder.

B. The Administrators group doesn't have Read access to the %SystemRoot%\System32\GroupPolicy folder.

C. The Group Policy snap-in has been removed.

D. The Administrative Templates node of the Group Policy snap-in is set to Not Configured.

70-220.03.01.003

Kate is configuring laptop computers for the sales department's traveling representatives. She must configure the computers to comply with the baseline specifications for laptop security, as directed by the network security administrator. The following guidelines have been established:

- All laptop computers will run Windows 2000 Professional

- Sensitive data on disk will be secured

- All communications to the company RRAS server will be secure and encrypted

- Installed Web browsers must be configured to access company sites securely

Which security components meet Kate's requirements for her laptop security design?

A. EFS, PPTP, SSL

B. EFS, SSL, MPPE

C. NTFS, PPTP, SSL

D. NTFS, PPP, HTTPS

Objective 3.1 Answers

70-220.03.01.001

▶ **Correct Answers: B and C**

A. **Incorrect:** Creating a custom IPSec policy and setting the Security Method to High (ESP) uses ESP, which, unlike AH, provides confidentiality (encryption). The predefined IPSec policy Secure Server (Require Security) does the same thing. In both situations, Network Monitor wouldn't be able to view the payload because it would be encrypted.

B. **Correct:** Administrators often need to test their IPSec policies to determine which policies are truly necessary. You can have three different types of IPSec policies: pass-through, blocking, and permit. During lab testing of deployment scenarios, it's important to simulate normal traffic as closely as possible to production levels to gain important performance and security feedback. Robert wants to monitor his IPSec traffic during the tests and view the packet contents with Network Monitor. To accomplish this, he must set the policy's security method to Medium security. This setting uses the AH protocol, which provides origination authentication, integrity, and antireplay for the entire packet (both the IP header and the data payload carried in the packet). Network Monitor can then view the AH packet's unencrypted payload. A way to accomplish this goal in this scenario is to use the predefined IPSec policy Server (Request Security).

C. **Correct:** Administrators often need to test their IPSec policies to determine which policies are truly necessary. During lab testing of deployment scenarios, it's important to simulate normal traffic as closely as possible to the production levels to gain important performance and security feedback. Robert wants to monitor his IPSec traffic during the tests and view the packet contents with Network Monitor. To accomplish this, he must set the policy's security method to Medium security. This setting uses the AH protocol, which provides origination authentication, integrity, and antireplay for the entire packet (both the IP header and the data payload carried in the packet). Network Monitor can then view the unencrypted payload of the AH packet. A way to accomplish this goal is to create a custom IPSec policy. From the Security Method tab, select Medium (AH).

D. **Incorrect:** The security zone level setting for different browser zones is a security mechanism employed by Microsoft Internet Explorer and doesn't relate directly to IPSec policy.

E. **Incorrect:** This answer is incorrect for the reasons stated in A.

70-220.03.01.002

▶ **Correct Answers: A**

A. **Correct:** Local Group Policy doesn't allow you to apply security filters or to have multiple sets of Group Policy objects, unlike Active Directory–based Group Policy objects. Policies set at the site, domain, or OU level can override local group policies. You can, however, set discretionary access control lists (DACLs) on the Group Policy folder so that specified groups are either affected or not affected by the Local Group Policy object. This is useful if you administer computers that are used in situations such as kiosk environments, in which the computer isn't connected to a LAN.

The Local Group Policy object uses the Read attribute, which makes it possible for the Local Group Policy object to affect ordinary users but not local administrators. The local administrator can first set the policy settings and then set the DACLs to the Local Group Policy object folder so that administrators no longer have Read access. For the administrator to make subsequent changes to the Local Group Policy object, she must first take ownership of the directory to give her Read access, make the changes, and then remove Read access. After you make changes to the Group Policy object, remember to remove Read access for the group in which you're a member. If you fail to remove Read access, you may not be able to gain access to the Group Policy object. Therefore, it appears that Patricia has Read access to the Group Policy folder. Not having Read access to this folder makes you immune to the Group Policy settings in it—a good thing for an administrator. You can make all these previously mentioned changes through the Microsoft Management Console (MMC) by adding the Group Policy snap-in.

B. **Incorrect:** This answer is incorrect for the reasons stated in A.

C. **Incorrect:** Removing the Group Policy snap-in wouldn't be catastrophic because it doesn't affect any of the current settings. Simply put back the snap-in.

D. **Incorrect:** You can extend the Administrative Templates node of the Group Policy snap-in by using a custom administrative template (.adm) file. An administrative template is essentially a file that consists of a grouping of categories that define how options are displayed through the Group Policy console. Unlike other Group Policy snap-in extensions, however, it isn't extensible by an MMC snap-in extension. The node itself wouldn't be set to Not Configured. The actual settings listed inside the .adm files would have that setting applied.

70-220.03.01.003

▶ **Correct Answers: A**

A. **Correct:** You can use EFS to encrypt NTFS files to provide confidentiality for the file contents. EFS uses the Expanded Data Encryption Standard (DESX) 56-bit encryption algorithm to generate symmetric key encryption in conjunction with public key technology. These components protect the file and ensure that only the file's owner can access the file.

A VPN enables you to send data between two computers across a shared or public internetwork in a way that emulates a point-to-point private link. To ensure confidentiality, the sender encrypts the data and the receiver decrypts it. PPTP takes the existing Point-to-Point Protocol (PPP) frames, encapsulates them into an IP datagram, and provides encryption services.

The SSL protocol provides communications privacy, authentication, and message integrity by using a combination of public-key and symmetric encryption. In order to put SSL into effect, you must implement both an SSL-based server and an SSL-enabled application. By using this protocol, clients and servers can communicate in a way that prevents eavesdropping, tampering, or message forgery. In the case of an SSL connection between a Web browser and Web server, you must type **https://** for Hypertext Transfer Protocol Secure (HTTPS) rather than **http://** for Hypertext Transfer Protocol (HTTP) as the protocol type in the URL. This will instruct the Web browser to use a different port for the communication; the Web server will be listening on this port for SSL requests. By default, Web data (HTTP) uses Transmission Control Protocol (TCP) port 80, and SSL (HTTPS) uses TCP port 443.

In this scenario, Kate needs to configure EFS, PPTP, and SSL.

B. **Incorrect:** You can use EFS to encrypt NTFS files to provide confidentiality for the file contents. EFS uses symmetric key encryption in conjunction with public key technology to protect the file and ensure that only the file's owner can access the file.

Microsoft Point-to-Point Encryption (MPPE) is the encryption method used by PPTP. By itself, MPPE doesn't satisfy the requirement for secure communications.

C. **Incorrect:** This answer is incorrect for the reasons stated in A.

D. **Incorrect:** The PPP is an industry standard method of using point-to-point links to transport multiprotocol datagrams. PPP normally is used over dial-up modem connections. It doesn't provide the encryption capabilities required by our scenario.

NTFS is required for EFS to work, but it doesn't provide the required data encryption services by itself.

HTTPS is the protocol you use with an SSL-enabled connection. You don't configure the browser specifically to support HTTPS; you configure the browser to enable SSL, which allows you to use the HTTPS protocol for secure Web site access.

O B J E C T I V E   3 . 2

Identify the required level of security for each resource.

The key idea in identifying the required security level for the various network components is **access controls**. Access controls are the parameters you specify for each user regarding which network resources he or she has access to. Each access control requires a definition for each resource you place on a network. This objective breaks down potential network resources and allows you to analyze them individually and then make the appropriate security choices.

With printer permissions, you need to decide who can print, who can manage a single printer or group of printers, and who has access for managing documents. You'll want to restrict printer usage to certain people, largely because of the sensitivity of certain documents. For example, you wouldn't require the human resources department to print salary records to a printer where anyone can come by and see them. On the other hand, you may reserve certain printer rights to certain users because of job type. You don't want to give everyone in the building access to a color laser printer; you'd probably reserve that permission for the graphic design user group.

File systems are another network resource. With Windows 2000 you can have the use of three separate file systems: NTFS, file allocation table (FAT), and FAT32. In most circumstances you'll be using NTFS in order to allow Windows 95 and 98 the same file access over the network as Windows 2000.

With dial-up access, begin the security setup by deciding which dial-up clients have network access at all. Once they're connected, the next step is deciding which network resources they have access to. With Windows 2000, the RRAS console lets you create and maintain dial-up client policies. So, you'd structure access through the dial-in properties of each user account and the users' respective policies. These policies are created and stored in the Remote Access Policies component of RRAS.

Finally, with Internet access you begin by isolating the point of access and then you move on from there. You first need to understand how clients access the Internet. Is it remote access by means of a modem, or a more permanent connection such as T1 or digital subscriber line (DSL)? Are firewalls in place? Does the system make use of a proxy server to control access? Knowing all these parameters will make it easier to define how you'll enable security.

Objective 3.2 Questions

70-220.03.02.001

You operate a small publishing company from your home office. You publish a daily local computer industry newsletter. You have a computer running Microsoft Windows 2000 Professional operating as your print server and configured for Internet printing using the Internet Printing Protocol (IPP). You often initiate a print job from a remote location using a Microsoft Internet Explorer–equipped laptop. You also accept Internet print requests from your correspondents, many of whom use non-Microsoft software.

How should you configure security to allow access to your printing resources only to authorized users?

A. Using Peer Web Services (PWS), select Basic Authentication. Remove the group Everyone and assign the Print permission to authorized users.

B. Using IIS, select Microsoft Challenge/Response. Remove the group Everyone and assign the Manage Documents permission to authorized users.

C. Using IIS, select Kerberos V5. Remove the group Everyone and assign the Manage Printer permission to the Print Operators group.

D. Using PWS, select Microsoft Challenge/Response or Kerberos V5 authentication. Remove the group Everyone and assign the Print permission to the Authenticated Users group.

70-220.03.02.002

Amy has just performed a clean installation of Windows 2000 Server on an NTFS partition. This server will function as a file server and won't be a domain controller. Barbara, a user in the department, has been assigned to help Amy support and maintain the file server. She needs sufficient access to install and maintain applications that will be used by all users in the department, but she doesn't need broad administrative powers. Barbara hasn't been assigned to any groups. How can Amy accomplish this objective with minimum administrative overhead?

A. Assign Barbara to the Power Users group. Assign the Power Users group Full Control permission to the All Users, All Users/Documents, and All Users/Application Data file system objects.

B. Assign Barbara Full Control permission to the %UserProfile% file system object.

C. Assign Barbara to the Server Operators group.

D. Assign Barbara to the Power Users group.

70-220.03.02.003

Kelly is assigning shared folder permissions to apply security to the folders on her file servers. One of her servers, MARKETING1, contains a FAT volume and an NTFS volume. Kelly assigns the Change shared folder permission to the group Marketing Users for the Public folder on the FAT volume. She assigns the Read shared folder permission to the Marketing Users group for the Market_Research folder on the NTFS volume.

Karen, a member of the Marketing Users group, can connect to the Public share and can perform all the activities associated with the Change permission. She can also connect to the Market_Research share but can't successfully perform activities associated with the Read permission. What's the most likely reason that Karen is having this problem?

A. Shared folder permissions are sufficient to gain access to files and folders on a FAT volume but not on an NTFS volume.

B. Kelly has moved the Market_Research folder to a different location on the volume.

C. Karen is logged on using cached credentials.

D. Kelly created the Market_Research shared folder as an Administrative share by mistake.

Objective 3.2 Answers

70-220.03.02.001

▶ **Correct Answers: A**

A. **Correct:** Internet printing, a new feature in Windows 2000, allows you to submit print jobs to a printer across the Internet. It also provides clients with information on the status of print jobs, as well as whether or not printers are available. Depending on the platform, print server security is provided by PWS. In our scenario, PWS is the correct choice because the print server is running on a Windows 2000 Professional computer. For authentication purposes, you must select Basic Authentication because you need to support a range of browsers and Internet clients. Because these correspondents only need to print, the Print permission is appropriate.

B. **Incorrect:** IIS would provide security if the print server were running Windows 2000 Server, Advanced Server, or Datacenter Server. Microsoft Challenge/Response would limit you to Microsoft Internet Explorer browsers, which is too limiting for our scenario. Manage Documents or Manage Printer permissions would give your clients too much control. With these permissions they'd be able to alter printer settings and make changes to document and printer pooling.

C. **Incorrect:** IIS would provide security if the print server were running Windows 2000 Server, Advanced Server, or Datacenter Server. Kerberos V5 would limit you to Microsoft Internet Explorer browsers, which is too restrictive for our scenario. Manage Documents or Manage Printer permissions would give your clients too much control.

D. **Incorrect:** In our scenario, PWS would be the correct choice because the print server is running on a Windows 2000 Professional computer, but Microsoft Challenge/Response or Kerberos V5 would limit you to Microsoft Internet Explorer browsers, which is too restricting for our scenario. Manage Documents or Manage Printer permission would give your clients too much control.

70-220.03.02.002

▶ **Correct Answers: D**

A. **Incorrect:** Assigning the Power Users group Full Control permission to these objects isn't correct. It would give this group more power than is required by our scenario. Also, it would require Amy to make these changes, adding to the administrative burden.

B. **Incorrect:** Barbara, and every other user, already has Full Control permission to the %UserProfile% object. This object represents user-specific settings that each user has complete control over (unless that control is revoked by the administrator). The use of the % character represents a system variable that's interpreted at logon time by the system and applied to the appropriate user.

C. **Incorrect:** The Server Operators group is to domain controllers what the Power Users group is to member servers. Membership in the Server Operators group gives a user similar abilities at the domain level than what the Power User enjoys at the local computer level. Because Amy's server isn't a domain controller, it doesn't have a Server Operators group.

D. **Correct:** With a clean installation of Windows 2000, certain default access control settings are assigned to the Power Users and the Users groups on an NTFS partition. Power User privileges are by default backward compatible with the Windows NT 4 Users group. The primary difference is that the Power Users group is given sufficient access to install computer-wide applications. The important detail to remember here is that applications that a Power User installs can write files into system directories but can't modify Windows 2000 system files. Power Users also can't install Windows 2000 services. Specifically, this group is given the following permission structure for the relevant file system objects: All Users: Modify, All Users/Documents: Modify, All Users/Application Data: Modify.

The Users group is given Read access to these same objects (plus Create File for the All Users/Documents object).

All that needs to be done to satisfy the conditions of our scenario is to assign Barbara to the Power Users group.

70-220.03.02.003

▶ **Correct Answers: A**

A. **Correct:** In our scenario, it's most likely that the appropriate NTFS permissions haven't been set to allow access to members of the Marketing Users group. As stated in the correct answer, shared folder permissions are sufficient to gain access to files and folders on a FAT volume but not on an NTFS volume.

B. **Incorrect:** If you move a shared folder to someplace else, it's no longer shared. We know this isn't Karen's problem, however, because she's able to attach to the share.

C. **Incorrect:** If Karen is logged on using cached credentials, it means that a domain controller wasn't available to service her logon request. Consequently, she doesn't have access to network resources, which she has in our scenario.

D. **Incorrect:** Administrative shares are created automatically by Windows 2000, not the administrator. Only if Karen were an administrator would she be able to access administrative shares.

Designing a Windows 2000 Security Solution

So far in this book, the domains have been largely theoretical. That is, we've been going over various strategies and discussing what we think might work best. In the designing domain, however, we begin to put some of these ideas to the test.

In designing a security solution, you need to keep in mind that security is relative to the location, the level of risk involved, and the sensitivity of the information you're trying to protect. Some companies are hardly concerned with security because they have a relatively small number of users who deal with information that's largely inconsequential to others.

Other organizations, however, such as financial institutions and research firms, consider computer security one of their top priorities because they have data that's extremely sensitive. The path to designing and implementing good security comes from understanding network security in general. Only by knowing your options can you be certain of making the right security choices for your network.

This portion of the exam tests your knowledge of creating an adequate security solution. It takes you through such topics as creating an audit policy so that you can understand which events will require reporting to the administrator. Designing a delegation of authority strategy allows you to decide which levels of security to assign. Designing the placement and inheritance of security policies allows you to get a grasp of the larger issue of implementing policy at the site, domain, and **OU (organizational unit) level**. By designing an **Encrypting File System (EFS)** strategy, you'll understand how to secure complete file systems from attack and theft. Designing an authentication strategy illustrates the different types of authentication and how to use them. Designing a security group strategy gives you an understanding of security groups, and designing a **Public Key Infrastructure (PKI)** moves you along to implementing a PKI design.

Finally, designing Windows 2000 network services security gets you through securing various network components, such as **DNS**, **VPN**, and **Terminal Services**.

Tested Skills and Suggested Practices

The skills that you need to successfully master the Designing a Windows 2000 Security Solution objective domain on the *Designing Security for a Microsoft Windows 2000 Network* exam include:

- **Designing an audit policy.**

    - Practice 1: In the Local Security Policy window of the Windows 2000 Administrative Tools snap-in, find the Audit Account Logon Events component and check its parameters.

    - Practice 2: Audit the Active Directory directory by enabling the Audit directory service access. Audit the success or failure to directory service access in order to open up the Active Directory auditing options.

- **Designing a delegation of authority strategy.**

    - Practice 1: Walk through the process of delegating authority by using the Delegation of Control Wizard.

    - Practice 2: Delegate the control of a single security group to a specific administrator of your choosing. Here's a hint: with built-in security groups, the permissions will already be in place.

- **Designing the placement and inheritance of security policies for sites, domains, and organizational units.**

    - Practice 1: Open the Active Directory Users And Computers snap-in, and then go to View and choose Advanced Features. Take a look at the predefined security groups located in the Built-In and Users Folders.

    - Practice 2: Use the Group Policy tab in the Site Domain Properties page to specify user properties such as Read and Write access for a user.

- **Designing an Encrypting File System strategy.**

    - Practice 1: Encrypt a file or folder by right-clicking on it in Windows Explorer, then following the correct tabs. Encrypt on NTFS partition as well.

    - Practice 2: Enable remote encryption on your Windows 2000 server. Remember that to do so you must designate the file server as Trusted For Delegation.

- **Designing an authentication strategy.**

  - Practice 1: Use the Certification Authority console in the MMC to specify certificate types that are to be issued by each Certificate Authority.

  - Practice 2: Use the Windows 2000 Authentication Service Exchange to change a user's password for an application server, or service, or both.

- **Designing a security group strategy.**

  - Practice 1: Come up with a Deployment Planning checklist. Topics should include: deciding which security risks affect your network, describing security and remote-access strategies, verifying network access authentication, and understanding your access-control policies, among others.

  - Practice 2: Describe the domains, domain trees, and forests that you've included within your domain. Describe the trust relationships that exist among them.

- **Designing a Public Key Infrastructure.**

  - Practice 1: Illustrate which settings are required for the following certificate factors: cryptographic algorithms that are coupled with certificates and public key length.

  - Practice 2: EFS Recover, Domain Controller, Machine, and Administrator are all Windows 2000 certificate templates. For each, state whom the template should be issued to (User or Computer), and define its purpose.

- **Designing Windows 2000 network services security.**

  - Practice 1: Define the computer naming policy through the use of the Active Directory Computers And Users console.

  - Practice 2: Use the Add/Remove Programs option in Control Panel to install applications on Terminal Services.

Further Reading

This section lists supplemental readings by objective. We recommend that you study these sources thoroughly before taking exam 70-220.

Objective 4.1

Microsoft Corporation. *MCSE Training Kit: Designing Microsoft Windows 2000 Network Security*. Redmond, Washington: Microsoft Press, 2000. Review Chapter 5, "Designing Group Security," Lesson 1, "Designing Microsoft Windows 2000 Security

Groups." After completing this lesson you should be able to determine how to best use custom groups in your Windows 2000 environment.

Microsoft Corporation. *MCSE Training Kit: Designing Microsoft Windows 2000 Network Security*. Redmond, Washington: Microsoft Press, 2000. Review Chapter 5, "Designing Group Security," Lab 5-1, "Designing Security Groups and User Rights." This is a hands-on lab that covers the design and application of Windows 2000 security groups.

Objective 4.2

Microsoft Corporation. *MCSE Training Kit: Designing Microsoft Windows 2000 Network Security*. Redmond, Washington: Microsoft Press, 2000. Review Chapter 2, "Designing Active Directory for Security," Lesson 3, "Designing an OU Structure." This lesson covers the decisions that you will need to make to design and deploy an OU structure in your organization.

Microsoft Corporation. *MCSE Training Kit: Designing Microsoft Windows 2000 Network Security*. Redmond, Washington: Microsoft Press, 2000. Review Chapter 2, "Designing Active Directory for Security," Lesson 2, "Designing Your Domain Structure." This lesson covers how to design a domain structure to suit the needs of your organization.

Objective 4.3

Microsoft Corporation. *MCSE Training Kit: Designing Microsoft Windows 2000 Network Security*. Redmond, Washington: Microsoft Press, 2000. Review Chapter 8, "Securing Microsoft Windows 2000-Based Computers," Lesson 3, "Planning the Deployment of Security by Using Security Templates." In this lesson you will learn how to deploy security templates across your network.

Microsoft Corporation. *MCSE Training Kit: Designing Microsoft Windows 2000 Network Security*. Redmond, Washington: Microsoft Press, 2000. Review Chapter 8, "Securing Microsoft Windows 2000-Based Computers," Lab 8-1, "Planning Security Templates." This lab takes you through the process of planning, creating, and deploying security templates.

Objective 4.4

Microsoft Corporation. *MCSE Training Kit: Designing Microsoft Windows 2000 Network Security*. Redmond, Washington: Microsoft Press, 2000. Review Chapter 6, "Securing File Resources," Lesson 3, "Planning EFS Security." This lesson details the deployment of EFS for a Windows 2000 network.

Microsoft Corporation. *MCSE Training Kit: Designing Microsoft Windows 2000 Network Security*. Redmond, Washington: Microsoft Press, 2000. Review Chapter 6, "Securing File Resources," Exercise 3, "Planning EFS for Laptops." This exercise covers the steps in a plan for EFS deployment on laptops.

Objective 4.5

Microsoft Corporation. *MCSE Training Kit: Designing Microsoft Windows 2000 Network Security*. Redmond, Washington: Microsoft Press, 2000. Review Chapter 3, "Designing Authentication for a Windows 2000 Network," Lesson 1, "Designing Authentication in a Microsoft Windows 2000 Network." This lesson details how to determine the business and technical requirements that will affect a Windows 2000 network design.

Microsoft Corporation. *MCSE Training Kit: Designing Microsoft Windows 2000 Network Security*. Redmond, Washington: Microsoft Press, 2000. Review Chapter 3, "Designing Authentication for a Windows 2000 Network," Lab 3-1, "Designing Authentication on the Network." This hands-on lab contains exercises on designing authentication for a Windows 2000 network.

Objective 4.6

Microsoft Corporation. *MCSE Training Kit: Designing Microsoft Windows 2000 Network Security*. Redmond, Washington: Microsoft Press, 2000. Review Chapter 5, "Designing Group Security," Lesson 1, "Designing MS Windows 2000 Security Groups." After completing this lesson you should be able to determine how to best use custom groups in your Windows 2000 environment.

Microsoft Corporation. *MCSE Training Kit: Designing Microsoft Windows 2000 Network Security*. Redmond, Washington: Microsoft Press, 2000. Review Chapter 6, "Securing File Resources," Lesson 1, "Securing Access to File Resources." This lesson covers how to design security for file resources on a Windows 2000 network.

Objective 4.7

Microsoft Corporation. *MCSE Training Kit: Designing Microsoft Windows 2000 Network Security*. Redmond, Washington: Microsoft Press, 2000. Review Chapter 10, "Planning a Public Key Infrastructure," the section titled "Determining the Certification Authority Structure." This section reviews several CA structures and the factors you should consider in deciding which is the best for your deployment.

Microsoft Corporation. *MCSE Training Kit: Designing Microsoft Windows 2000 Network Security*. Redmond, Washington: Microsoft Press, 2000. Review Chapter 10, "Planning a Public Key Infrastructure," Lesson 2, "Managing Certification Authorities." This lesson covers the design of a management strategy for a CA deployment.

Objective 4.8

Microsoft Corporation. *MCSE Training Kit: Designing Microsoft Windows 2000 Network Security*. Redmond, Washington: Microsoft Press, 2000. Review Chapter 9, "Designing Microsoft Windows 2000 Services Security," Lesson 1, "Designing DNS Security." Lesson 1 details how to design security for your DNS deployment.

Microsoft Corporation. *MCSE Training Kit: Designing Microsoft Windows 2000 Network Security*. Redmond, Washington: Microsoft Press, 2000. Review Chapter 9, "Designing Microsoft Windows 2000 Services Security," Lesson 3, "Designing RIS Security." This lesson covers the secure deployment of Windows 2000 Professional through RIS.

Microsoft Corporation. *MCSE Training Kit: Designing Microsoft Windows 2000 Network Security*. Redmond, Washington: Microsoft Press, 2000. Review Chapter 9, "Designing Microsoft Windows 2000 Services Security," Lesson 4, "Designing SNMP Security." This lesson details the factors involved in a secure deployment of SNMP.

Microsoft Corporation. *MCSE Training Kit: Designing Microsoft Windows 2000 Network Security*. Redmond, Washington: Microsoft Press, 2000. Review Chapter 9, "Designing Microsoft Windows 2000 Services Security," Lesson 5, "Designing Terminal Services Security." This lesson covers the security for a Terminal Services deployment on your Windows 2000 network.

OBJECTIVE 4.1

Design an audit policy.

This objective tests your knowledge of how to track security-related events, otherwise known as **auditing**. The reason for the "design" title is that you always need to develop the audit feature and test it in a laboratory environment before exposing it to your actual network. Unless you design and test it, the feature that you implement can end up causing more problems than it solves.

When Windows 2000 Server is initially installed, the default setting for auditing categories is Off. You can design specific security requirements by enabling various auditing event categories. You need to have your design laid out correctly so that you can select the correct events to be audited. Once you've enabled various audit policies, you'll then need to decide which option you'll take: successes, or failures, or both. In the end, you'll need to view the results of your audits. You can do this by using the Event Viewer, which provides you with information regarding the status of your audits.

Objective 4.1 Questions

70-220.04.01.001

You run a high-security network. You want to ensure that the system halts if the security log becomes full. You're a member of the Administrators group. You've selected Do Not Overwrite Events (Clear Log Manually) from the General tab of the Event Viewer Properties dialog box. You've used the registry editor to create the CrashOnAuditFail registry key. As a test, you allow the security log to become full. The system displays the Audit Failed message and the system stops responding. You clear the security log and restart the system. You repeat the test. This time the system doesn't stop when the security log becomes full. What's the most likely cause of the problem?

A. You must repeat the initial procedure if you want a full log to stop the computer.

B. You should select Overwrite Events Older Than N Days (Select An Appropriate Number Of Days) instead of Do Not Overwrite Events (Clear Log Manually).

C. You must be logged on as an administrator when you clear the security log.

D. You induced an error when you created the CrashOnAuditFail registry entry.

70-220.04.01.002

Sarah suspects that a virus outbreak on her network is imminent. She wants to protect network integrity and minimize downtime and inconvenience. She elects to modify the audit policy for her domain controllers and all public access servers. She plans on actively monitoring the system log for the next 48 to 72 hours. Which events should she incorporate into her audit policy? (Choose all that apply.)

A. Logon events

B. Process tracking

C. Privilege use

D. Policy change

E. Write access for program files (.exe and .dll extensions)

70-220.04.01.003

Joseph is a member of the Administrators group. To guard against improper access to sensitive files, Joseph wants to establish an audit policy for his local application server. When he uses Windows Explorer to navigate to a folder containing sensitive material, Joseph navigates to the Auditing tab but is unable to set auditing options for the folder. What's the likely cause of the problem?

A. He must first enable the Audit Object Access setting in the audit policy.

B. He must first be granted the Manage Auditing And Security Log right in Group Policy.

C. The folder is on a FAT32 volume.

D. He must be a member of the Power Users group.

Objective 4.1 Answers

70-220.04.01.001

► **Correct Answers: A**

A. **Correct:** To halt the computer when the security log fills up, perform the following steps:

First, open Event Viewer. Then, in the console tree, right-click Security Log, and then click Properties. In the General tab of the Properties screen, click either Overwrite Events Older Than N Days or Do Not Overwrite Events (Clear Log Manually). Finally, use Registry Editor to create or assign the following registry key value:

```
HKEY_LOCAL_MACHINE\SYSTEM\CurrentControoSet\Control\Lsa\CrashOnAuditFail
```

Now you should restart the computer.

You must be logged on as an administrator to complete these steps. If Windows 2000 halts as a result of a full security log, you must restart the system and repeat this procedure if you want a full log to stop the computer in the future.

B. **Incorrect:** Selecting either Overwrite Events or Do Not Overwrite Events is correct. This isn't the cause of the problem.

C. **Incorrect:** Although it's true that you must be logged on as an administrator when you clear the security log, there's no indication that you would have logged on otherwise during an ongoing test procedure. This isn't the most likely cause of the problem.

D. **Incorrect:** If you had induced an error with a registry setting, it would most likely have manifested itself during the initial system restart. You must not use the Registry keys to perform any kind of manual change to a machine's security settings. If you improperly configure security settings at the Registry level, you may end up doing irreparable damage to the operating system. Because the system restarted successfully following the edit, this isn't the most likely cause of the problem.

70-220.04.01.002

▶ **Correct Answers: B and E**

A. **Incorrect:** Logon events are tracked whenever a user logs on or off. Tracking logon events is most useful in fighting password attacks.

B. **Correct:** You can specify that an audit entry be written to the security event log whenever certain actions are performed or certain files are accessed. The audit entry shows the action performed, the user who performed it, and the date and time of the action. You can audit both successful and failed attempts at actions, so the audit trail can show who performed actions on the network and who tried to perform actions that aren't permitted. You can view the security log in the Event Viewer.

For Sarah's situation, it would be most useful to utilize process tracking. Process tracking is used to watch what a program does while it executes. She should run any suspect programs and then examine the security log for unexpected attempts to modify program files or create unexpected processes. While performing these audits, she should run them only when actively monitoring the system log, as our scenario specifies.

C. **Incorrect:** Tracking privilege use would show Sarah who is exercising various user rights. User rights are different from permissions because user rights apply to user accounts and permissions are attached to objects. Examples of privilege use would be loading device drivers or taking ownership of objects.

D. **Incorrect:** Auditing policy change events would give another indication of a possible misuse of privileges but wouldn't be useful in tracking a possible virus threat.

E. **Correct:** For Sarah's situation, it would be most useful to track Write access for program files. She should run any suspect programs and then examine the security log for unexpected attempts to modify program files or create unexpected processes. While performing these audits, she should run them only when actively monitoring the system log, as our scenario specifies.

70-220.04.01.003

▶ **Correct Answers: A**

A. **Correct:** The Audit Object Access category is created whenever a user or computer gains access to an object. An auditing policy specifies categories of security-related events that you want to track. These activities include such things as List Folder/Read Data, Read Attributes, and Create Files/Write Data. When Windows 2000 is first installed, auditing is disabled by default. By enabling various auditing event categories, you can implement an auditing policy that suits your security needs. If you choose to audit access to objects as part of your audit policy, you must turn on either the Audit Directory Service Access category (for auditing objects on a domain controller), or the Audit Object Access category (for auditing objects on a member server). Once you've turned on the correct object access category, you can use each individual object's properties to specify whether to audit successes or failures for the permissions granted to each group or user.

In our scenario, Joseph needs to audit file and folder access on his application (member) server. So he first needs to enable the Audit Object Access setting.

B. **Incorrect:** To audit files and folders, you must be logged on as a member of the Administrators group or have been granted the Manage Auditing And Security Log right in Group Policy. Since Joseph is a member of the Administrators group, he doesn't need to be assigned the Manage Auditing And Security Log right.

C. **Incorrect:** Files and folders must be on an NTFS volume for auditing to be available. In our scenario the Auditing tab was visible, clearly indicating that the folder was on an NTFS volume, not a FAT32 volume.

D. **Incorrect:** There's no requirement that he be in the Power Users group, especially if he's already in the Administrators group.

OBJECTIVE 4.2

Design a delegation of authority strategy.

The most secure way of delegating control within a Windows 2000 Server framework lies in creating **organizational units (OUs)**. By using OUs, you can create a tree structure in which OUs lie within each domain. With this in place, you can then delegate authority to specific users and groups that reside within specific organization unit **subtrees**. By using OUs to delegate authority, you can give administrative rights of varying levels to users within a specific department. For example, you can give specific administrative rights to a few people in the human resources department. In addition to this, you may have users with administrative rights to only a subunit of this human resources unit, for example, the insurance and benefits departments. In this manner, you can give users administrative rights to certain components of an OU, while restricting them in another. While the Insurance and Benefits users might have free rights to their OU, they still don't have complete clearance within the larger realm of the human resources OU.

By delegating authority, you can keep a specific degree of control over a limited set of objects to specific users or groups. Remember that the appropriate **Active Directory directory service** objects such as **files**, **objects**, and **directories**, must be in place before you can perform this type of delegation.

Objective 4.2 Questions

70-220.04.02.001

Your existing structure consists of a Windows NT 4 master accounts domain and two resource domains, Project A and Project B. You're preparing for a Windows 2000 migration. Currently, the administrators for Project A and Project B are responsible for two things: creating computer accounts for project members and using group membership to regulate access to file share resources. After the migration, you want to delegate authority for the administration of resources in Project A and Project B in a manner consistent with the current level of administration. What strategy should you follow to achieve the desired result?

A. Retain the existing domain structure. Within the Project A domain, add appropriate members to the Domain Admins group. Repeat for the Project B domain.

B. Replace the resource domains with OUs. Create four administrative groups: A_compadmin, A_grpadmin, B_compadmin, and B_grpadmin. Grant A_compadmin Full Control Of This Object And All Child Objects and grant A_grpadmin Full Control Of This Object And All Child Objects at the Project A OU. Make similar assignments for the Project B groups.

C. Replace the resource domains with OUs. Create two administrative groups: A_Admins and B_Admins. Grant A_Admins Full Control Of Computer Objects and Full Control Of Group Objects at the Project A OU. Make similar assignments for the Project B groups.

D. Consolidate Project A and Project B into a single Projects domain under the XYZ domain. Within the Projects domain, create an OU structure for each project. Within the Projects domain, create four administrative groups: A_compadmin, A_grpadmin, B_compadmin, and B_grpadmin. Grant A_compadmin Full Control Of Computer Objects and grant A_grpadmin Full Control Of Group Objects at the Project A OU. Make similar assignments for the Project B groups.

70-220.04.02.002

Rob, the network administrator, manages an Active Directory containing about 15,000 user objects distributed over 5 OUs. Rob has recently been assigned a project that consumes about 30 percent of his time. He, as well as his user population, has noticed that his response time for network support issues has increased, sometimes dramatically. Concerned about the level of service, Rob has analyzed the demands on his time and has discovered that he spends an inordinate amount of time responding to password change requests from users who have forgotten their passwords. Most of the requests come from the Distribution OU, which accounts for about 8,000 users.

Mark, a shop supervisor in Distribution, has expressed interest in becoming a network administrator. Rob agrees to give Mark a trial period as an assistant administrator. Initially, Rob wants to limit Mark's activities to reading technical materials and responding to password change requests. Rob's first official act is to send e-mail to everyone in the Distribution OU providing Mark's name and phone extension as the contact for password change requests. What should Rob do next?

A. Create a Dist-Admins group. Delegate permissions for creating and deleting user objects in the Distribution OU to the Dist-Admins group. Add Mark to the group.

B. Create a Dist-Admins group. Delegate permissions allowing the Dist-Admins group to update the password property on User objects in the Distribution OU. Delegate permissions at the User objects themselves. Add Mark to the group.

C. Create a Dist-Admins group. Delegate permissions allowing the Dist-Admins group to update the password property on User objects in the Distribution OU. Delegate permissions at the Distribution OU level. Add Mark to the group.

D. Create a Dist-Admins group. Delegate permissions for the Dist-Admins group to change properties on the Distribution OU. Add Mark to the group.

70-220.04.02.003

The Aspen location for the 3-D Graphics unit of the Adventure Works software company contains two Windows NT 4 resource domains—Backgrounds and Explosions. As part of a planned Windows 2000 upgrade, these domains will be consolidated into the *adventure-works.com* domain.

The Backgrounds and Explosions administrators currently use their domains for two main purposes:

- Creating computer accounts for new designers

- Sharing file system space on Windows NT 4 member servers, where access to the file system and shares are controlled by local group membership

Suki, the administrator for the 3-D Graphics unit, created the directory structure within Active Directory to reflect the new hierarchy. The Backgrounds and Explosions OUs are peers, each directly below the 3D Graphics OU. Suki assigns all subordinate administrators to either of the two resource domains.

How should Suki structure security so that the administrators for Backgrounds and Explosions can continue to function as they had before without giving them administrative access to objects outside their span of control?

A. Create the following local groups in the 3D Graphics OU: BG-grp-admins, BG-comp-admins, EX-grp-admins, and EX-comp-admins. Place the appropriate administrators in the appropriate groups. In the Backgrounds OU, make two ACL entries: Allow BG-Grp-Admins Full Control Of Group Objects and Allow BG-Comp-Admins Full Control Of Computer Objects. Make similar entries for the Explosions OU.

B. Create the following local groups in the 3D Graphics OU: BG-admins and EX-admins. Place the appropriate administrators in the appropriate groups. In the Backgrounds OU, make one ACL entry: Allow BG-Grp-Admins Full Control Of This Object And All Child Objects. Make a similar entry for the Explosions OU.

C. Create the 3d-admins local group in the 3D Graphics OU. Add the administrators for the Backgrounds and Explosions OUs to 3d-admins. In the Backgrounds OU, make two ACL entries: Allow 3d-Admins Full Control Of Group Objects and Allow 3d-Admins Full Control Of Computer Objects. Make similar entries for the Explosions OU.

D. Create the following local groups in the Backgrounds OU: BG-grp-admins and BG-comp-admins. Place the appropriate administrators in the appropriate groups. In the Backgrounds OU, make two ACL entries: Allow BG-Grp-Admins Full Control Of Group Objects and Allow BG-Comp-Admins Full Control Of Computer Objects. Repeat the process for the Explosions OU.

Objective 4.2 Answers

70-220.04.02.001

▶ **Correct Answers: C**

A. **Incorrect:** Unless there's a specific reason to do so, you're not required to retain a master/resource domain layout after a Windows 2000 migration. In fact, the OU capabilities of the Windows 2000 domain structure are designed as a replacement for the old structure and make domain administration more efficient.

B. **Incorrect:** Our scenario doesn't indicate a need for four administrative groups. Since each set of administrators handles computer accounts and file share access, this is most efficiently handled with one administrative group for each OU. Also, the Full Control Of This Object And All Child Objects permission granted at the OU level gives the OU administrators far more administrative rights than they currently possess, in violation of our scenario requirements.

C. **Correct:** In Windows NT, delegation of authority within a domain was achieved using built-in local groups. This often didn't meet the situation's exact needs. In Windows 2000, delegation of administration is more powerful and flexible. This flexibility is achieved through a combination of OUs, per-attribute access control, and access control inheritance. For our scenario, consolidating the resource domains into the existing master domain and replacing them with OUs makes the most sense. This will then allow this group to take advantage of the OU capabilities that exist in Windows 2000 that were not available in Windows NT. Since there are two discrete subsets of administrative responsibility, creating two security groups to handle administration is correct. The appropriate permissions to grant are Full Control Of Computer Objects and Full Control Of Group Objects, based on the descriptions of job duties.

D. **Incorrect:** In Windows 2000, there are several reasons to create additional domains. In our scenario no reason is apparent, so the resource domains should be replaced by OUs. Also, this answer suggests the creation of unnecessary administrative groups, which would only lead to greater access control problems in the future.

70-220.04.02.002

▶ **Correct Answers: C**

A. **Incorrect:** Giving the group permissions to create and delete User objects would give Mark too much control. Although he can change the password property of any user he creates, he can also perform other, less desirable, activities.

B. **Incorrect:** Remember, the OU is the lowest level to which you can delegate authority. This means you can't delegate authority all the way down to User objects, as suggested by the answer.

C. **Correct:** By delegating authority to administer the rights for a container, you can decentralize administrative operations and minimize overhead. This reduces the cost of ownership by distributing administration closer to the resources. You define delegation of responsibility at the level of the OU, or container, where the accounts are created. An OU is the smallest scope or unit to which you can assign Group Policy settings or delegate administrative authority. However, policy settings that are domain-wide and permissions that are defined at higher levels in the directory tree can apply throughout the tree by using inheritance of permissions. You can delegate administration of a domain or OU by using the Delegation of Control Wizard available in Active Directory Users And Computers.

In Rob's case, he should restrict the delegation of permissions for the Dist-Admins group to updating just the specific property, the password property, of User objects in the OU. This way, Mark can't inadvertently apply unsound administrative practices during his apprenticeship.

D. **Incorrect:** Giving the group permissions to change properties of the OU would extend Mark's reach beyond mere User objects, allowing him to make changes that would have an adverse effect on the OU as a whole.

70-220.04.02.003

▶ **Correct Answers: A**

A. **Correct:** In Windows 2000, delegation of administration is more powerful and flexible than it was with its predecessor, Windows NT 4. This is achieved through a combination of OUs, per-attribute access control, and access control inheritance. Administration can be delegated arbitrarily by granting a set of users the ability to create specific objects or to modify attributes of objects.

In our scenario the appropriate choice is for Suki to create four groups in the 3D Graphics OU and make ACL entries in the child OUs limiting the administrators, capabilities to full control over groups and full control over computers in their own specific OUs. This solution has several advantages. By creating the groups in the 3D Graphics OU, their span of control is limited to OUs in only this portion of the hierarchy. By creating separate groups to administer groups and computers, she's able to exercise a more granular level of control than she would easily be able to otherwise. In this manner, if Suki wants to add administrator assistants for specific jobs, she's able to limit their influence to either the Grp-admins group or the Comp-admins group.

B. **Incorrect:** Creating just two groups, BG-admins and EX-admins, isn't optimal because it gives both the Backgrounds and the Explosions administrators too much power. This answer also gives those groups full control over the OU and all child objects. This is the real issue. In addition to controlling file access with groups and creating computer accounts, these administrators would now be able to create and modify any object at all, including additional OUs, which is too much control over other administrative functions that they shouldn't have access to.

C. **Incorrect:** One solution for delegation of administration was to put all the admins in a group at the 3D Graphics level and then create ACL entries at the child OUs. This would work, but it would allow the Backgrounds admins to make changes to the Explosions OU, and vice versa. This violates our scenario.

D. **Incorrect:** Creating the admin groups in the child OU violates our scenario. In our situation, Suki makes all the administrator assignments. The guideline is, if the OU is allowed to set its administrative membership, place the OU's admins group into the OU. If the OU isn't allowed to set its own administrative membership, leave the group outside of the OU.

OBJECTIVE 4.3

Design the placement and inheritance of security policies for sites, domains, and organizational units.

In this objective you'll need to know how to correctly place security policies on your network. You'll want to organize them in such a fashion that policies are efficiently routed from one machine to the other throughout your network's entire area. The important component to remember with security policies is that the design is crucial to success. Once you've enabled inherited security policies, they'll be harder to reverse down the road if the situation calls for it. Good planning, though, will alleviate most backtracking of this sort in the future.

With sites, domains, and OUs, you'll need to have a complete understanding of your network's potential complexity. Sites will have specific parameters largely because of physical location. Having separate LANs in different locations calls for specific security requirements. Although domains can be separated by physical distance, they will most likely be separated by department or team. Because of this, you must ensure that inherited policies are intrinsic to specific departments so that the right user can gain appropriate access.

With OUs, you can break up different locations that may have the same structure. For example, you may have human resources departments in offices located in Seattle, London, and New York. Again, you'll need to make a decision about breaking down your organization by physical location or by business structure. This goes back to the idea of creating a good solid security design.

Objective 4.3 Questions

70-220.04.03.001

Your Active Directory tree structure includes the ABC domain, the XYZ domain, and the 123 domain. XYZ and 123 are in the West site, and ABC is in the East site. A Group Policy object is linked to the West site that specifies red Windows wallpaper. A Group Policy object linked to XYZ that specifies Active Desktop Wallpaper is disabled. A Group Policy object linked to the Marketing OU in XYZ specifies green wallpaper.

What color is the wallpaper on Marketing OU computers?

A. No wallpaper is displayed

B. Green

C. Red

D. Windows default

70-220.04.03.002

Katie is designing her company's Active Directory structure. She has certain sensitive materials and specialized hardware on her network that she wants to effectively "hide" from all but authorized users. She wants to ensure that a casual user will never become aware of their existence. How can Katie accomplish her objective with the least amount of administrative overhead?

A. Create a separate resource domain and move the sensitive objects to this new domain. Create local groups in the new domain for access control. Add users in the original domain to the appropriate global group and assign that global group to the new local groups.

B. Create an OU. Move the sensitive objects into the OU. From the Security tab on the OU Properties sheet, remove the existing permissions from the OU and add new permissions as appropriate. In the Advanced dialog box, clear the Inherit Permissions From Parent check box.

C. Modify the ACL entries for each of the designated objects to remove the List Contents right from the Everyone group. Then apply new ACL entries as appropriate.

D. Create a security group. Place the sensitive objects into the group. Define a Group Policy to apply to your new group and implement it at the domain level.

70-220.04.03.003

Doug is supervising a Windows 2000 migration. The company's organizational structure consists of five departments: marketing, sales, production, operations, and administration. Five corresponding OUs will be created, containing the appropriate user accounts. With the exception of the operations department, all servers, printers, and other hardware assets will also be placed into their respective OUs. Because of higher security requirements for the servers in the operations department, they'll be placed into a separate OU, Ops_SVR.

All communications with servers in the operations department must be secured and encrypted to protect against network attacks.

How should Doug implement security for the operations department?

A. Assign the Secure Server (Require Security) and the Client (Respond Only) IPSec policies to the Marketing, Sales, Operations, Production, and Administration OUs.

B. Assign the Server (Request Security) IPSec policy at the Operations OU and the Client (Respond Only) IPSec policy at the domain level.

C. Assign the Server (Request Security) IPSec policy at the Ops_SVR OU and the Client (Respond Only) IPSec policy at the Operations OU.

D. Assign the Secure Server (Require Security) IPSec policy at the Ops_SVR OU and the Client (Respond Only) IPSec policy at the domain level.

Objective 4.3 Answers

70-220.04.03.001

▶ **Correct Answers: A**

A. **Correct:** You can apply Group Policy in four places: the local computer, the site, the domain, and the OU. The local Group Policy object is applied first. Then site-linked policies are applied in administrator-specified order, followed by domain-linked policies, also in specified order. Finally, OU-linked policies are applied, starting at the top of the Active Directory hierarchy and ending with the OU actually containing the user or computer. The setting in the child policy takes priority, although in one case this isn't true. If the parent disables a setting and the child makes a change to that setting, the child's change is ignored. In other words, the disabling of a setting is always inherited down the hierarchy. So in this case no wallpaper is displayed.

B. **Incorrect:** If a parent Group Policy object hadn't disabled the Active Desktop Wallpaper setting, the child policy (OU, in this case) would have been applied, making the wallpaper green.

C. **Incorrect:** Based on the order in which settings are applied, the wallpaper would have been red only if Group Policy objects were linked to the domain or OU with different settings.

D. **Incorrect:** No situation related to the application of Group Policy objects would have caused the computers to have Windows default wallpaper applied. This answer tricks many people, though, because they think that the default is reverted to in this instance.

70-220.04.03.002

▶ **Correct Answers: B**

A. **Incorrect:** You could create a separate resource domain, but there would be significantly more administrative overhead, not to mention additional hardware requirements, to implement that option.

B. **Correct:** As part of your OU structure plan, you create OUs for three purposes: delegation of authority, hiding objects, and Group Policy.

Even if a user doesn't have the right to read an object's attributes, that user can still see that the object exists by viewing the contents of the parent container. The easiest and most efficient way to hide an object or set of objects is to create an OU for those objects and limit the set of users who have the List Contents right for that OU. In this way you have only one group of ACL settings to manage, whether you need to hide 1 object or 1,000.

C. **Incorrect:** You could (eventually) accomplish the same goal by going to each and every object you want to "hide," and individually manipulating their ACLs. In addition, this incorrect response also refers to removing the List Contents right from the Everyone group. List Contents would only apply to container objects. If one of your objects were, for example, a server, there wouldn't be a List Contents right.

D. **Incorrect:** A security group is designed to simplify providing access for large numbers of users. In addition to designing security groups, Windows 2000 has certain default security groups available that include their own preset rights and access privileges. Examples of security groups include local groups, global groups, and universal groups. You wouldn't be able to place other random types of objects into a security group. (Note that List Contents only applies to container objects, not leaf objects.)

70-220.04.03.003

▶ **Correct Answers: D**

A. **Incorrect:** Because of the requirement for all operations department servers to communicate securely at all times, the Secure Server (Require Security) IPSec policy should be implemented. Placing the high security servers into a separate OU allows for ease of administration, as well as enhanced security. By applying this IPSec policy to the Ops_SVR OU, all servers in the OU are affected.

Applying the Secure Server (Require Security) policy to the Marketing, Sales, Operations, Production, and Administration OUs would have the unfortunate effect of requiring secure communications for servers that don't need it and not requiring them for servers that do. Applying the Client (Respond Only) policy to those same OUs would work, but applying this policy at the domain level is better.

B. **Incorrect:** The Server (Request Security) IPSec policy isn't strict enough. In our scenario all communications from operations department servers must be secure. With this policy the server can fall back to nonsecure if the client can't respond securely.

C. **Incorrect:** This answer is incorrect for the reasons stated in B.

D. **Correct:** To ensure that client computers are properly configured to respond securely if attempting communications with operations department servers, employ the Client (Respond Only) IPSec policy at the domain level. The policy will propagate down through the Active Directory structure to all client computers in all subordinate OUs. In this way, if changes are made to the AD structure (like adding a new OU), the security policy won't be affected.

Applying the Client (Respond Only) policy to the Marketing, Sales, Operations, Production, and Administration OUs would work, but applying this policy at the domain level is better.

O B J E C T I V E   4 . 4

Design an Encrypting File System strategy.

The **Encrypting File System (EFS)** is a component that's new to Windows 2000 Server. When implemented properly, it can severely cut down on data theft and loss, which is largely caused by remote or roving clients. The administrative side is largely hands-free, as this gives users the ability to encrypt files and folders of their choosing.

From a design standpoint, you need to consider how much you'll allow your users to use EFS. If you give users too much EFS control, you run the risk that overencryption will result in files not being available to users who require them. If you don't give your users the right to encrypt files, you risk leaving sensitive data and files exposed to whomever wants to view them.

In terms of overall EFS design, you need to keep a few things in mind. Determine who has the ability to encrypt files and who does not. You need to decide who will be in charge of recovery keys, as well as where those recovery keys will be stored and with whom.

Objective 4.4 Questions

70-220.04.04.001

You have EFS enabled. You want to transfer an encrypted file to an NTFS partition on another computer. You're unsuccessful. What is the most likely cause of your problem?

A. You attempted the transfer using the Windows 2000 Backup utility.

B. The file is decrypted for transfer across the network. You must use SSL or IPSec to encrypt the transmitted file.

C. The sender's public key isn't available on the target computer.

D. The other computer isn't trusted for delegation.

70-220.04.04.002

Peter must implement a procedure to ensure that internal communications between the production server, PRODUCTION1 and the research server, RESEARCH1, are secure and confidential. The data on these servers is highly sensitive and must not be compromised by unauthorized or malicious network users.

Peter's network is a native-mode Windows 2000 environment, with PRODUCTION1 and RESEARCH1 located on geographically separated subnets and a T1 connection linking the routers between them.

Which primary technology must Peter employ?

A. EFS with centralized recovery agent

B. DFS with CryptoAPI (CAPI)

C. IPSec with ESP

D. IPSec with AH

70-220.04.04.003

Lisa, the network administrator, is concerned about laptop security for her traveling sales representatives. Just last year, 12 laptop computers were stolen from airports or client sites. Recognizing that this problem is likely to continue, Lisa wants to protect the integrity of the stolen data, rendering it useless to the thief. She has recently upgraded all client computers to Windows 2000 Professional. Lisa wants to accomplish the following:

- Protect files and folders with encryption

- Prevent unauthorized users from accessing encrypted files

- Provide recovery capability for administrators

To accomplish the stated objectives, what should Lisa incorporate into her security plan?

A. EFS and NTFS5

B. IPSec

C. L2TP

D. PPTP

E. NTLM

F. Kerberos V5

Objective 4.4 Answers

70-220.04.04.001

▶ **Correct Answers: D**

   A. **Incorrect:** Transferring encrypted files using Windows 2000 Backup isn't a problem. Normally, if you transfer an encrypted file to any other media, you lose the encryption. This isn't true if you use Windows 2000 Backup.

   B. **Incorrect:** While it's true that the file is transmitted as clear text, as long as the target volume is Windows 2000 NTFS, the file should be encrypted at the target, subject to the conditions listed above. SSL would be used more to authenticate a browser with its corresponding Web server using public key encryption. Therefore, it doesn't apply here.

   C. **Incorrect:** The sender's public key doesn't have to be on the target to support encryption. However, if the user wants to decrypt the file on the target computer, the user's private key must be available.

   D. **Correct:** EFS determines when an encrypted file is being moved or copied to another drive. EFS always decrypts and sends files as plaintext. The file is reencrypted if the target drive supports EFS. If the target drive has EFS but is on a different computer, the file is reencrypted with the sender's public key. The target computer must be trusted for delegation or the transfer fails. To determine whether the target computer is trusted, select the computer in Active Directory and select the General tab of the Properties dialog box. If the computer is trusted, the Trusted For Delegation check box will be selected.

70-220.04.04.002

▶ **Correct Answers: C**

   A. **Incorrect:** EFS provides encryption services for file systems, ensuring that only authorized users may access these files. Although EFS is certainly a technology Peter should employ, it isn't warranted in our scenario because it doesn't encrypt transmission of data. The problem in this scenario is that each subnet is located in a different geographical location, which makes EFS an invalid option.

   B. **Incorrect:** DFS is a service that combines elements from different file systems into a single logical tree structure. DFS has no inherent security capabilities, but it will incorporate EFS to provide encryption. EFS requires an NTFS partition to work, but DFS doesn't. However, no file system protection is available on any part of a DFS tree that's located on a FAT volume.

C. **Correct:** Peter has two concerns: integrity and encryption. The communications must be secure, meaning they must be verified and unchanged at the destination. Also, they must be confidential (encrypted). The primary technology that assures these requirements will be met is IPSec. IPSec policies allow secure, end-to-end communication between two computers on an IP network. Optionally, Peter can encrypt his IPSec traffic using ESP.

D. **Incorrect:** Peter has two concerns: integrity and encryption. The communications must be secure, meaning they must be verified and unchanged at the destination. Also, they must be confidential (encrypted). The primary technology that assures these requirements will be met is IPSec. IPSec policies allow secure, end-to-end communications between two computers on an IP network. Optionally, Peter can encrypt his IPSec traffic using ESP. Authentication Header (AH) provides data origination authentication, integrity, and antireplay service. It doesn't provide encryption.

70-220.04.04.003

▶ **Correct Answers: A**

A. **Correct:** Lisa needs to implement EFS. EFS protects sensitive data on disk using the NTFS5 (the new Windows 2000 version of NTFS) file system. You can't implement EFS on a non-NTFS formatted drive. EFS uses symmetric key encryption and public key technology to provide confidentiality for files. EFS runs as a system service, meaning it's easy to manage, difficult to attack, and transparent to the file's owner and to applications the user is running. Only the owner of a protected file can access the file, just like a normal document. Other users simply receive an Access Denied message. However, recovery administrators (whom you can designate) have the ability to recover protected files if that becomes necessary. This protects the user in case the user's key gets lost or it becomes corrupted in some way.

B. **Incorrect:** IPSec is a technology that incorporates data encryption, but it involves encrypted transmissions, not encrypted files.

C. **Incorrect:** L2TP is a technology that incorporates data encryption, but it involves encrypted transmissions, not encrypted files.

D. **Incorrect:** PPTP is a technology that incorporates data encryption, but it involves encrypted transmissions, not encrypted files.

E. **Incorrect:** Windows NT Lan Manager (NTLM) authentication is an authentication technology. It verifies a user's identity, but it doesn't encrypt the user's files.

F. **Incorrect:** Kerberos V5 is an authentication technology. It verifies a user's identity, but it doesn't encrypt the user's files.

O B J E C T I V E   4 . 5

Design an authentication strategy.

With Windows 2000 Server, the idea of authentication becomes a new and interesting component of computer networking. Before, it was easy to just create the requisite firewall and keep everyone out. Now clients need to access your site for product information, remote sales people and workers need to make on-time checks of inventory, as well as a host of other things. No longer is a network some island in a vast ocean. Now networks more resemble a subway station. Information is continually going in and out of the station. The important thing to remember is who gets off the train, who doesn't, and why.

By designing a correct authentication strategy, you'll be able to make sure that people are who they say they are from a network analysis perspective. To design an authentication strategy, you must take users with various parameters, profiles, and possibly operating systems and make sure that everyone gets where they need to go along your network's path, or more importantly, that they get where they should go and nowhere else.

Objective 4.5 Questions

70-220.04.05.001

You want to enable authentication for your remote access users using the Windows 2000 IAS, the Microsoft implementation of RADIUS. How does the authentication request process originate?

A. The RADIUS server sends an access-request packet to the RADIUS client.

B. The remote access client sends a RADIUS access-request packet to the NAS.

C. The NAS attempts to negotiate a secure connection with the remote access client using the most secure protocol first.

D. The remote access client sends a digital signature to a domain controller.

70-220.04.05.002

You maintain a Novell NetWare network for file and print services. This network shares infrastructure with your Windows 2000 network. There is no immediate plan to migrate the Novell network resources to your Windows 2000 network. Your client computers have been upgraded to Windows 2000 Professional. To lessen the burden of maintaining parallel networks, you use synchronized passwords and pass-through authentication to access NetWare services. What must you install to enable this capability?

A. Client Service for NetWare (CSNW) on the Windows 2000 Professional computers

B. CSNW on one or more Windows 2000 Server computers

C. File and Print Service for NetWare (FPNW) on the Windows 2000 Professional computers

D. Gateway Service for NetWare (GSNW) on the Windows 2000 Professional computers

70-220.04.05.003

Kimberly is configuring VPN connectivity for her mobile sales representatives.

They require the ability to transmit data using 128-bit encryption techniques. Because some of the laptop computers are older and aren't scheduled to be upgraded soon, Kimberly has elected to configure the VPN to use PPTP tunneling.

For extra security, Kimberly requires that both the client and the server mutually verify their identities. Which authentication methods can Kimberly implement?

A. Extensible Authentication Protocol-Message Digest 5 Challenge Handshake Authentication Protocol (EAP-MD5 CHAP)

B. Microsoft Challenge Handshake Authentication Protocol version 2 (MS-CHAP v2)

C. Smart card and other certificate authentication

D. Extensible Authentication Protocol-Transport Layer Security (EAP-TLS)

E. SPAP

F. PAP

G. CHAP

Objective 4.5 Answers

70-220.04.05.001

▶ **Correct Answers: C**

A. **Incorrect:** The RADIUS server doesn't send an access-request packet to the RADIUS client. The RADIUS server verifies the requestor's identity by validating the user's credentials against a domain controller.

B. **Incorrect:** The NAS sends a RADIUS access-request packet to the IAS server. The NAS originates the access-request packet; it doesn't receive the packet from the client attempting to access the network.

C. **Correct:** IAS performs centralized connection authentication, authorization, and accounting for dial-up and VPN remote access and for router-to-router connections. IAS can authenticate a whole host of users and computers using several different protocols such as Password Authentication Protocol (PAP), Challenge Handshake Authentication Protocol (CHAP), Microsoft Challenge Handshake Authentication Protocol (MS-CHAP), and Extensible Authentication Protocol (EAP). The use of RADIUS allows this data to be maintained in a central location, rather than on each NAS. Users connect to RADIUS-compliant NASs, such as a Windows 2000–based computer that's running RRAS. The NASs then forward authentication requests to the centralized IAS server. The first step in the process is for the NAS to negotiate a secure connection with the remote access client (user). For example, a Windows 2000 remote access server tries to negotiate EAP, MS-CHAP v2, MS-CHAP, CHAP, Shiva Password Authentication Protocol (SPAP), and lastly PAP.

D. **Incorrect:** The remote access client doesn't send a digital signature to a domain controller. The IAS server uses the digital signature to verify that the request came from a NAS.

70-220.04.05.002

▶ **Correct Answers: A**

A. **Correct:** Computers running Windows 2000 Server with Gateway Service for NetWare and computers running Windows 2000 Professional with CSNW can use pass-through authentication. If a user has the same credentials for a Windows 2000 network and a NetWare network, and the password is synchronized, the user can log on to both networks at once.

B. **Incorrect:** CSNW runs only on client machines, not servers.

C. **Incorrect:** FPNW is an added cost component to allow NetWare users to gain access to Microsoft file and print services.

D. **Incorrect:** GSNW runs only on servers.

70-220.04.05.003

▶ **Correct Answers: D**

A. **Incorrect:** EAP-MD5 CHAP uses the same challenge handshake protocol as PPP-based CHAP, but the challenges and responses are sent as EAP messages.

B. **Incorrect:** Kimberly would use MS-CHAP v2 only if all her clients were running Windows 2000 on their laptops. Because the laptops are older, they're most likely running Windows 95 or another vendor's operating system (OS), such as MacOS. In this case, she should use MS-CHAP, but not MS-CHAP v2.

C. **Incorrect:** If a certificate is installed either in the certificate store on your computer or on a smart card and EAP is enabled, you can use certificate-based authentication in a single network logon process.

D. **Correct:** To enable MPPE-based data encryption for VPN connections, you must select the MS-CHAP, MS-CHAP v2, or EAP-TLS authentication methods. These authentication methods generate the keys used in the encryption process. However, our scenario specifies mutual client/server verification, which eliminates MS-CHAP.

E. **Incorrect:** SPAP is a vendor solution for use when connected to Shiva LAN Rover hardware. It's more secure than plaintext but less secure than CHAP.

F. **Incorrect:** PAP uses plaintext passwords and is the least sophisticated authentication method. Normally, you'd use PAP only if the client and the remote access server were unable to negotiate anything better.

G. **Incorrect:** CHAP is an industry-standard authentication protocol used by many non-Microsoft clients.

OBJECTIVE 4.6

Design a security group strategy.

In designing a cohesive security group strategy, you're going to be faced with the task of laying out your security deployment plan for all the world to see. The core of designing an appropriate security group strategy lies in your Group Policy settings. You'll need to decide to what degree you will need to alter the standard Group Policy settings to fit your specific network requirements.

A solid security group strategy is projective in that it should identify the additional security groups that you'll need to create in the future. You'll need to establish the range of influence they'll have and identify the various membership requirements that they'll require.

Windows 2000 supports four types of built-in security groups, differentiated by scope. Those groups are:

- **Domain local groups**   These groups are typically used to assign permissions to specific resources, such as printers and file systems.

- **Global groups**   These groups are used to logically organize users by function or resource access needs. The preferred method to grant user access is to assign global groups to the appropriate local groups that define the access. In Windows 2000 you can nest global groups to make administration simpler.

- **Universal groups**   These groups are used in larger, multidomain environments where you have users in different domains requiring similar levels of access to resources. The normal technique is to place global groups into universal groups, and then add the universal group to the local group. Note: A single domain model doesn't support universal groups.

- **Computer local group**   This group exists for access control that's specific to one computer that isn't recognized elsewhere in the domain.

With the previous objectives, you've made arrangements so that your users get access to all the systems they want. With this objective, you'll take that line of thinking one step further and give your various users the access they require. To do this, you'll need to have a clear understanding of these options in Windows 2000 in regard to security groups: the privilege assignment, the security group, and the security principal.

Objective 4.6 Questions

70-220.04.06.001

You're the administrator for a small, native-mode Windows 2000 network. Currently, you use universal groups to handle all of your access control needs.

Your organization is growing rapidly through internal growth, acquisitions, and mergers. What access control strategy should you adopt?

A. Reduce reliance on universal groups and use a combination of global groups and local groups to assign access permissions.

B. Carefully plan your universal group growth strategy to leverage the advantages of nesting groups.

C. Use universal groups for all access across domain boundaries and global and local groups for all intra-domain access.

D. In a multidomain environment, eliminate global groups where there are access requirements across domain boundaries.

70-220.04.06.002

Daniel is supervising the Windows 2000 upgrade of his existing Windows NT 4 network. Before the upgrade, Daniel had a Headquarters domain located in Atlanta and two resource domains in Chattanooga and Savannah. After the upgrade, Daniel retained the Headquarters domain and merged the resource domains into OUs under Headquarters. No user accounts will be in the resource OUs. How should Daniel define his security group strategy to allow authorized users access to resources in Chattanooga and Savannah?

A. Create local groups in the resource OUs and grant them appropriate permissions to the resources located within. Create global groups at Headquarters containing logical groupings of users. Place the appropriate global groups into the appropriate local groups.

B. Create global groups in the resource OUs and grant them appropriate permissions to the resources located within. Create the necessary local groups at Headquarters containing the logical groupings of users. Place the local groups into the appropriate global groups.

C. Create local groups in the resource OUs, and grant them appropriate permissions to the resources located within. Create universal groups at Headquarters containing predefined global groups. Add the appropriate universal groups to the local groups.

D. Modify the ACLs of the resources in the OUs granting the appropriate permissions to the Users, the Power Users, and the Administrators groups. Create a transitive, two-way trust between the OUs and Headquarters.

70-220.04.06.003

You manage a large, complex network with thousands of users. Dozens of Group Policy objects apply to these users in multiple configurations. There are instances where large groups of users experience logon delays primarily because they are included in Group Policy objects that really don't apply to them.

What is the best way to exempt members of a given security group from a Group Policy object? (Choose all that apply.)

A. Set the Apply Group Policy permission to Deny

B. Set the Read permission to Deny

C. Set the Apply Group Policy permission to Allow

D. Set the Read permission to Allow

E. Set the Apply Group Policy permission to neither Deny nor Allow

F. Set the Read permission to neither Deny nor Allow

Objective 4.6 Answers

70-220.04.06.001

▶ **Correct Answers: A**

A. **Correct:** Some small organizations in a native-mode Windows 2000 environment use universal groups to handle their access requirements. As an organization grows, it's prudent to reduce reliance on universal groups and instead implement an access control strategy based on global groups and local groups. Global groups are good for organizations where membership is expected to change frequently, and local groups are good for protecting resources because local domain group members can be either inside or outside the same existing domain. Because universal groups are listed in the global catalog database, a large number of universal groups—especially where membership changes frequently—can cause a lot of replication traffic.

B. **Incorrect:** Nesting is the ability to include one group in the membership of another. This is a real benefit to administrators in terms of organization. However, because universal groups are listed in the global catalog database, every logon is subject to a search of the database to verify any universal group membership. You still have to deal with the ramifications of increased replication traffic. Nesting universal groups doesn't alleviate this concern.

C. **Incorrect:** You have no assurance that a strategy involving universal groups for interdomain access will be free of the concerns stated earlier. As an organization grows, reliance on universal groups should diminish.

D. **Incorrect:** Eliminating global groups would have a harmful effect on network access. If you eliminate global groups, you must use universal groups or domain local groups for access control. It's always recommended that you populate domain local groups with global groups instead of individual users. The argument against the proliferation of universal groups has previously been advanced.

70-220.04.06.002

▶ **Correct Answers: A**

A. **Correct:** In Daniel's situation, the correct approach would be to create domain local groups and add the global groups. These groups are typically used to assign permissions to specific resources, such as printers and file systems.

B. **Incorrect:** Although you can add a global group to a domain local group, you can't add a domain local group to a global group. Global groups are used to logically organize users by function or resource access needs. The preferred method to grant user access is to assign global groups to the appropriate local groups that define the access. In Windows 2000 you can nest global groups to make administration simpler.

C. **Incorrect:** Although you can add a global group to a domain local group, you can't add a domain local group to a global group. Universal groups are used in larger, multidomain environments where you have users in different domains requiring similar levels of access to resources. The normal technique is to place global groups into universal groups, and then add the universal group to the local group.

D. **Incorrect:** Trusts are created between domains, not within a single domain. Also, granting access permissions to only the Users, Power Users, and Administrators groups wouldn't give you granular enough control over domain resources.

70-220.04.06.003

▶ **Correct Answers: A and B**

A. **Correct:** A powerful capability of Windows 2000 Group Policy is the ability to filter the application of Group Policy using security groups. If you want to exempt the members of a particular security group from a certain Group Policy object, you open the Group Policy object whose scope is to be filtered. From the Properties sheet, select the Security tab, and then select the security group through which to filter this Group Policy object. For our scenario, set the Apply Group Policy permission to Deny. This setting ensures that this Group Policy object never applies to members of this security group regardless of the permissions those members might have in other security groups.

B. **Correct:** A powerful capability of Windows 2000 Group Policy is the ability to filter the application of Group Policy using security groups. If you want to exempt the members of a particular security group from a certain Group Policy object, you open the Group Policy object whose scope is to be filtered. From the Properties sheet, select the Security tab, and then select the security group through which to filter this Group Policy object. For our scenario, set the Read permission to Deny. This setting ensures that this Group Policy object never applies to members of this security group regardless of the permissions those members might have in other security groups.

C. **Incorrect:** Setting the Apply Group Policy permission to Allow specifically applies this Group Policy object to members of this security group (unless they are members of at least one other security group covered by the provisions in the answer explanation for B).

D. **Incorrect:** Setting the Read permission to Allow specifically applies this Group Policy object to members of this security group (unless they are members of at least one other security group covered by the provisions in the answer explanation for B).

E. **Incorrect:** By setting the Apply Group Policy permission to neither Deny nor Allow, this Group Policy object will apply to members of this security group only if they have both the Apply Group Policy permission and the Read permission set to Allow as members of at least one other security group. They also must not have the Apply Group Policy permission or the Read permission set to Deny as members of any other security group.

F. **Incorrect:** By setting the Read permission to neither Deny nor Allow, this Group Policy object will apply to members of this security group only if they have both the Apply Group Policy permission and the Read permission set to Allow as members of at least one other security group. They also must not have the Apply Group Policy permission or the Read permission set to Deny as members of any other security group.

OBJECTIVE 4.7

Design a Public Key Infrastructure.

When PKI was first introduced, it was heralded as the final wave of network security. Like a lot of ideas, it didn't catch on fast, but there's considerable interest in it today. PKI is the whole combination of components and services that uses public and private key pairs as the authentication process between servers and clients.

In regard to Windows 2000 Server, EFS implements PKI to encrypt and decrypt information stored within files and folders. For the exam, it's important to remember various aspects of PKI. You need to make sure that you know how to implement the hierarchical structure of certificate authorities (CAs). In order to obtain a digital certificate, a user must generate a private key. After its identity is verified with the CA, the CA then assigns a private root key to the user's public key.

You'll also need to know the difference between the various types of certificate server roles, such as stand-alone, issuing, and enterprise CAs. For instance, Active Directory must be present when using enterprise CAs, and stand-alone CAs are used when Active Directory isn't present on your system.

Objective 4.7 Questions

70-220.04.07.001

You're the Certificate Services manager for your organization. Your organization is a large, multinational conglomerate with complex and extensive PKI and Certificate Services requirements. You're keenly aware of the danger of physical compromise or network attack on your certificate-related hardware.

You've established a multiple-level certification hierarchy to enhance centralized control and ensure high security and integrity coupled with operational flexibility. You want to strike a balance between usability and security. After careful consideration, you've decided to protect certain assets with specialized crypto-graphic hardware, highly secure locked vaults, and offline operation. For the sake of usability, which category of assets should not normally be secured in this manner?

A. Root CAs

B. Issuing CAs

C. Enterprise CAs

D. Stand-alone CAs

70-220.04.07.002

You're the certificate manager for your company's Windows 2000 Active Directory–enabled network. You've installed an enterprise CA as the root CA. You want to have the capability of issuing a certificate for a subordinate CA with a lifetime of 10 years. Which statement applies?

A. Given the present configuration, certificate lifetime for the subordinate CA is limited to two years.

B. Given the present configuration, certificate lifetime for the subordinate CA is limited to five years.

C. You must change the registry settings for ValidityPeriod and ValidityPeriodUnits for the root CA to 10 years or more.

D. A subordinate CA certificate can never be issued for more than five years.

70-220.04.07.003

Salman's company is in a partnering relationship with another, much larger company. Salman needs to set up certificate-based secure e-mail with the partner company. As it happens, the partner company is a CA and is capable of issuing certificates for server authentication, client authentication, code signing, and secure e-mail. Salman would like to use the partner company's certificates only for secure e-mail. He wants to ensure that any certificates issued for another purpose aren't accepted.

Salman's network houses internal CAs installed for other purposes, some on Windows 2000 servers and some on Windows NT 4 servers. Salman's network uses Active Directory.

How should Salman proceed?

A. Salman shouldn't use the partner's CA because of the increased security risks from the external CA's unwanted capabilities. Salman should find another external CA that can issue certificates only for secure e-mail.

B. Salman should use the enterprise trust policy to create certificate trust lists.

C. Salman should use the "Using the Advanced Certificate Request" Web page at the partner site, and set the following option: under Intended Purposes select E-Mail.

D. Salman should use the trusted root certification authority policy to distribute the external root certificates.

Objective 4.7 Answers

70-220.04.07.001

▶ **Correct Answers: B**

A. **Incorrect:** Because the enterprise root CA is the top level, it's capable of signing its own certificate. Therefore, in a multiple-level CA hierarchy, you can tailor the CA environment to provide a balance between security and usability. For example, for a root CA, you might choose to use special purpose cryptographic hardware, maintain it in a locked vault, and operate it in offline mode.

B. **Correct:** The issuing CA is the CA that actually gives out the certificate. In a multiple-level CA hierarchy, you can tailor the CA environment to provide a balance between security and usability. For an issuing CA, crypto-hardware, locked vaults, and offline operations are costly. They make the CA difficult to use and reduce the CA's performance and effectiveness.

C. **Incorrect:** Windows 2000 Server and Certificate Services support two types of CAs: enterprise CAs and stand-alone CAs. You can install a root CA or a subordinate CA as an enterprise CA or a stand-alone CA. These answers wouldn't be correct because you wouldn't install these types of CAs as issuing CAs.

D. **Incorrect:** This answer is incorrect for the reasons stated in C.

70-220.04.07.002

▶ **Correct Answers: A**

A. **Correct:** Enterprise CAs require Active Directory in order to be available for use. Enterprise CAs publish certificates and certificate revocation lists (CRLs) to Active Directory. Enterprise CAs use certificate template information, user account information, and security group information stored in Active Directory to approve or deny certificate requests. The template for subordinate CAs has an absolute maximum life cycle of five years. In our scenario we must assume the enterprise CA was installed with the default two-year certificate lifetime. That means that, given the circumstances, the subordinate CA certificate is limited to two years.

B. **Incorrect:** To extend the subordinate CA certificate to five years, the enterprise CA must have its registry settings for ValidityPeriod and ValidityPeriodUnits extended to five or more years. Extending the enterprise CA certificate to 10 years wouldn't change the subordinate CA hard limit of 5 years.

C. **Incorrect:** This answer is incorrect for the reasons stated in B.

D. **Incorrect:** If your root CA is a stand-alone CA, the hard time limits associated with enterprise CAs no longer exist. Stand-alone CAs don't use templates and don't need Active Directory or membership in a Windows 2000 domain to be used, but all certificates that the stand-alone CA issues have the lifetime specified by the values of its ValidityPeriod and ValidityPeriodUnits registry entries. To issue certificates with different lifetimes, deploy enterprise CAs, multiple stand-alone CAs, or third-party CAs.

70-220.04.07.003

▶ **Correct Answers: B**

A. **Incorrect:** If he follows the proper guidelines, Salman shouldn't have to worry about increased security risks due to unnecessary capabilities of the external CA.

B. **Correct:** A certificate trust list (CTL) is used to establish trust between your organization and another, and it allows you to control trust of the purpose and validity period of certificates issued by external CAs. If your trusted CA trusts their root CA, CTL isn't necessary. However, you want to limit the trust of certificates issued by a particular CA, especially if the CA is external. This is where creating a certificate trust list and using it through Group Policy is useful.

In our scenario the external CA is capable of issuing certificates for e-mail, server and client authentication, and code signing. Salman wants to trust only certificates issued for the purpose of secure e-mail. He can create a CTL and limit the purpose for which he trusts certificates issued by the external CA so that they're valid only for secure e-mail. Any certificates issued for another purpose won't be accepted for use by any computer or user in the scope of the Group Policy object to which the certificate trust list is applied.

C. **Incorrect:** This option is limited to internal stand-alone CAs.

D. **Incorrect:** Trusted root certification authority policy only applies to internal CAs, not external.

OBJECTIVE 4.8

Design Windows 2000 network services security.

The path toward gaining network access (either honestly or dishonestly) is a short but important one. In order to have network availability, you need to be authenticated in some manner. In order to be authenticated, you need to locate a domain controller. If you're working in a Windows 2000 environment, you have just one choice. DNS is the path through which network access is achieved.

In addition to DNS, Windows 2000 Server utilizes a complete host of services for managing, or protecting your network, or both. Whether for this exam or for the real world, you need to understand how each service works and how they interrelate. The interrelation should be stressed because as new applications come about, they continually require the presence of various Windows 2000 services in order to work effectively. If one of these services fails, it might affect services down the line. Think of it like the popular party game where if you pull the wrong block of wood from the center structure, you risk having the whole tower collapse.

You need to have a good understanding of the following services: DNS, Remote Installation Services (RIS), Simple Network Management Protocol (SNMP), and Terminal Server. You can't work for a company that only utilizes kiosks in some public capacity and think that all the knowledge you'd require is on Terminal Services. In order to keep those machines free from harm, you must know their relationship to the entire network. Understanding that relationship comes from understanding these aforementioned network subsystems.

Objective 4.8 Questions

70-220.04.08.001

You're the network administrator. You maintain a high security native-mode Windows 2000 network. You make the following registry entry on the DNS server:

```
HKEY_LOCAL_MACHINE\SYSTEM\CurrentControlSet\Services\Tcpip\Parameters
\UpdateSecurityLevel=256
```

Later, you discover that the dynamic update process has failed. Which of the listed failure scenarios is most likely?

A. The prerequisites for the dynamic update haven't been met.

B. The primary server that's authoritative for the name doesn't respond.

C. The server isn't accepting dynamic updates because the zone is being transferred.

D. The server accepts only secure dynamic updates, and the insecure dynamic update operation failed.

70-220.04.08.002

Leonard is the network administrator for the southeast region of his company. His LAN consists of a mix of Windows 2000 and non-Windows 2000 computers. He has several Windows 2000 DHCP servers installed for fault tolerance and securing dynamic updates. One of his DHCP servers (DHCPMAIN) failed. Three days later, a user informed Leonard that he was having problems with DNS addressing. Leonard pieced together the following facts:

- DHCPMAIN registered the name *bob.marketing.fabrikam.com* on behalf of a non-Windows 2000 client.

- DHCPMAIN went down.

- An administrator upgraded the user's computer to Windows 2000.

- The user can no longer dynamically update his host A record in DNS.

Leonard called Tech Support for assistance and was instructed to add all of his DHCP servers to the security group DNSProxyUpdate. How will this solve Leonard's problem?

A. Any object created by a member of this group has no security and the first user (who isn't a member of the DNSProxyUpdate group) to modify the set of DNS records becomes the owner.

B. Membership in this group causes the DHCP servers to emulate the DHCP/DNS interaction behavior for non-Windows 2000 clients.

C. By default, the DHCP server sends updates for clients who don't support the Client Fully Qualified Domain Name (FQDN) option (option 81). Members of this group will *not* send updates for these clients.

D. Membership in this group enables full control over all DNS objects stored in Active Directory.

70-220.04.08.003

Fidelma is concerned with SNMP security because, under normal circumstances, community names are transmitted in cleartext format, creating an unacceptable security risk. She has decided that she wants to protect SNMP messages with IPSec. How should Fidelma configure her IPSec policy?

A. Edit the appropriate IP filter list. Add two sets of filter specifications, one for typical SNMP traffic, and one for SNMP trap messages. For the first filter, specify a port source and destination address of 161 for TCP and UDP traffic. For the second filter, specify a port source and destination address of 162 for TCP and UDP traffic. Mirror both.

B. Add a new IP filter list called All SNMP Traffic. In the Filter Properties dialog box, select Any from the Select A Protocol Type drop-down list. Select From Any Port and To Any Port in the Set The IP Protocol Port section.

C. In the SNMP Service Properties dialog box, select the Security tab. Select the Send Authentication Trap check box. Select the Public community and change the Community Rights drop-down list to None.

D. Use the Server (Require Security) predefined IPSec policy, which encrypts the SNMP protocol by default.

Objective 4.8 Answers

70-220.04.08.001

▶ **Correct Answers: D**

   A. **Incorrect:** This answer represents legitimate failure conditions for DNS dynamic updates, but nothing in our scenario suggests any of them is likely.

   B. **Incorrect:** This answer is incorrect for the reasons stated in A.

   C. **Incorrect:** This answer is incorrect for the reasons stated in A.

   D. **Correct:** DNS dynamic updates allow clients, even DHCP clients, to dynamically register address (A) and pointer (PTR) records with a primary name server, which reduces the administrative effort required to maintain those records manually. In addition, DHCP servers can use dynamic updates to register these records on behalf of clients who can't do it themselves, further reducing administrative overhead. Secure dynamic update works the same way, except authorization is required before the records can be modified. By default, a dynamic update is attempted first, followed by a secure dynamic update attempt if the first attempt fails. By manipulating the UpdateSecurityLevel registry key, you can specify either Always Attempt An Insecure Update or Always Attempt A Secure Update. A value of 256 means always attempt a secure update. This indicates that the most likely cause for our failure is that the server accepts only secure dynamic updates.

70-220.04.08.002

▶ **Correct Answers: A**

   A. **Correct:** You can configure a Windows 2000 DHCP server to dynamically register A and PTR resource records on behalf of DHCP clients. Using secure dynamic update with Windows 2000 DNS servers might cause problems with this configuration. Consider, for example, that a Windows 2000 DHCP server performs a secure dynamic update on behalf of a client for a specific DNS name. Then the DHCP server becomes the owner of the name. Now only that DHCP server can update the DNS name.

   The problem comes when the DHCP server fails and a subsequent update request from the original client will fail because the failed DHCP server owns the name. To solve this problem, a new security group called DNSProxyUpdate is provided. Any object (DNS record) created by a member of this group has no security. The first client (who isn't a member of this group) to request an update becomes the owner. Note: If you're using multiple DHCP servers, add them all to the DNSProxyUpdate group.

The DNSProxyUpdate group raises a couple of security issues that you have to deal with. First, any DNS names registered by the computer running the DHCP service aren't secure. This is important if the DHCP server is on a domain controller. Also, the DHCP server has full control over all DNS objects stored in the Active Directory because the DHCP server runs under the computer (in this case, the domain controller) account. Therefore, it's highly recommended that you not run DHCP servers on domain controllers.

B. **Incorrect:** Membership in this group does *not* cause the DHCP servers to emulate the interaction behavior for non-Windows 2000 clients.

C. **Incorrect:** By default, the DHCP server does indeed send updates for clients who don't support the Client FQDN option (option 81).

This allows the server to perform proxy updates in DNS for all of its non-Windows 2000 DHCP clients. This doesn't, however, have anything to do with the DNSProxyUpdate security group.

D. **Incorrect:** It is true that membership in the DNSProxyUpdate group enables full control over all DNS objects stored in Active Directory. But the reason this answer is incorrect is because this is a problem, not a solution!

70-220.04.08.003

▶ **Correct Answers: A**

A. **Correct:** SNMP service gives you the ability to monitor and communicate status information between a variety of hosts. SNMP performs its management services by using a distributed architecture of management systems and agents. Two components are required to use SNMP—an SNMP management system and an SNMP agent. The SNMP management system can request a variety of information from managed computers (SNMP agents).

The SNMP service provides a basic form of security through the use of community names and authentication traps. You can restrict SNMP communications for the agent and allow it to communicate with only a prescribed list of SNMP management systems.

To add the security our scenario dictates, you'd edit the existing IPSec policy to add two sets of filter specifications to the appropriate IP filter list (normally something like All IP Traffic). For typical SNMP traffic, you'd specify port 161 for both TCP and UDP protocols. SNMP uses port 161 for general messages and port 162 for trap messages.

B. **Incorrect:** The Filter Properties dialog box doesn't list SNMP as an option in the drop-down list.

C. **Incorrect:** You use the SNMP Service Properties dialog box to configure the SNMP service, not to modify IPSec.

D. **Incorrect:** IPSec does *not* encrypt the SNMP protocol by default.

Designing a Security Solution for Access Between Networks

In order to create and secure communication and data transfer from network to network, you need to know which tools are available to achieve these connections as well as how to utilize and implement them.

In the previous domains, we've covered a considerable number of tools that you can use toward this end. Knowing how and where they work will allow you to make better choices when it comes to your network design. Some of the services you can use to create secure network communication include:

- **Routing and Remote Access Service (RRAS)**

- **Virtual private networking (VPN)**

- **Terminal Services**

- **Proxy server**

- **NAT** and **Internet Connection Sharing (ICS)**

- **Internet Authentication Service (IAS)**

In order to successfully establish secure network links, you'll need to know these components. In this domain, you'll find many questions devoted to their use and to which circumstances each tool works best in.

In addition to knowing these components, you'll need to be able to implement certain networking situations. For example, this domain covers how to provide secure public network access from a private network. It also covers how to provide external users with secure access to the private network. This could be anything from accessing e-mail remotely to sending in weekly sales reports. This domain also covers the topic of providing secure access between networks. This last item plays a major role because many companies often form temporary partnerships with other companies and need secure private network access for a limited time.

Tested Skills and Suggested Practices

The skills that you need to successfully master the Designing a Security Solution for Access Between Networks objective domain on the *Designing Security for a Microsoft Windows 2000 Network* exam include:

- **Providing secure access to public networks from a private network.**

  - Practice 1: Set up RRAS to connect your users to the Internet, making sure that routing is enabled. In this scenario your user is using an ISP, so a static IP will be given.

  - Practice 2: Determine a security solution that employs the various technologies available to you (NAT, VPN, RRAS, IAS, ICS, proxy servers, and Terminal Services) to prevent the following problems: (1) company information, such as addressing schemes, are being exposed; (2) viruses are appearing on the company network; and (3) internal machines are being attacked from outside sources.

- **Providing external users with secure access to private network resources.**

  - Practice 1: Perform both a RAS and VPN setup, thus converting a single machine into a VPN and RAS server. Start this process from the Routing And Remote Access snap-in located under the Administrative Tools section of Start.

  - Practice 2: Illustrate three different ways in which proxy servers (with the use of third-party software) can mimic the functions of firewalls.

- **Providing secure access between private networks.**

  - Practice 1: Describe the different strategies a network administrator would use to secure access between private networks within a LAN, within a WAN, and across a public network, such as the Internet.

  - Practice 2: Create a network solution in which you would use a VPN to link to private networks in two different cities.

- **Designing Windows 2000 security for remote access users.**

    - Practice 1: You have a Windows 2000 server that's configured as a RAS server. It's part of a native mode domain. Use the Active Directory Users And Computers snap-in to set up the required RAS rights in order to manage access through RAS policies.

    - Practice 2: Enable remote access permission for each user individually. Implement this from the appropriate tab for the correct user account in Active Directory directory service.

Further Reading

This section lists supplemental readings by objective. We recommend that you study these sources thoroughly before taking exam 70-220.

Objective 5.1

Microsoft Corporation. *MCSE Training Kit: Designing Microsoft Windows 2000 Network Security.* Redmond, Washington: Microsoft Press, 2000. Review Chapter 15, "Securing Internet Access," Lesson 1, "Designing an Internet Acceptable Use Policy." This lesson covers how to determine the contents of your organization's acceptable use policy.

Microsoft Corporation. *MCSE Training Kit: Designing Microsoft Windows 2000 Network Security.* Redmond, Washington: Microsoft Press, 2000. Review Chapter 15, "Securing Internet Access," Lesson 3, "Restricting Access to Content on the Internet." This lesson covers the steps involved in restricting access to content on the Internet in order to enforce your organization's policies.

Objective 5.2

Microsoft Corporation. *MCSE Training Kit: Designing Microsoft Windows 2000 Network Security.* Redmond, Washington: Microsoft Press, 2000. Review Chapter 13, "Securing Access for Remote Users and Networks," Lesson 1, "Planning Remote Access Security." This lesson covers the differences between the possible solutions available for remote access and how to plan each type of solution.

Microsoft Corporation. *MCSE Training Kit: Designing Microsoft Windows 2000 Network Security.* Redmond, Washington: Microsoft Press, 2000. Review Chapter 14, "Securing an Extranet," Lesson 1, "Identifying Common Firewall Strategies." This lesson covers topics such as the use of NAT and comparing DMZ configurations.

Objective 5.3

Microsoft Corporation. *MCSE Training Kit: Designing Microsoft Windows 2000 Network Security*. Redmond, Washington: Microsoft Press, 2000. Review Chapter 16, "Securing Access in a Heterogeneous Network Environment," Lesson 1, "Providing Interoperability Between Windows 2000 and Heterogeneous Networks." This is a discussion of the Microsoft services that provide interoperability with several alternative network operating systems.

Microsoft Corporation. *MCSE Training Kit: Designing Microsoft Windows 2000 Network Security*. Redmond, Washington: Microsoft Press, 2000. Review Chapter 16, "Securing Access in a Heterogeneous Network Environment," Lesson 4, "Securing Access to Windows 2000 Resources." This covers how to secure file and print resources on a Windows 2000 network in a heterogeneous environment.

Objective 5.4

Microsoft Corporation. *MCSE Training Kit: Designing Microsoft Windows 2000 Network Security*. Redmond, Washington: Microsoft Press, 2000. Review Chapter 13, "Securing Access for Remote Users and Networks," Lesson 2, "Designing Remote Access Security for Users." This covers the planning and configuration for secure remote client access.

Microsoft Corporation. *MCSE Training Kit: Designing Microsoft Windows 2000 Network Security*. Redmond, Washington: Microsoft Press, 2000. Review Chapter 13, "Securing Access for Remote Users and Networks," Lesson 4, "Designing Remote Access Policy." This lesson covers the design and planning stages for implementing a remote access policy.

OBJECTIVE 5.1

Provide secure access to public networks from a private network.

This is probably one of the most serious and time-consuming components of network security. One reason is the misuse of Internet privileges by various users in many companies. After the problem is recognized, you, as the network administrator, will have everyone looking to you to do something about it. The following are some options covered in this objective that you'll need to know for the test.

Using proxy servers is one way you can protect the company. You do this by using some type of censoring function. Remember, though, that proxy servers aren't firewalls and that you'll need to know the various functions that proxy servers perform.

The other component that relates to this subject is VPN. This might be implemented in your organization for telecommuters. Within a VPN scenario, you have several elements of the connection: the client, the server, the tunnel, the connection, tunneling protocols, tunneled data, and the transit network. For the exam, make sure that you know all these components and how each functions in terms of the actual VPN connection.

Objective 5.1 Questions

70-220.05.01.001

Joe needs secure access to data on Bob's computer. You've analyzed the situation and have correctly determined that you need to set up a pass-through VPN connection. What general statement can you make regarding Joe and Bob's networking environment?

A. Joe and Bob are on separate intranets using the Internet to connect.

B. Joe is a remote user using an ISP to connect to the Internet. Bob is another remote user using an ISP to connect to the Internet.

C. Joe is a remote user using an ISP to connect to the Internet. Bob is on his company's intranet connected to Joe using a VPN server.

D. Joe and Bob are on two physically isolated subnets of the same network.

70-220.05.01.002

Salman must configure his network to allow the research department, located in Atlanta, to establish secure communications with the development department, located in San Diego. Both networks maintain a dedicated WAN connection to the company headquarters intranet located in Denver. Because of the sensitive nature of the material on the servers in the research and development departments, this data must not be accessible to users in Denver. How should Salman proceed?

A. Schedule all communication between the research and development departments to take place during off-peak hours.

B. Connect the two networks over the intranet with a router-to-router VPN connection.

C. Create global groups containing the members of the research and development departments. Exclude Denver users from this group. Assign this group Modify permissions to the shared resources on the servers in Atlanta and San Diego.

D. Require Kerberos V5 authentication for all users from the research and development departments. Require reauthentication prior to each data exchange.

70-220.05.01.003

One of your traveling sales representatives is visiting Contoso, Ltd. She needs to communicate securely with Fabrikam, Inc., to transfer confidential sales quotes and confirmations. Her laptop has Windows 2000 Professional installed. It's equipped with a network card and a 56 Kbps dial-up modem. The laptop has a dial-up networking entry configured with the IP address of a VPN server at Fabrikam. The sales representative has limited access to Contoso's internal network, but this access includes unrestricted Internet access.

Both Contoso and Fabrikam are protected by firewalls. Fabrikam has a VPN server behind the firewall, whereas Contoso has no VPN capability. Contoso maintains a RRAS server, but Fabrikam doesn't.

While attached to Contoso's network, the sales representative is unable to establish a VPN connection with Fabrikam. What should be done to enable secure communication?

A. Ensure that Contoso's proxy server is equipped with packet filters to allow VPN traffic to pass through.

B. Install VPN services on a server at Contoso.

C. Use an analog phone line at Contoso to dial in to Fabrikam's VPN server.

D. Use a Terminal Services client machine at Contoso using guest credentials to log on.

Objective 5.1 Answers

70-220.05.01.001

▶ **Correct Answers: A**

    A. **Correct:** A VPN connection is a networking tool that can provide secure point-to-point connections in a variety of configurations. A combined Internet and intranet VPN connection, called a pass-through VPN connection, allows a remote access client connected to a company's intranet to access the resources of another company's intranet using the Internet. In this scenario a remote access VPN connection passes through one intranet and the Internet to access a second intranet.

    In this situation it's important to remember that the appropriate firewall settings are in place so that the VPN server that's connected to the Internet is accepting and forwarding just VPN traffic and not anything else. To do this, you need to look in the RRAS snap-in in order to configure the correct firewall filters.

    B. **Incorrect:** If Joe and Bob were both properly configured remote users, you'd use their respective ISPs to establish the VPN connection between them. This is an example of an Internet-based VPN connection.

    C. **Incorrect:** If Joe were remote and Bob were on his company's intranet, Joe's ISP would set up one end of the VPN connection and a VPN server attached to Bob's intranet would establish the other end. This is an example of an Internet-based VPN connection.

    D. **Incorrect:** If Joe and Bob were on physically isolated subnets of the same network, a VPN connection could be established between them using two VPN servers. This would be an example of an intranet-based VPN connection. This network segment would be hidden from view from those who don't have the correct permissions to this connection.

70-220.05.01.002

▶ **Correct Answers: B**

    A. **Incorrect:** Scheduling communication at only specific times doesn't address the issue of securing the data.

    B. **Correct:** Salman's big problem is allowing the research and development departments to communicate securely using the company's intranet as an intermediary. The best choice is to create a VPN connection router-to-router. In this scenario the two networks are connected to the common intranet with computers that can act as VPN clients or VPN servers. When the VPN connection is established, users on computers on either network will be able to exchange sensitive data across the corporate intranet, exposing only encrypted data to anyone attempting a network attack on the transmission. This scenario also eliminates the need for additional expensive leased line connections.

C. **Incorrect:** Creating the proper level of access control is necessary, but it doesn't address the issue of sending secure communication. Denying access to a given resource doesn't prevent a malicious user from mounting network attacks in an attempt to gain access to sensitive data flowing across the intranet.

D. **Incorrect:** Kerberos authentication is the standard authentication mechanism for Windows 2000. Authentication only proves who you are; it doesn't provide the encryption services this scenario demands.

70-220.05.01.003

▶ **Correct Answers: A**

A. **Correct:** A VPN connection encrypts the data payload and enables secure communication using public media such as the Internet. The two essential components, the VPN server and the VPN client, are in place. The likely source of our connectivity problem is the firewall at Contoso. Fabrikam is configured for VPN communications, so it's a foregone conclusion that the required packet filters are in place at Fabrikam to allow VPN connections to pass through. Because Contoso doesn't have a VPN infrastructure in place, it's likely that the firewall is filtering out the VPN traffic. By creating packet filters to allow VPN traffic to pass through the firewall at Contoso, you should be able to establish connectivity while leaving Contoso's network integrity intact.

B. **Incorrect:** The IT staff at Contoso doesn't need to dedicate additional resources simply to support an external user. Besides, our scenario doesn't require any VPN services at Contoso.

C. **Incorrect:** Using a phone line to dial in to Fabrikam's VPN server wouldn't work because Fabrikam has no dial-up capability. It would be possible for the sales representative to dial up a local ISP, and then activate her existing VPN dial-up networking entry using the connection to the ISP (as long as the ISP supports VPN connections).

D. **Incorrect:** There would be no benefit in our scenario to using a Terminal Services client with guest credentials. First, the packet filtering issue is the real problem. After that's solved, the sales representative could log on from any machine at Contoso because the VPN connection would prompt her for her Fabrikam credentials to establish the link. There's also the issue of necessary encryption that wouldn't be provided by the Terminal Services component.

O B J E C T I V E   5 . 2

Provide external users with secure access to private network resources.

In today's fast-paced business world, the need to provide external users with access to internal network resources is at an all-time high. Many organizations have decentralized structures in which remote users in the field provide products and services at a fast pace. Obtaining resources on demand while being outside the network framework is a necessity for any large-scale network environment. Giving those users the access they require without leaving the network's back door open to malicious users is essential. Through dial-up services, VPNs, and other options, you can use Windows 2000 to provide a complete remote access solution for any network environment.

One of the most popular solutions for this is RAS. Although you may choose to use either VPN or RAS, some situations might call for both. Be on the lookout for scenario questions that will request the use of one or the other, or perhaps both. If your needs specify giving this option to a small number of remote access users, such as a small sales force, you might consider the RAS option. Conversely, if the dial-in population would incur large long-distance costs, then perhaps the VPN connection would be the choice. Understanding what will work where is the key to success with this portion of the exam.

Objective 5.2 Questions

70-220.05.02.001

You're the network administrator for a large multinational conglomerate. In addition to your company's Web presence (which is handled by another administrator), you must accommodate secure network access for 15,000 remote users worldwide.

To enhance the availability of VPN servers, you've created a network load-balancing cluster of 32 PPTP servers using Microsoft Windows 2000 Advanced Server. In addition, you used network load balancing to create a cluster of IAS servers to handle authentication. Finally, you've contracted with three major ISPs to outsource all remote access. Now a remote client dials up one of the contract ISPs before establishing a VPN connection using the ISP's NAS.

In this scenario, what's the primary benefit of outsourcing remote access?

A. Increased security

B. Better centralized control

C. Cost savings

D. Load balancing

70-220.05.02.002

Derik is the network administrator for Northwind Traders. The company's products are sold through a network of job-lot wholesalers and warehouse-style club stores. At last count, Northwind Traders merchandise was being sold in over 8,000 retail outlets worldwide.

The individual retail locations periodically need to check inventory status with their wholesaler. Each wholesaler has an inventory software program provided by Northwind for this purpose. When the wholesaler needs to check order status, the program dials up a server at Northwind, authenticates, and downloads the information. Each wholesaler location has been allocated a generic ID and password with which to contact Northwind Traders.

Derik wants to maintain centralized management of remote access because of the large numbers of external remote users involved. What scheme should Derik employ to handle the wholesalers' communication needs?

A. RRAS with Windows 2000 authentication

B. RRAS with RADIUS authentication

C. VPN with Windows 2000 authentication

D. VPN with RADIUS authentication

70-220.05.02.003

Holly is in the process of evaluating ISPs. A sales representative for one of them, Litware, Inc., informs Holly that her ISP offers an encrypted PPP dial-up connection for no additional charge. None of the other providers Holly is considering offers this feature. Also, Litware is running a promotion and is offering the whole package at a substantial discount. Holly must support several remote users who require secure communications to the company intranet and these users require user authentication and encryption features. Given the circumstances, what action should Holly take regarding Litware?

A. Sign up, but don't employ the encrypted PPP connection feature.

B. Sign up with the encrypted PPP connection feature enabled. All tunneling protocols are supported.

C. Sign up with the encrypted PPP connection feature enabled, even though PPTP is the only tunneling protocol supported.

D. Sign up with the encrypted PPP connection feature enabled, even though L2TP over IPSec is the only tunneling protocol supported.

Objective 5.2 Answers

70-220.05.02.001

▶ **Correct Answers: C**

A. **Incorrect:** Most of the network security is realized in your banks of IAS servers and PPTP servers. The ISP simply provides the connectivity infrastructure (and one end of a VPN tunnel) while you handle all the authentication tasks. When a remote user connects to the ISP's NAS, the authentication and usage records are forwarded to your IAS server. The IAS server utilizes remote access policies in order to accept or reject connection attempts. The IAS server allows the company to control user authentication, track usage, and manage which employees are allowed to access the ISP's network.

B. **Incorrect:** In this situation better centralized control is going to originate with remote access policies, which are implemented at the IAS server level. It would be difficult to administer this type of centralized control if 15,000 users were dialing in worldwide.

C. **Correct:** The primary benefit of outsourcing remote access is cost savings. By using an ISP's routers, network access servers, and T1 lines instead of buying your own, you could save a tremendous amount on infrastructure costs. By dialing into the ISPs with worldwide connections, you could significantly decrease your long-distance phone bill. Also, the provider now handles the technical support costs, potentially eliminating a large amount of your administrative budget.

D. **Incorrect:** The benefits of network load balancing are realized with your IAS and PPTP server "farms." The outsourced remote access simply funnels thousands of users for you, and the load-balanced servers in your network eliminate bottlenecks and smooth out traffic flow.

70-220.05.02.002

▶ **Correct Answers: B**

A. **Incorrect:** There are two dial-up scenarios Derik might consider in this case: RRAS and VPN. RRAS provides the ability to handle incoming calls from clients without the overhead of a VPN connection. Security and encryption aren't specified in our requirements, so a VPN isn't indicated.

In small network situations with no requirements for centralized management of remote access, RRAS can be configured to use Windows authentication. However, in situations like this one greater control and flexibility are achieved through centralized authentication using RADIUS.

B. **Correct:** Our dial-in clients have two ways to authenticate: Windows 2000 authentication and RADIUS authentication. Because we have provided network server access to users outside our network, RADIUS is the better choice. The RADIUS server has access to user account information and can check remote access authentication credentials. If the user's credentials are authentic and the connection attempt is authorized, the RADIUS server authorizes the user's access based on specified conditions and logs the remote access connections as accounting events. Remote access policies provide a more powerful and flexible way to manage remote access permission. An example is support for callback functionality. By establishing a remote access policy that expects a client to be at a certain phone number, you can guard against that type of unauthorized access attempt.

C. **Incorrect:** This is incorrect for the reasons stated in A.

D. **Incorrect:** This is incorrect for the reasons stated in A.

70-220.05.02.003

▶ **Correct Answers: A**

A. **Correct:** Holly shouldn't use the encrypted PPP connection feature.

Although it's possible to negotiate an encrypted PPP connection for the dial-up connection with an ISP, it's neither necessary nor recommended. The private data being sent, the tunneled PPP frame, is already encrypted. The additional level of encryption isn't needed and can impact performance. Even though both tunneling protocols, PPTP and L2TP over IPSec, are compatible with the encrypted PPP connection feature, you still shouldn't use it.

B. **Incorrect:** This is incorrect for the reasons stated in A.

C. **Incorrect:** This is incorrect for the reasons stated in A.

D. **Incorrect:** This is incorrect for the reasons stated in A.

OBJECTIVE 5.3

Provide secure access between private networks.

With private networks, it seems like the administrator could assume that the security risk is low because the possibility of an outside threat is low. But with more risks originating from within organizations, it's important for the administrator to understand how to keep information from being stolen or lost by employees.

One of the most important ways to provide secure access is through the use of **certificate authority (CA) servers**. You can utilize CA servers in a variety of setups to provide enterprise-wide solutions. Within the context of a LAN, you, as the administrator, can create a CA server and therefore control digital certificates of the entire organization at the site, domain, or OU level. Within the context of a WAN, you can utilize IPSec to secure exchange by means of a site-to-site VPN connection. If you must take your Windows 2000 framework and incorporate it into third-party situations, you can utilize IPSec in tunnel mode. This encapsulates IP packets and also encrypts them if necessary when you encounter routers or gateways that don't support the L2TP/IPSec structure.

Objective 5.3 Questions

70-220.05.03.001

Joe and Bob are users on isolated subnets of the same TCP/IP network. Joe and Bob need to communicate securely. Because of the nature of the data being exchanged, they require mutual computer authentication and mutual user-level authentication. Which combination of factors should you employ to meet these requirements?

A. L2TP using IPSec with MS-CHAP v2 authentication.

B. L2TP using IPSec with any valid PPP authentication protocol.

C. PPTP using MPPE with EAP-TLS or MS-CHAP authentication.

D. PPTP using MPPE with EAP-TLS or MS-CHAP authentication and PPTP packet filtering at the firewall.

70-220.05.03.002

You're configuring a VPN server on your network to allow secure access from authorized Internet users. You select PPTP for your VPN. What must you do to prevent potentially malicious Internet users from gaining access to your intranet?

A. Enable PPTP packet filtering on either the VPN server or an intermediate firewall.

B. Disable forwarding between the public and private interfaces on the VPN server.

C. Use the strongest user authentication protocol your network will support.

D. Ensure the user authentication protocol you select supports encryption.

70-220.05.03.003

Simi has two users in different departments who need to communicate securely. These users need their communications to each other on the LAN to be both mutually authenticated and encrypted. However, they both need to communicate in the clear with other users on the LAN. How should Simi proceed?

A. Use VPN features to create a PPTP tunnel between the users' computers.

B. Secure the shared resources on both users' computers with local groups and restrict access to the shared resources to the two users.

C. Put the two users on an isolated subnet. Enable packet filtering at the switch.

D. Define and implement an IPSec policy for both users' computers.

Objective 5.3 Answers

70-220.05.03.001

▶ **Correct Answers: A**

  A. **Correct:** To establish secure connectivity between two isolated subnets on the same network, set up a VPN connection. This will provide security for the data as it traverses the "common" portion of the network. VPNs come in two types—PPTP and L2TP. Both protocols provide for user authentication, but only L2TP provides for mutual computer authentication. To provide mutual user-level authentication, you can use either EAP-TLS or MS-CHAP v2 authentication.

  B. **Incorrect:** Several PPP authentication protocols don't allow for mutual user authentication. These include EAP, MS-CHAP, CHAP, SPAP, and PAP.

  C. **Incorrect:** PPTP doesn't provide mutual computer authentication.

  D. **Incorrect:** This is incorrect for the reasons stated in C.

70-220.05.03.002

▶ **Correct Answers: A**

  A. **Correct:** To protect the intranet from all traffic not sent by a VPN client, you must configure PPTP packet filtering so that the VPN server only performs routing between VPN clients and the intranet. Make sure that you configure both the input and output filters with the appropriate filter action set. This will effectively block all other forms of IP traffic from breaching security. PPTP packet filtering can be configured either on the VPN server or on an intermediate firewall.

  B. **Incorrect:** If you disable forwarding, no packets, not even authorized PPTP packets, can cross the VPN server to the other side. Because forwarding must be enabled, it's important to apply PPTP packet filtering.

  C. **Incorrect:** Authentication and encryption are important VPN issues but don't address the requirement of blocking non-VPN traffic from accessing your intranet resources.

  D. **Incorrect:** This is incorrect for the reasons stated in C.

70-220.05.03.003

▶ **Correct Answers: D**

A. **Incorrect:** A VPN is designed to provide secure communication for remote users and users on different networks. In our scenario the users are on the same physical network.

B. **Incorrect:** Securing resources with access control is good practice but doesn't address the issues of authentication and encryption.

C. **Incorrect:** Segmenting the users on an isolated subnet may be a good idea, but it doesn't address the issues of authentication and encryption. Also, packet filtering would control the flow of communication from one side of the switch to the other, but this wouldn't be necessary if they were both on the same side, and it might harm their ability to communicate in the clear with other users.

D. **Correct:** In this case both users are on the same LAN and have different communication needs with different users. The best way for Simi to accomplish her objective would be for her to implement IPSec policies. This way she can configure communications between their computers to require mutual authentication and provide encryption based on IP filters in the policy. This type of setup would require a negotiated policy. Remember that every different packet type used requires a specific filter that's part of the communication applied to the associated rule. Communications to other users would be unaffected by this policy because there would be no matching filter.

O B J E C T I V E   5 . 4

Design Windows 2000 security for remote access users.

Remote access users can come in all shapes and sizes. They could be telecommuters or salespeople who need to dial in to check order and part status. They might be users who have offices or workplaces in other company locations. This won't be the first time you've come into contact with remote users. In previous objectives we've covered topics related to this objective, such as securing information flow across networks and protecting data that's moved around by mobile users. This objective tests your knowledge of using various technologies in order to achieve a complete network solution.

Previous objectives have covered such topics as remote authentication; SSL, PKI, and EFS solutions; and domain trust policies and procedures. This objective will lead you into more robust authentication solutions, such as RRAS coupled with IAS. Although previous objectives have indicated how these various technologies work, the following questions test your knowledge of integrating them into your overall security solution.

Objective 5.4 Questions

70-220.05.04.001

You want to allow remote access users entry to your native-mode Windows 2000 network with the capability of sending encrypted PPP packets. Users must be authenticated, but no other security requirements would affect them. How should you enable this capability with the minimum administrative effort?

A. Set up a PPTP server and enable MS-CHAP authentication.

B. Set up a RRAS server and enable MS-CHAP authentication.

C. Set up a L2TP server using IPSec. Enable MS-CHAP v2 authentication.

D. Set up a PPTP server using MPPE. Enable MS-CHAP authentication.

70-220.05.04.002

You're troubleshooting remote access for one of your Windows 2000 Professional clients. The remote access server offers callback, the client declines, and the remote access server disconnects the connection. How are callback settings configured?

A. The client is set to No Callback. The remote access server is set to Always Call Back To with the client's phone number specified.

B. The client is set to No Callback. The remote access server is set to Set By Caller.

C. The client is set to Ask Me During Dialing When The Server Offers. The remote access server is set to Set By Caller.

D. The client is set to Ask Me During Dialing When The Server Offers. The remote access server is set to Always Call Back To with the client's phone number specified.

70-220.05.04.003

Tanya is designing a security plan for her Windows 2000 remote access users. Her network contains highly sensitive information, and all users, even remote users, must use smart cards in order to authenticate. Tanya's remote access server is in a Windows 2000 native mode domain. What authentication method must Tanya select?

A. MS-CHAP v2

B. EAP-MD5 CHAP

C. MS-CHAP

D. CHAP

E. SPAP

F. PAP

G. EAP-TLS

Objective 5.4 Answers

70-220.05.04.001

▶ **Correct Answers: B**

A. **Incorrect:** PPTP would accomplish the objective of allowing encrypted packets, but it requires substantially more administrative effort than a simple RRAS server does.

B. **Correct:** The key to this question is the authentication protocol. If you use MS-CHAP, you can use MPPE to send encrypted data over a PPP or PPTP connection. The answer that supports this with the least amount of administrative overhead is to set up a RRAS server using MS-CHAP authentication.

C. **Incorrect:** L2TP would accomplish the objective of allowing encrypted packets, but it requires substantially more administrative effort than a simple RRAS server does.

D. **Incorrect:** This answer is redundant because MPPE is an integral part of PPTP and doesn't need to be enabled separately. It's simply the encryption mechanism used by the tunneling protocol.

70-220.05.04.002

▶ **Correct Answers: A**

A. **Correct:** You specify callback options on the client computer in the Dial-Up Preferences menu of Network And Dial-Up Connections. The settings in Callback indicate the conditions under which you want to use that feature. For secure callback, Callback is always set to call back a single number. Callback options are also configured on the remote access server by the network administrator. For example, if the client is configured for No Callback, but the remote access server is set to Always Call Back To, you can't connect. With this combination of settings, the remote access server requests callback, your computer refuses, and the remote access server disconnects your connection.

B. **Incorrect:** With a client setting of No Callback and a server setting of Set By Caller, the remote server offers callback, but the client declines. In this case the connection stays open.

C. **Incorrect:** If the client is set to Ask Me During Dialing When The Server Offers and the server is set to Set By Caller, the Callback dialog box appears on the client. The client enters the current callback number in the dialog box and waits for the server to disconnect and return the call. Or the client can cancel the callback process and remain connected.

D. **Incorrect:** When the client is set to Ask Me During Dialing When The Server Offers, and the server is set to Always Call Back To, the remote access server disconnects and then returns the call, using the number specified on the remote access server. Although this would work as the solution, it might confuse the users.

70-220.05.04.003

▶ **Correct Answers: G**

A. **Incorrect:** The other protocols listed provide authentication services in decreasing levels of strength. MS-CHAP is normally used in conjunction with MPPE to encrypt data sent through a PPP or PPTP connection. Windows 2000 adds support for MS-CHAP v2, which addresses some shortcomings in MS-CHAP. While MS-CHAP v2 is a strong authentication protocol it does not support smart cards or certificates.

B. **Incorrect:** This is incorrect for the reasons stated in G.

C. **Incorrect:** This is incorrect for the reasons stated in A.

D. **Incorrect:** CHAP is an industry-standard authentication protocol used by many non-Microsoft clients, but it does not support certificate-based authentication.

E. **Incorrect:** SPAP is a vendor solution for use when connected to Shiva LAN Rover hardware. It's more secure than plaintext but less secure than CHAP and it has no support for smart cards.

F. **Incorrect:** PAP uses plaintext passwords and is the least sophisticated authentication method. Normally, PAP would be used only if the client and the remote access server were unable to negotiate anything better.

G. **Correct:** If you're using smart cards for remote access authentication, you must use the EAP-TLS authentication method.

With the EAP, an arbitrary authentication mechanism validates a remote access connection. The exact authentication scheme to be used is negotiated by the remote access client and the authenticator. EAP in Windows 2000 is a set of internal components that provide architectural support in the form of a plug-in module. For successful authentication, both the remote access client and authenticator must have the same EAP authentication module installed. Windows 2000 provides two EAP types: EAP-MD5 CHAP and EAP-TLS. The components for an EAP type must be installed on every remote access client and every authenticator.

EAP-TLS is an EAP type that's used in certificate-based security environments. EAP-TLS is supported only on a remote access server running Windows 2000 that's a member of a Windows 2000 mixed-mode or native-mode domain. A remote access server running stand-alone Windows 2000 doesn't support EAP-TLS.

EAP-TLS provides the strongest authentication and key exchange method.

Designing Security for Communication Channels

Because this is the end of the exam and the last domain, some of this material is devoted to unifying what's been previously presented. Using IPSec for secure **VPN** connections has already been covered to a degree in the objectives devoted to creating secure access channels on the network.

That said, this last domain has a fundamentally different focus than the others: communication. Previous domains analyzed security either from the client level, the server level, or both. This domain covers the idea that the communication itself needs to be monitored and secured to a degree stipulated by your network security design. Not all communications will receive the same level of security or require the same amount of attention.

This domain is at the end because you should use your knowledge of security levels and policies to implement secure communications. If you've coordinated users, computers, and servers into their correct security groups, it simply becomes a matter of configuring the correct policies. In other words, if you've paid close attention to the preceding domains, hopefully this one will reveal itself as a matter of filling in blanks and combining your knowledge into a cohesive whole.

In this domain the two most important routes to secure communications are SMB signing and IPSec. SMB stands for server message block, and it serves as the digital signature that's carried with each packet that's sent. You can use IPSec to provide authentication, data integrity, and confidentiality. With IPSec, you can safely establish communications between your various servers. Understanding these two fundamental components will allow you to achieve success in this area.

Tested Skills and Suggested Practices

The skills that you need to successfully master the Designing Security for Communication Channels objective domain on the *Designing Security for a Microsoft Windows 2000 Network* exam include:

- **Designing an SMB-signing solution.**

  - Practice 1: List the four types of policy security options you have available regarding the use of SMBs. Here's a hint: two are for the client side and two are for the server side. Briefly explain how they function to digitally sign the transfer packet.

  - Practice 2: Implement an SMB-signing solution. Do this through the local computer policy snap-in located in the MMC.

- **Designing an IPSec solution.**

  - Practice 1: Configure the IP Security Monitor. Do this so you can monitor the connections that will be created through the IPSec policy. You'll need to utilize IPSECMON.EXE to accomplish this task.

  - Practice 2: Configure the filter action that will be applied to the IP packets after you've set the IP security levels for each packet. Use the Use Add Wizard to do this.

Further Reading

This section lists supplemental readings by objective. We recommend that you study these sources thoroughly before taking exam 70-220.

Objective 6.1

Microsoft Corporation. *MCSE Training Kit: Designing Microsoft Windows 2000 Network Security*. Redmond, Washington: Microsoft Press, 2000. Review Chapter 11,"Securing Data at the Application Layer," Lesson 1, "Planning Authenticity and Integrity of Transmitted Data." This lesson covers both SMB signing and Digital signing.

Microsoft Corporation. *MCSE Training Kit: Designing Microsoft Windows 2000 Network Security*. Redmond, Washington: Microsoft Press, 2000. Review Chapter 11, "Securing Data at the Application Layer," Lesson 2, "Planning Encryption of Transmitted Data." In Lesson 2 the encryption of e-mail and application-level encryption with SSL/TLS is covered.

Objective 6.2

Microsoft Corporation. *MCSE Training Kit: Designing Microsoft Windows 2000 Network Security*. Redmond, Washington: Microsoft Press, 2000. Review Chapter 12, "Securing Data with Internet Protocol Security (IPSec)," Lesson 1, "Designing IPSec Policies." This lesson discusses the design of IPSec policies, covering such topics as modes, filters, and authentication.

Microsoft Corporation. *MCSE Training Kit: Designing Microsoft Windows 2000 Network Security*. Redmond, Washington: Microsoft Press, 2000. Review Chapter 12, "Securing Data with Internet Protocol Security (IPSec)," Lesson 2, "Planning IPSec Deployment." Lesson 2 is about the deployment of IPSec policies in different types of environments.

OBJECTIVE   6.1

Design an SMB-signing solution.

SMB isn't new to the Microsoft Windows NT and Windows 2000 arena. Known previously as the Common Internet File System (CIFS), it's been available for use with Windows NT 4 since the release of Service Pack 3.

SMB is especially helpful when it comes to mutual authentication. It prevents problems associated with mutual authentication by alleviating the danger of any traffic between the server and client from being intercepted and altered. For example, hackers may want to disrupt communication between the server and the client. They do this by placing their machines "between" the client and the server it's calling. By doing so, they can imitate either machine and therefore have access to the information that's coming across. SMB requires digital signatures on all packets, therefore making it extremely difficult for imposters to portray themselves as legitimate users.

When designing this type of solution, keep in mind a couple of things: SMB doesn't work with direct host IPX protocol. This is because SMB modifies IPX and leaves it unable to complete an SMB-signing structure. Also, keep in mind that in terms of machine resources, CPU performance is significantly reduced when SMB is enabled.

Objective 6.1 Questions

70-220.06.01.001

Kevin is the administrator for the finance department. He's responsible for his department's server, and he'd like to apply security settings to it. This server has a freshly installed version of Windows 2000 and isn't a domain controller. Kevin wants to ensure that all inbound and outbound server and client communication traffic is digitally signed, and he wants to ensure that no unsigned device drivers can be installed. What should Kevin do?

A. Import the HISECWS.INF security template into the Security Configuration And Analysis snap-in of the MMC.

B. Import the HISECDC.INF security template into the Security Templates snap-in of the MMC.

C. Import the SECUREWS.INF security template into the Group Policy snap-in of the MMC.

D. Import the COMPATWS.INF security template into the Security Templates snap-in of the MMC.

70-220.06.01.002

You're the network administrator. Your personal workstation is running Windows 2000 Advanced Server. This server was upgraded from Windows NT 4 Server. Following the upgrade, you applied the BASICWK.INF security template to this computer to bring it in line with the security settings of clean-installed Windows 2000 computers.

You've recently acquired a new personal workstation and you want to convert your existing workstation to a domain controller. Because it will remain in your office, you want to retain the option of logging on interactively and using it in a client capacity. You don't want to be overly restrictive, but you want the old machine to have both client and server signing enabled. What's the least restrictive template you should apply to enable these capabilities?

A. BASICDC.INF

B. SECUREDC.INF

C. HISECDC.INF

D. COMPATWS.INF

70-220.06.01.003

You're upgrading your Windows NT 4 servers to Windows 2000. The Windows NT domain controllers will all become Windows 2000 domain controllers.

Following the upgrade, what should you do to ensure that the Windows 2000 domain controllers require all incoming and outgoing traffic to be digitally signed?

A. Using the Domain Controller Security Policy snap-in, import the HISECDC.INF template.

B. Using the Domain Security Policy snap-in, import the SECUREDC.INF template.

C. Using the Active Directory Domains And Trusts snap-in, select Change Mode from the General tab of the Properties dialog box. Follow the on-screen instructions.

D. Apply the BASICDC.INF template to each domain controller.

Objective 6.1 Answers

70-220.06.01.001

▶ **Correct Answers: A**

A. **Correct:** After you've placed your users into the appropriate groups to allow access to supported applications, you can further define security settings by applying security templates. Windows 2000 provides a collection of security templates for setting up your network security environment. You can import security templates into the Security Configuration And Analysis or the Group Policy snap-in modules of the MMC. You can edit, view, define, and modify templates in the Security Templates snap-in, but you can't import them. Security templates are inactive until they're imported into the Security Configuration And Analysis snap-in or the Group Policy snap-in. Remember to use the SECEDIT.EXE command-line tool in Windows 2000 to assign security templates to individual machines.

There are four classes of security templates, which provide varying levels of security. These classes are Basic, Compatible, Secure, and High Secure. These classes contain templates specifically designed for domain controllers as well as templates for other computers. Note the use of "ws," "sv," "wk," and "dc" in the filenames: "dc" indicates a template designed for use on a domain controller, and "ws" is a template for computers that aren't domain controllers.

The Basic template (which isn't one of your choices) contains the default settings that Windows 2000 incorporates during a clean install. This template is normally used when upgrading from Windows NT 4 to ensure that the settings are consistent. It is the only template that has the "wk" and "sv" versions that denote workstations and non–domain controller servers respectively.

The High Secure template takes some of the settings from the SECUREDC.INF template and applies their extreme values to favor security over performance, ease of use, and connectivity. This template mandates digital signing of communications and blocks unsigned device drivers. The template file HISECWS.INF is the appropriate choice for us. HISECDC.INF is the High Secure template designed for domain controllers.

B. **Incorrect:** This answer is incorrect for the reasons stated in A.

C. **Incorrect:** The secure template modifies certain settings that wouldn't affect application functionality but would have more of an impact on operating system and network behavior. For example, this template incorporates settings that enable digital signing of communications, but it doesn't require it. SECUREWS.INF wouldn't apply in our scenario.

D. **Incorrect:** The Compatible template is designed for those situations in which you have legacy applications and want your users to be able to run them without making your users Power Users. Be aware that a computer that incorporates this template, COMPATWS.INF, isn't considered secure. This wouldn't work for our situation.

70-220.06.01.002

▶ **Correct Answers: B**

A. **Incorrect:** The BASICDC.INF template is used primarily to bring a machine that has been upgraded from Windows NT 4 up to the same security standards as a machine that has been clean-installed. It's also useful to set the security configuration settings back to the baseline for a machine that has had other security templates or custom security configurations applied. The BASICDC.INF template is designed for domain controllers in a less secure environment. The settings for this template assume that the computer is going to be functioning only as a domain controller and not as a client, so the only security option enabled is Digitally Sign Server Communication (When Possible).

B. **Correct:** Windows 2000 provides a set of security templates for your use in setting up your network environment. A security template is a profile of security settings considered appropriate to a specific level of security on a Windows 2000 domain controller, server, or client computer. Security templates are inactive until imported into a Group Policy object or the Security Configuration And Analysis snap-in to the MMC. There are four basic classes of security templates: Basic, Compatible, Secure, and High Secure. For our scenario, the SECUREDC.INF template is the least restrictive template that enables both of our requested capabilities. The SECUREDC.INF template modifies settings that have more of an impact on the operating system's operational behavior and network functionality than on application functionality.

C. **Incorrect:** The HISECDC.INF template, on the other hand, configures many operational parameters to their extreme values without regard for performance, operational ease of use, or connectivity with clients using third party or earlier versions of NTLM. IPSec is required for communications that utilize the HISECDC.INF template. This includes requiring client and server signing, not merely enabling signing.

D. **Incorrect:** The COMPATWS.INF template is designed for use in an environment where you're operating many legacy applications, and you don't want to require the users be in the Power Users group in order to run them. The COMPATWS.INF template "opens up" the default access control policy for this purpose. It doesn't meet our scenario's requirements.

70-220.06.01.003

▶ **Correct Answers: A**

A. **Correct:** For our scenario, the HISECDC.INF template requires all communications to be signed and is designed for use in a highly secure network. Import this template using the Domain Controller Security Policy snap-in. The HISECDC.INF template configures many operational parameters to their extreme values without regard for performance, operational ease of use, or connectivity with clients using third-party or earlier versions of NTLM.

B. **Incorrect:** The SECUREDC.INF template modifies settings that have more of an impact on the operating system's operational behavior and its network functionality than on application functionality. With the SECUREDC.INF template, permissions to file system objects aren't affected through its usage. Unmodified, this template doesn't specify that all communications be signed, only that communications will be signed if specifically asked to be signed. Also, the Domain Security Policy snap-in affects all computers in the domain, not just domain controllers.

C. **Incorrect:** Using the Active Directory Domains And Trusts snap-in is incorrect. The suggested action, selecting Change Mode from the General tab of the Properties dialog box, would change the network from mixed mode to native mode, which isn't the result we're looking for.

D. **Incorrect:** The BASICDC.INF template is used primarily to bring a machine that has been upgraded from Windows NT 4 up to the same security standards as a machine that has been clean-installed. The BASICDC.INF template allows you to return to the original installation defaults. The BASICDC.INF template is designed for domain controllers in a less secure environment. This template's settings assume that the computer is going to function only as a domain controller and not as a client, so the only security option enabled is Digitally Sign Server Communication (When Possible).

OBJECTIVE 6.2

Design an IPSec solution.

Although this isn't the first time that IPSec has been covered in this exam, this objective goes down to the level of cryptography and security that's provided by this suite of services and protocols. IPSec incorporates L2TP in order to protect any protocols that fall within the TCP/IP protocol suite. The L2TP component is responsible for securing Internet communications.

You can use IPSec to protect the network from a variety of attacks, whether they're external or internal. In addition, you can use IPSec to enable the following features:

- **Access control**

- Data authentication

- Outward protocol filtering

- Data integrity

With designing an encryption scheme, you should be able to define the level of encryption required. Regarding an IPSec management strategy, you should know what it takes to keep the system up and running while it deals with all the encryption it has to generate. With negotiating policies, you'll need to understand such things as key life, key length, and whether to utilize AH or ESP as the primary protocol. Make sure you understand the proper setting for IP filters so you can establish and maintain the correct communication channels. Finally, when defining security levels, you need to understand the types of security levels and where and how to implement each one.

Objective 6.2 Questions

70-220.06.02.001

Your Windows 2000 network hosts a variety of computers running various older Microsoft operating systems. You're considering applying IPSec policy to a domain controller on your network. This computer also functions as your DNS server. Before applying IPSec policy to this computer, what should you first ensure?

A. IPSec policy is configured to permit unsecured traffic.

B. IPSec policy isn't configured to permit unsecured traffic.

C. The domain controller isn't running DHCP.

D. All clients are IPSec-capable.

70-220.06.02.002

You maintain a firewall server, FIREWALL, that functions as a security gateway for your network. You must ensure that IPSec packets aren't rejected. What should you do?

A. Apply one of the predefined IPSec configurations to the firewall.

B. Click Start, and then click Run. Type **ipsecmon FIREWALL**.

C. No action is required. FIREWALL is an intermediary, not an endpoint.

D. Enable inbound and outbound packet filtering on the Internet interface for IPSec traffic.

70-220.06.02.003

You maintain a mixed-mode Windows 2000 network. A server, SERVER1, is configured with the Secure Server (Require Security) IPSec policy. This policy has been assigned to SERVER1 without modification. The Client (Respond Only) IPSec policy has been applied, unmodified, at the domain level.

Bob is on a different subnet than SERVER1 but on the same network. A router connects these segments. Bob can't establish communication with SERVER1. Why?

A. The router is running Microsoft Windows NT 4.

B. SERVER1 lacks inbound and outbound filters to specifically allow Bob's computer to communicate.

C. Bob is using a Microsoft Windows 98 SE workstation.

D. SERVER1 is a domain controller.

Objective 6.2 Answers

70-220.06.02.001

▶ **Correct Answers: A**

A. **Correct:** Before enabling IPSec for computers functioning as domain controllers or DHCP, DNS, or Windows Internet Naming Service (WINS) servers, you should determine if all the clients are also IPSec-capable. If they aren't, you must configure the server that is acting as the domain controller to permit unsecured traffic to accommodate older clients. Otherwise, secure negotiation might fail and access to these network services might be blocked.

B. **Incorrect:** This answer is incorrect for the reasons stated in A.

C. **Incorrect:** There's no IPSec-related restriction on running the DHCP service on a domain controller.

D. **Incorrect:** Based on the scenario, we already know that not all clients are IPSec-capable. They don't need to be, but the server must be configured to allow for unsecured traffic to accommodate these older clients.

70-220.06.02.002

▶ **Correct Answers: D**

A. **Incorrect:** In all likelihood, the firewall isn't an endpoint for IPSec communications, so you wouldn't need to apply IPSec policy. But even if you did, you'd still need to ensure that IPSec packets weren't being filtered out.

B. **Incorrect:** You can use the IP Security Monitoring tool to find out if IPSec policy is active (assigned) on a given computer. This tool can only monitor IPSec traffic, not solve the problem presented in our scenario. To use it, type **ipsecmon** at the Run prompt under the Start menu.

C. **Incorrect:** Even though the FIREWALL server might function only as an IPSec intermediary, action is definitely required.

D. **Correct:** In this scenario you must ensure that IPSec packets aren't inadvertently filtered out. Specifically, you must enable both inbound and outbound packet filtering on the Internet interface for AH, ESP, and IKE negotiation traffic.

70-220.06.02.003

▶ **Correct Answers: C**

A. **Incorrect:** In an IPSec environment, only the endpoint computers need to be IPSec-enabled. An intermediate router can forward IPSec traffic without being IPSec-enabled itself. A Windows NT 4 server falls into this category.

B. **Incorrect:** Applying filters wouldn't help in this case. Even if you were to apply appropriate filters and add filter rules, Bob still couldn't communicate as long as the Allow Unsecured Communication With Non IPSec-Aware Computer check box remains cleared on the property sheet for the policy.

C. **Correct:** SERVER1 is configured at the High Security level. The predefined policy, Secure Server (Require Security), requires IPSec protection for all traffic sent or received. This policy also includes strong confidentiality and integrity algorithms, Perfect Forward Secrecy, key lifetimes and limits, and strong Diffie-Hellman groups. Unsecured communication, because of non–IPSec-aware computers or failed security negotiation, is blocked. Since Windows 98 SE computers are non–IPSec-aware, Bob is unable to communicate.

D. **Incorrect:** SERVER1's functioning as a domain controller wouldn't affect Bob's ability to communicate. It's important, however, that you're aware that applying a policy this restrictive to a domain controller could block access to older clients, like Bob's workstation.

Blue Yonder Airlines

Background

Blue Yonder Airlines provides central support for corporate and governmental helicopter facilities throughout Texas and New Mexico. It provides all administrative and operational support for approximately 850 mechanics and pilots stationed at 17 airfields.

Organization

The corporate structure and logistics of Blue Yonder Airlines are summarized in the following sections.

Corporate Headquarters

The corporate headquarters are located in Dallas, Texas. The headquarters provides administrative, logistic, personnel, and communications support. Between 140 and 150 personnel are employed at the Dallas headquarters.

Airfield Offices

Offices are located at each airfield. Each office consists of about 50 personnel, including pilots, mechanics, and administrative support personnel. The director of flight operations reports directly to the vice president of operations in the Dallas office.

Remote Sites

Each airfield office has two or three remote offices maintaining auxiliary facilities in support of pilot training. Staffing support comes from the airfield offices, and these personnel occupy the outlying facilities for a shift lasting between one and two weeks, depending on the site's accessibility. Certain training sites can only be reached by helicopter.

Current Operating Procedures

Blue Yonder's operating procedures at the corporate headquarters, airfield offices, and remote sites are outlined in the following sections.

Corporate Headquarters

All IT functions are handled at the Dallas office. At the monthly staff meeting, all directors come to Dallas for a briefing. A portion of this briefing is confidential, and each director will sign for and hand carry any confidential materials back to the airfield office in a sealed courier pouch. This material includes operational schedules, personnel issues, and planning documents concerning upcoming training exercises. Only that portion of the plan actually relevant to a particular director is released to that director.

Airfield Offices

Airfield office computers are set up in a "workgroup" environment, allowing file and print sharing as well as e-mail and Internet access. The computer in the director's office isn't connected to the network, and it's the only computer on which classified material may be stored. Consequently, if the director needs something printed or needs to share a file, it cannot be transferred through the network.

Remote Sites

Any confidential information required by a remote site must arrive in one of two ways: through diskettes and documents physically hand carried by the oncoming shift at the beginning of the week or through the administrative director on an ad hoc basis. Because physical distances separate some sites from their parents, there can be a delay in receipt of up to 14 hours.

Existing IT Environment

The current IT environment of Blue Yonder Airlines is described in the following sections.

Computers

Users at the Dallas office use 60 Microsoft Windows 98 desktops. The network support staff uses six Windows NT 4 Workstation desktops.

The Dallas office maintains eight servers running Windows NT 4 Server.

Each airfield office has four computers running Windows 98. In addition to required programs supplied by Dallas, users are authorized to load personal applications. One desktop at each airfield office has a modem attached to it and is used to dial in to Dallas twice daily to send and receive unsecured administrative traffic and e-mail.

Remote sites have no computer assets available. Each site has two analog phone lines.

LAN Connectivity

Dallas operates a TCP/IP network at 100 Mbps. Airfield offices maintain 100 Mbps TCP/IP networks, and one computer dials in to a RAS server to access the Dallas LAN.

Network

All servers maintain static IP addresses. All workstations are dynamically assigned IP addresses.

Envisioned IT Environment

Blue Yonder plans to make upgrades and changes to its IT environment as described in the following sections.

Computers

First, upgrade to Windows 2000 incorporating Active Directory directory service. Create a single-tree structure. Upgrade all servers to Windows 2000 Server. Upgrade all desktops to Windows 2000 Professional. Incorporate NTFS on all computers.

Second, purchase laptop computers for remote sites. Perform a clean install of Windows 2000 Professional. Remote users will use smart cards for authentication.

WAN and LAN Connectivity

Add 256 Kbps dedicated WAN links from the airfield offices to Dallas. Each airfield office will maintain a dedicated router. Remote sites will dial in to their parent airfield offices not less than twice a day.

Network

Each airfield office will be on a separate subnet. All computers will have e-mail and Internet access.

Proposed Network Usage

Blue Yonder's proposed goals for network usage based on the envisioned IT environment are stated in the following sections.

Dallas Office Administration

Sensitive personnel data will be stored on a member server, ADMIN1, in a shared folder called Personnel.

Authority for creation and maintenance of user, group, and computer accounts will be delegated to the administrative staff at the airfield office level. Administrative personnel must not have administrative capabilities outside of their assigned airfield offices.

Airfield office operating procedures require 3DES encryption strength for all confidential communications. Mutual computer authentication must take place.

Dallas Office Operations

One of the operations department servers, OPS1, will contain highly confidential material, and all communication with OPS1 must be secure and encrypted. OPS1 will contain two folders, Schedules and Training, which will contain the confidential files. The Training folder will be further divided into 17 subfolders, each one corresponding to a particular airfield office.

Airfield Offices

The airfield office director requires access to confidential material that affects only that director's office. The material must be locally stored in a secure, confidential manner.

Remote Sites

All communications must be secured and confidential. All materials maintained locally must be secured and confidential. The airfield office director or designated personnel from Dallas must be able to recover any material stored on the laptop computers.

Problem Statement

The following sections contain the required outcomes from Blue Yonder's CEO, network manager, and operations manager.

CEO

Current procedures don't allow timely dissemination of critical data. This data must be delivered rapidly and securely throughout the company. Network technology must be used to its full potential.

With the upgraded infrastructure, it's critical that unauthorized users external to our network are denied access.

Network Manager

Access to the Personnel shared folder must be restricted to administration department personnel and airfield office directors. These users must be able to view and modify files, create files and subfolders, and delete files and subfolders. We must know who's attempting to access this resource.

Operations Manager

Access to OPS1 must be restricted to members of the Administrators group, designated operations department personnel, and airfield office directors. Administrators must be able to fully administer the server. Designated operations department personnel must be able to access and modify files and folders in both folders, as well as delete them. Directors must be able to view all files in Schedules. Directors must be able to view only their own subfolders in the Training folder.

We must know who is attempting to modify and delete resources from either folder.

Case Study 1 Questions

70-220.CS1.001

Which security requirement will directly affect the tree's design?

A. User and computer authentication requirement

B. Secure communication with OPS1

C. Physical location of outlying facilities

D. Requirement to maintain local security on laptop files

70-220.CS1.002

How would you define a security solution for communications between the remote sites and the airfield office?

A. VPN, EFS, give unique recovery key to each airfield office

B. IPSec, DFS, give unique recovery key to each airfield office

C. VPN, EFS, give common recovery key to each remote site

D. IPSec, DFS, give common recovery key to each remote site

70-220.CS1.003

How would you identify the existing and envisioned IT administrative model?

A. Existing—Centralized / Envisioned—Centralized

B. Existing—Centralized / Envisioned—Decentralized

C. Existing—Decentralized / Envisioned—Decentralized

D. Existing—Decentralized / Envisioned—Centralized

70-220.CS1.004

How would you identify the security method necessary to ensure data security between OPS1 and ADM3 (a server in the administration department)?

A. IPSec with AH

B. EFS

C. Group Policy for shared folders

D. IPSec with ESP

70-220.CS1.005

Which components are required to securely connect a remote site to the parent airfield office? (Choose all that apply.)

A. L2TP

B. EAP-TLS

C. MS-CHAP

D. PPTP

E. Secure DNS

70-220.CS1.006

How should you secure OPS1 in the Active Directory tree?

A. Place it in the OPS_Dept OU. Apply Group Policy at OPS1.

B. Place it in an OU under the domain. Apply Group Policy at the site level.

C. Place it in a separate OU under the OPS_Dept OU. Apply Group Policy at the OU level.

D. Place it in a separate Active Directory tree. Apply Group Policy at the domain level.

70-220.CS1.007

What action must you take before you can audit files and folders on OPS1?

A. Use Group Policy to enable auditing.

B. Place user accounts that will be conducting the audits into the domain Server Operators group.

C. Enable success and failure auditing for process tracking.

D. Install the Event Viewer security-logging feature into the administrator's workstation.

70-220.CS1.008

How should you grant permissions to airfield office administrative personnel?

A. Create an AFO_Admins group. Add existing administrative support personnel from all airfield offices to the group. Assign permissions to the group.

B. Create a new Administrator user account for each airfield office OU. Assign permissions to each Administrator account.

C. Create an Admins group for each airfield office OU. Add existing administrative support personnel from all airfield offices to each group. Assign permissions to the group.

D. Create an Admins group for each airfield office OU. Add existing airfield office administrative support personnel to the group. Assign permissions to the group.

70-220.CS1.009

How should you restrict access to the Training folder on OPS1?

A. Share the Training folder, granting Read access to the group AFO_Directors.

B. Share the Training folder, granting Read access to the group AFO_ Directors. Remove the Everyone group from the ACL of the subfolders. Grant the NTFS Read permission for each subfolder to the appropriate airfield office director.

C. Share the Training folder, granting Full Control to the group, AFO_Directors. Remove the Everyone group from each subfolder's ACL. Grant Read access to the group AFO_Directors.

D. Remove the Everyone group from the ACL of the subfolders. Grant the NTFS Read permission for each subfolder to the appropriate airfield office director.

70-220.CS1.010

What protocols should be implemented in order to secure network communications with OPS1?

A. IPSec with AH

B. IPSec with ESP

C. L2TP over IPSec

D. SSL

70-220.CS1.011

How should you configure IPSec policy as it relates to OPS1?

A. Create an OU to contain OPS1. Apply the Secure Server (Require Security) IPSec policy at this OU. Apply the Client (Respond Only) IPSec policy at the domain level.

B. Create an OU to contain OPS1. Apply the Secure Server (Require Security) IPSec policy at this OU. Apply the Client (Respond Only) IPSec policy at the Ops_Users OU.

C. Apply the Secure Server (Require Security) and Client (Respond Only) IPSec policies at the domain level.

D. Apply the Server (Request Security) IPSec policy at OPS1. Apply the Client (Respond Only) IPSec policy at the domain level.

70-220.CS1.012

How should the remote users authenticate with the airfield office?

A. EAP-MD5 CHAP

B. MS-CHAP v2

C. EAP-TLS

D. MS-CHAP

70-220.CS1.013

How should you regulate access to the Personnel shared folder?

A. Create a domain local group ADM1_Personnel. Grant this group Change permissions to the Personnel shared folder. Add the AFO_Directors and Admin_Users global groups to ADM1_Personnel. Remove the Everyone group from the Personnel share.

B. Create a domain local group ADM1_Personnel. Grant this group Full Control permissions to the Personnel shared folder. Add the Domain Users global group to ADM1_Personnel. Remove the Everyone group from the Personnel share.

C. Grant the Admin_Users global group Full Control permissions to the Personnel shared folder. Grant the individual airfield office director user accounts Change permissions to the Personnel shared folder. Remove the Everyone group from the Personnel share.

D. Create a universal group called ADM1_Personnel. Add the AFO_Directors and Admin_Users global groups to ADM1_Personnel. Grant ADM1_Personnel the Full Control permission to the Personnel shared folder.

70-220.CS1.014

Which authentication method should users at the Dallas office use to gain access to the LAN?

A. NTLM

B. Basic authentication with SSL

C. Kerberos

D. RADIUS

70-220.CS1.015

What audit policy should you establish for the Personnel folder?

A. Success and Failure for Object Access

B. Failure for Logon Events

C. Success and Failure for Directory Service Access

D. Success for Process Tracking

Case Study 1 Answers

70-220.CS1.001

▶ **Correct Answers: B**

A. **Incorrect:** Kerberos is the default Windows 2000 authentication mechanism. It'll adapt to whatever forest structure you design.

B. **Correct:** In our scenario server security requirements have the most direct impact on our tree design. If you have servers that must communicate securely, it's generally advised to place them into their own OU, allowing you to apply the appropriate security policies at the OU level. It's important to remember that OUs can be broken down by either physical locations or network sites. This allows an administrator to "lock down" a particular OU and all the resources it contains. In this way, if you were to gain an additional resource (a file server, for instance) that required the same security policy, you'd simply add it to the existing high-security container.

C. **Incorrect:** In our scenario the physical location of the outlying facilities is inconsequential because the only connectivity comes from standard analog phone lines. Technically, they'd be treated as dial-up clients and wouldn't be a direct element of the tree design.

D. **Incorrect:** The requirement to maintain local security on laptop files can be implemented through EFS, and this doesn't affect placement of resources within the tree structure.

Domain objective addressed by this question: 4.3.

70-220.CS1.002

► **Correct Answers: A**

A. **Correct:** The remote sites need to dial in securely to their airfield office. This can easily be accomplished using VPN features. Further, based on our scenario's requirements, the type of VPN support we require is L2TP because we require 3DES encryption strength, which is available with L2TP. Technically, we require L2TP over IPSec to provide the encryption services.

We also require EFS to provide local security for the laptop files and folders. Protection with EFS spans the entirety of the network regardless of the data's location, as long as the data is located somewhere on the network. A significant benefit of this technology is that it provides built-in data recovery support. You can use file encryption only if the system is configured with one or more recovery keys. EFS allows recovery agents to configure public keys that are used to enable file recovery. Both the user and the recovery agent's public keys are stored on the originating encryption computer as X.509 version 3 certificates. After an employee leaves, data recovery enables an organization to recover data encrypted by that employee. It also provides the ability to recover data when encryption keys are lost. The recovery policy is under the control of domain administrators. Further, recovery can be delegated to designated administrator accounts. This provides better and more flexible control of who is authorized to recover encrypted data. EFS also supports multiple recovery agents, allowing data recovery to be controlled centrally but delegated to lower level administrators, as in our example. By distributing the appropriate unique recovery keys to the appropriate airfield office administrators, we meet our scenario's objective.

B. **Incorrect:** IPSec, by itself, wouldn't be the best choice for our remote sites. Only in the context of a VPN would mention of IPSec be appropriate. In addition, DFS is a tool to combine parts of multiple file systems into a single logical hierarchy. It's very convenient but doesn't offer us the encryption support we require.

C. **Incorrect:** A common recovery key would allow one airfield office to decrypt files from another airfield office.

D. **Incorrect:** IPSec, by itself, wouldn't be the best choice for our remote sites. Only in the context of a VPN would mention of IPSec be appropriate. In addition, DFS is a tool used to combine parts of multiple file systems into a single logical hierarchy. Although it's very convenient, this doesn't offer us the encryption support we require. A common recovery key would allow one airfield office to decrypt files from another airfield office.

Domain objective addressed by this question: 4.4.

70-220.CS1.003

▶ **Correct Answers: A**

A. **Correct:** With the existing structure, the Dallas office retains all IT control. All administrative functions are handled centrally, rendering a clear picture of a classic centralized administrative model.

With the envisioned model, Active Directory provides the ability for higher level administrators to delegate control for specific elements within Active Directory to individuals or groups. This eliminates the need for multiple administrators to have authority over an entire domain. Don't be fooled by the relative autonomy afforded the airfield offices. IT functions remain centralized and authority is delegated to the local level.

B. **Incorrect:** Neither of the IT environments is an example of a decentralized model. The existing processing structure doesn't support a decentralized model, and the envisioned Windows 2000 model would have to be structured in such a way as to have separate, independent IT departments at the airfield office level, which we don't have.

C. **Incorrect:** This answer is incorrect for the reasons stated in B.

D. **Incorrect:** This answer is incorrect for the reasons stated in A and B.

Domain objective addressed by this question: 1.2.

70-220.CS1.004

▶ **Correct Answers: D**

A. **Incorrect:** The AH protocol provides authentication and integrity but not encryption, so it wouldn't be sufficient for our scenario.

B. **Incorrect:** EFS encrypts the data locally, which is a good idea. However, EFS does nothing to secure the communication channel.

C. **Incorrect:** Group Policy can regulate access to resources by controlling how a workstation functions and acts. It doesn't provide encryption services.

D. **Correct:** Because all the servers are on the same network, the appropriate strategy would be to employ IPSec policies. IPSec allows you to secure data that's in transit on end-to-end systems. Authenticated users are the only ones who have access to those system resources. To provide encryption services, use ESP. ESP will support data encryption and authenticate the sending resource as well.

Domain objective addressed by this question: 6.2.

70-220.CS1.005

► **Correct Answers: A and B**

A. **Correct:** The requirement to support 3DES encryption strength and require mutual computer authentication makes L2TP the correct choice. PPTP doesn't meet these requirements.

B. **Correct:** Because our remote users will be using smart cards to authenticate, EAP with TLS is required.

C. **Incorrect:** MS-CHAP can't be used because it doesn't support 3DES encryption strength or smart card authentication.

D. **Incorrect:** PPTP doesn't meet these requirements.

E. **Incorrect:** Secure DNS updates ensure that only authorized users can modify DNS entries. With our VPN connectivity setup, secure DNS isn't required. A DHCP server issues each client an IP address upon dial-in.

Domain objective addressed by this question: 5.2.

70-220.CS1.006

► **Correct Answers: C**

A. **Incorrect:** The OU is the lowest level at which you can apply Group Policy. You can't apply Group Policy at an individual computer, as this answer suggests. You have to apply the Group Policy to the OU of which the computer is a member.

B. **Incorrect:** Applying Group Policy at the site level isn't correct for our scenario.

C. **Correct:** When you are working in a Windows 2000 environment, Group Policy lets you define a user's environment and then rely on the operating system to enforce the policies. Group Policy is different from profiles. Users have control over profile settings, but administrators control and implement Group Policy.

By default, Group Policy is inherited from the site, to the domain, and finally to the OU level. The order in which you apply Group Policy objects determines the Group Policy settings that a user or computer actually receives. By default, Group Policy affects only computers and users in the site, domain, or OU and doesn't affect any other objects.

By placing OPS1 in an OU separate from other operations department resources, an administrator is able to apply Group Policy at the OU level. This applies the policy to OPS1 without affecting users and other servers in the department.

D. **Incorrect:** Applying Group Policy at the domain level isn't correct for our scenario. Additionally, creating a separate Active Directory tree for this purpose isn't supported by unit requirements.

Domain objective addressed by this question: 4.3.

70-220.CS1.007

▶ **Correct Answers: A**

A. **Correct:** Before Windows 2000 will audit access to files and folders, you must use the Group Policy snap-in to enable the Audit Object Access setting in the Audit Policy. Once auditing is enabled, you can select specific events to be audited. Otherwise you receive an error message when you attempt to set up auditing for files and folders. Once auditing is enabled in Group Policy, view the security log in Event Viewer to review successful or failed access attempts.

B. **Incorrect:** To audit files and folders, you must be logged on as a member of the Administrators group or have been granted the Manage Auditing And Security Log right in Group Policy. No requirement or particular benefit is associated with the Server Operators group in this situation. It's important to remember, though, that excessive auditing requires memory and processor usage, which can hurt system performance.

C. **Incorrect:** If you were concerned about a virus outbreak, you'd want to enable auditing for process tracking as well as have virus detection software already in place. Then you could observe whether any unexpected processes were created. This isn't required for file and folder auditing.

D. **Incorrect:** The security log is an integral part of the Event Viewer tool. It doesn't need to be installed separately.

Domain objective addressed by this question: 4.1.

70-220.CS1.008

▶ **Correct Answers: D**

A. **Incorrect:** Populating a single AFO_Admins group with support personnel from all the airfield offices would create a situation in which a person in Airfield Office 2 would have administrative privileges to resources in Airfield Office 8.

B. **Incorrect:** There's no need to create 17 new Administrator accounts. Simply create the individual airfield office administrator security groups and add existing user accounts as necessary. In addition, this answer is incorrect because it advocates assigning permissions to the individual user accounts as opposed to using groups.

C. **Incorrect:** Creating Admins groups for each airfield office is a good idea, but populating each group with support personnel from *all* airfield offices is a bad idea. For instance, this would give the manager from Airfield Office 5 administrative privileges over the resources in Airfield Office 10.

D. **Correct:** Although you can give permissions to individual users, it's more efficient to give them to a security group. That way you can grant permission once to the group rather than several times to each individual. You can also specifically deny a user the right to access an object, even if the user is a member of a group that does have access. Using this component, you can specifically deny permissions when needed.

Every user added to a security group receives the permissions defined for that group. In our scenario each airfield office has administrative support personnel. The correct setup would be to create an Admins group for each airfield office and populate each group with the appropriate support people from the corresponding airfield office. Then grant permissions allowing administration of airfield office resources to the appropriate Admins group. In this way, when personnel transfer out of the airfield office, simply remove them from the group. Conversely, when new personnel arrive, add them to the group.

Domain objective addressed by this question: 4.2.

70-220.CS1.009

▶ **Correct Answers: B**

A. **Incorrect:** Simply sharing the Training folder and assigning the directors the Read permission doesn't provide adequate security. Unless you apply NTFS permissions to the individual subfolders, any director would have Read access to any subfolder.

B. **Correct:** To access the Training folder through the network, the folder must first be shared. Grant the airfield office directors permission to the Read shared folder. Then grant NTFS Read permission to the individual subfolders to the specific director. When shared folder permissions and NTFS permissions are combined, the effective permission is the *more* restrictive of the two. In this case you could have granted a higher level of access to the shared folder, because access was further restricted with NTFS permissions. Good practice, however, dictates that you grant only the permissions you need in order to get the job done.

It's worthwhile to note here that while NTFS prevents unauthorized users from gaining access, data can still be compromised. The hard disk can be removed and placed on a computer on which an unauthorized user has administrative privileges. From there an unauthorized user can gain access to the data on the drive.

Also, remove the Everyone group from each subfolder's ACL. By default, the Everyone group is granted Full Control.

C. **Incorrect:** Granting Full Control to the AFO_Directors group isn't a good strategy, but it's not fatal—at least not yet. The problem arises when the AFO_Directors group is given Read access to the subfolders. Even though the effective permission structure of the combined shared folder/NTFS permissions would limit them to Read, they still have Read access to material they shouldn't be reading.

D. **Incorrect:** Assigning the appropriate NTFS permissions without creating a shared folder gives the directors no way to navigate to the subfolders. Without a share, they wouldn't be able to access the subfolders from the network.

Domain objective addressed by this question: 3.2.

70-220.CS1.010

▶ **Correct Answers: B**

A. **Incorrect:** If encryption weren't required, we could provide authentication and data integrity using the AH protocol. But it is required in this scenario.

B. **Correct:** IPSec enables encrypted network communication. IPSec uses cryptography-based protection services, security protocols, and dynamic key management to accomplish two goals: protect IP packets and provide a defense against network attacks. IPSec is based on an end-to-end security model, meaning that the sending computer encrypts the packet before it's ever placed on the wire and the receiving computer decrypts the packet only after it's been received. IPSec also uses an algorithm to generate the same encryption key at each end of the connection. Therefore, the key is never transported on the network. The underlying assumption is that the communication medium is inherently insecure.

Because any communication with OPS1 needs to be secured and confidential, we need to use ESP to provide encryption services.

A primary benefit of IPSec is that it operates at the network layer of the TCP/IP protocol stack and any upper layer protocols or applications don't have to be concerned with IPSec.

C. **Incorrect:** L2TP is a VPN tunneling protocol. This would be appropriate to connect the remote sites to the airfield offices, but OPS1 doesn't need to participate in a VPN, so this wouldn't be a correct choice.

D. **Incorrect:** SSL operates at the application layer of the TCP/IP protocol stack. It provides communications privacy, authentication, and message integrity by using a combination of public-key and symmetric encryption. SSL requires that applications be specifically written to support SSL. This is commonly used to provide authentication and encryption services to Web site users.

Domain objective addressed by this question: 6.2.

70-220.CS1.011

▶ **Correct Answers: A**

A. **Correct:** This policy is for computers that normally don't secure communications. This policy enables affected computers to respond to requests for secured communications. It contains a default response rule, which enables negotiation with computers requesting IPSec. Only the requested protocol and port traffic for the communication is secured. In our scenario, because all communications with OPS1 must be secured, applying this IPSec policy at the domain level ensures that all clients will respond securely.

The Client (Respond Only) policy ensures that all computers can respond as required to requests for secure transfers.

The Server (Request Security) policy is for computers that normally perform secure communications, such as servers that transmit sensitive data.

The Secure Server (Require Security) policy is for computers that always require secure communications, such as a server that transmits highly sensitive data. You can assign IPSec policies through the Group Policy features of Active Directory. This allows the IPSec policy to be assigned at the site, domain, or OU level, which eliminates the administrative overhead of configuring each computer individually. You should use the IP Security Monitor to monitor the connections that the IPSec policy creates.

B. **Incorrect:** The problem with applying the Client (Respond Only) policy at the Ops_Users OU is that it's too restrictive. By not applying the policy at the domain level, you're restricting communications with OPS1 to only users and computers in the Ops_Users OU, a condition not specified in our scenario.

C. **Incorrect:** If you apply the Secure Server (Require Security) policy at the domain level, *all* communications between anybody in the entire domain must be secured. This is not a requirement of our scenario.

D. **Incorrect:** The Server (Request Security) doesn't provide the required level of IPSec security for OPS1. Also, in an Active Directory structure, you apply policy at the OU (or higher) level, not at an individual computer.

Domain objective addressed by this question: 6.2.

70-220.CS1.012

▶ **Correct Answers: C**

A. **Incorrect:** A typical use for EAP-MD5 CHAP is to authenticate the credentials of remote access clients by using user name and password security systems.

B. **Incorrect:** MS-CHAP v2 is an additional form of an encrypted, password-based authentication mechanism.

C. **Correct:** You can use EAP to support authentication schemes such as Generic Token Card, MD5-Challenge, and Transport Level Security (TLS) for smart card support. In our scenario, remote users authenticate using smart cards. If you're using smart cards for remote access authentication, you must use EAP-TLS because the other choices do not support smart card authentication.

D. **Incorrect:** MS-CHAP is an additional form of an encrypted, password-based authentication mechanism.

Domain objective addressed by this question: 5.3.

70-220.CS1.013

▶ **Correct Answers: A**

A. **Correct:** Windows 2000 gives an administrator tremendous flexibility in regulating resource access. One such technique is the use of security groups. Security groups let you assign the same security permissions to large numbers of users in one operation. Security groups are listed in DACLs that define permissions on resources and objects. Each security group has a scope that identifies the extent to which the group is applied in the domain tree or forest. There are three different scopes: universal, global, and domain local.

Domain local groups can contain accounts, global groups, and universal groups from any domain, as well as domain local groups from the same domain. The purpose of a domain local group is to provide a convenient place to assign access control permissions. Domain groups are best used for granting resource access to such things as file systems or printers.

Given this information, the appropriate strategy for our scenario is to create a domain local group (ADM1_Personnel) for assigning access control permissions. Assigning the Change permission provides all the administrative capabilities necessary. Creating the appropriate global groups (AFO_Directors and Admin_Users) provides the logical grouping. Adding these two groups to the domain local group is a very effective access control strategy. Finally, don't forget to remove the Everyone group from the ACL. This system group is assigned Full Control by default, which would violate the conditions of our scenario.

B. **Incorrect:** Adding the Domain Users group to the ADM1_Personnel local group would allow personnel outside the designated groupings to have inappropriate access. Also, the Full Control permission is too broad, allowing for administrative action beyond our scenario's scope. In addition to all the capabilities of the Change permission, Full Control allows users to change permissions and take ownership of the resource.

C. **Incorrect:** Global groups can be granted permissions anywhere in the forest, but they can contain only groups and user accounts as members from the domain in which the global group was defined. Global groups are primarily used to logically group users from within the same domain who have common access needs. Also, global groups are typically used by organizations that need to frequently change memberships between various groups. Two such logical groupings, airfield office directors and administration department users, are obvious choices for this scenario.

This answer suggests giving the Admin_Users group Full Control permissions to the shared folder directly, without the use of a local group. Technically, this is possible, but it's not recommended. The reason the answer is wrong is that we've assigned Full Control instead of Change. In addition, there are disadvantages associated with assigning permissions to a resource directly to individual user accounts. Strictly from an administrative perspective, this approach requires much more management overhead than does the recommended method of using global groups. While this will work (technically), it's still considered bad form.

D. **Incorrect:** Not only is this answer incorrect, but it also suffers from bad form. A universal group isn't indicated in this scenario, and the Full Control permission is too broad. Also, we haven't removed the Everyone group, allowing access by inappropriate users.

Universal groups can contain groups and accounts from any Windows 2000 domain in the domain tree or forest structure. Universal groups are often used to contain global groups from different domains within the forest structure that have common access needs. In order to use universal security groups, a Windows 2000 domain must be in native mode.

Domain objectives addressed by this question: 3.1, 4.6.

70-220.CS1.014

▶ **Correct Answers: C**

A. **Incorrect:** NTLM is included with Windows 2000 for mixed-mode environments where remnants of a previous operating system exist, such as Windows NT 4, that don't support Kerberos. Once all devices are capable of using Kerberos to authenticate, it's recommended that you no longer use NTLM. In our scenario, there's no benefit to using NTLM authentication.

B. **Incorrect:** Basic authentication with SSL would be appropriate for Web clients who need to conduct business over the Internet securely. This isn't one of the authentication choices available for the LAN environment.

C. **Correct:** As defined in the scenario, we have a Windows 2000 native-mode environment. Within the LAN, all users will access the network from a Windows 2000 device. The default (and preferred) authentication method for this situation is Kerberos.

Pervasive throughout Windows 2000, Kerberos authentication is a technically advanced solution to the authentication requirement and provides interoperability with UNIX systems. Kerberos provides authentication in this context through the use of secret key cryptography. It's strongly recommended that you use Kerberos in your Windows 2000 environment.

D. **Incorrect:** RADIUS provides a way to authenticate dial-up and VPN users. The RADIUS server is an IAS server that provides RADIUS authentication. This isn't an available technology for LAN-based authentication.

Domain objective addressed by this question: 4.5.

70-220.CS1.015

► **Correct Answers: A**

A. **Correct:** Personnel is a network shared folder on a member server. This folder contains files and sub-folders. The appropriate audit policy to establish would be success and failure audits for Object Access. Success auditing allows you to track who is doing what to the protected files. Failure auditing allows you to observe who is trying to access the resource, such as someone instigating a random-password hack. A well-balanced audit policy will be concerned with both eventualities.

B. **Incorrect:** Tracking failure for logon events would be an appropriate strategy to protect against such things as password attacks on the network. This wouldn't let us know who is attempting to access resources once inside the network.

C. **Incorrect:** You should audit directory service access if you're monitoring object access on domain controllers. ADMIN1 is a member server, so this policy wouldn't apply.

D. **Incorrect:** Auditing process tracking would be useful to guard against virus and Trojan horse programs. To do this you should run suspect programs and examine the security log for unexpected attempts to modify program files or create unexpected processes. However, this wouldn't address our requirement.

Domain objective addressed by this question: 4.1.

Adventure Works

Background

The background for Adventure Works, Tailspin Toys, and their joint project is summarized in the following sections.

Adventure Works

Adventure Works is the predominant manufacturer of computer game software. Its flagship game uses a proprietary, in-house–developed graphics rendering engine to provide realistic motion and lighting effects on Pentium-class PCs.

Adventure Works' headquarters is in Ridgecrest, California, and employs 450 people.

Its Web site currently receives about one million hits a day. In addition to state-of-the-art graphic content, visitors enjoy secure e-commerce capabilities, technical support, chat rooms, and an extensive download area. Users must register (it's free) to use most of the special features the site offers. The large majority of visitors to the site do register. Visitors are advised that the site is optimized for Microsoft Internet Explorer 4.01 or later, and 800-by-600 pixel resolution is recommended.

Tailspin Toys

Tailspin Toys also writes computer game software. It has 30 employees in its Skeeter Flats, Louisiana, facility.

Joint Project

Adventure Works and Tailspin Toys are collaborating on a follow-up to Adventure Work's flagship game. Software developers from both companies will work together on the project. The two companies will need to communicate daily. Some developers from Tailspin Toys will spend time on-site at Adventure Works' headquarters.

The release date for the new game, code-named "D3," is three months after the project starts, at which time the joint project will be officially terminated.

Existing IT Environment

The following sections describe the existing IT environment for each company.

Adventure Works' Computers

All computers attached to the LAN run Microsoft Windows 2000 in a single Active Directory directory service tree. Several client computers run a variety of Microsoft Windows client operating systems for testing purposes, but they are stand-alone machines not connected to the LAN.

Adventure Works has a production server named PRODUCTION, a Web server named WEBSERVER, a Quality Assurance server named QA, and a development server named DEVELOPMENT. QA must communicate securely with PRODUCTION, and vice versa.

WEBSERVER runs IIS 5.0 and has e-commerce capabilities. When visitors register, a cookie is created containing user-preference information. When a registered visitor makes an on-line purchase, the visitor becomes a customer. At this point, information about the visitor, including username and password, is stored in a database. There is also a private area of the Web site for use by Adventure Works software developers. They require Modify rights to the files in this area.

Adventure Works utilizes certificate services for a variety of activities. It maintains its enterprise root CA offline for security reasons. The root CA has a certificate with a five-year expiration date. One subordinate CA issues certificates specifically for developer access needs. The other subordinate CA issues certificates company-wide for many purposes, such as secure e-mail, IPSec, and EFS recovery. These CAs have certificates valid for two years.

The Guest user account is disabled for security reasons.

Adventure Works' WAN Connectivity

Adventure Works maintains a RRAS server to accommodate dial-up users.

Tailspin Toys' Computers

All servers run Windows NT 4. The client computers run a variety of Microsoft Windows client operating systems for testing purposes. Developer laptop computers run Windows 2000 Professional.

Tailspin Toys' WAN Connectivity

Tailspin Toys maintains a RAS server to accommodate dial-up users.

Envisioned IT Environment

Adventure Works and Tailspin Toys need to modify their existing IT environments to accommodate their joint project. Their vision of this new environment is outlined in the following sections.

Both Companies' Computers

Developers will have a D3 folder on their laptops containing up-to-date information on the joint project. This folder must be encrypted and secured. Updates to this folder will be made when the developers dial in to their company LAN. Both companies will have a VPN server to facilitate secured dial-in connections.

The development server at both companies will have a shared folder, D3Project, containing information about the project. Only the development manager at each company will have Write access to this folder on his or her respective development server. These folders will be synchronized daily at 10:00 P.M. Pacific Standard Time. Developers will have Read access to this folder.

Both Companies' WAN Connectivity

Demand-dial VPN support will be added to connect Adventure Works and Tailspin Toys for the project's duration. Remote users will connect through a VPN.

Adventure Works' Computers

A third issuing CA needs to be configured in the development department to issue certificates for Tailspin Toys access. Certificates must be distributed through secure e-mail, and all certificates from this CA must be revoked at the end of the joint venture.

Tailspin Toys developers need Read access to the private developer-only area on the Web server. This data is located in the Private folder on the Web server.

Problem Statement

Adventure Works' CEO, CIO, and Webmaster describe their concerns and project requirements in the following sections.

Adventure Works' CEO

The only reason we're working with Tailspin Toys is because they have a really good graphics guy over there. I don't trust them. Even though our developers must work with theirs, we must ensure that their people have only enough access to do their job and no more. PRODUCTION and QA contain proprietary information. Their people must not have *any* access to these servers. Moreover, I want to know who's attempting to access project resources. If our proprietary technology becomes public, we'll be out of business by Christmas!

Adventure Works' CIO

During the joint project, both companies must share resources. For example, Tailspin Toys personnel at our facility must have access to printers, and vice versa. Any files leaving our facility must be transmitted securely and confidentially, and data must be stored in the same manner.

Adventure Works' Webmaster

Developers must be authenticated to use special secured areas of the Web server. We want to use certificate-based authentication for Tailspin Toys developers who need access to this information. On the public part of the site, we use in-house developed custom ActiveX controls to provide user interactivity. Our controls must have public credibility to encourage users to trust and download our content.

Case Study 2 Questions

70-220.CS2.001

What type of CA should Adventure Works use to sign its custom ActiveX controls?

A. Enterprise subordinate

B. Microsoft Authenticode 2.0

C. Stand-alone root

D. Third party

70-220.CS2.002

Which types of CA should Adventure Works implement for internal use? (Choose all that apply.)

A. Enterprise subordinate CA

B. Stand-alone root CA

C. Stand-alone subordinate CA

D. Enterprise root CA

E. Third-party CA

70-220.CS2.003

How should Adventure Works regulate Tailspin Toys' access to the developer-only area of the Adventure Works Web site?

A. Issue X.509 client certificates to the Tailspin Toys developers. Map their certificates to the IUSR_WEBSERVER account.

B. Issue S/MIME client certificates to the Tailspin Toys developers. Then map their certificates on a one-to-one basis to a designated user account on the Adventure Works network. Assign the NTFS Read permission to the virtual directory.

C. Issue X.509 client certificates to the Tailspin Toys developers. Map their certificates on a many-to-one basis to a designated user account on the Adventure Works network. Assign Read permissions to this account.

D. Create user accounts for the Tailspin Toys developers. Issue X.509 client certificates to the Tailspin Toys developers. Map their certificates on a one-to-one basis to the newly created user accounts. Map the user accounts on a many-to-one basis to the IUSR_WEBSERVER account.

70-220.CS2.004

How should you authenticate previously registered visitors to your Web site?

A. Anonymous

B. Cookies

C. Basic

D. Integrated Windows authentication

E. Digest

F. Client certificate mapping

70-220.CS2.005

When a customer purchases one of the game's action figures from your Web site, how should you protect the customer's personal financial data during the transaction?

A. Authenticode 2.0

B. EFS

C. SSL

D. L2TP

70-220.CS2.006

How should you set up auditing on the Web server to track access attempts to the Private folder?

A. Navigate to the Auditing tab. Add the Domain Users group. Select Successful and Failed for the following: Traverse folder/Execute file, List folder/Read data, Create files/Write data.

B. Navigate to the Auditing tab. Add the Network group. Select Successful for the following: Traverse folder/Execute file, List folder/Read data, Create files/Write data, Delete subfolders and files, Delete.

C. Navigate to the Auditing tab. Add the Interactive group. Select Failed for the following: Traverse folder/Execute file, List folder/Read data, Create files/Write data, Delete.

D. Navigate to the Auditing tab. Add the Everyone group. Select Successful and Failed for the following: Traverse folder/Execute file, List folder/Read data, Create files/Write data.

70-220.CS2.007

Joe, a user at Tailspin Toys, needs to access a resource at Adventure Works. When the demand-dial VPN connection is established, Joe retrieves his document. Doris, another user at Tailspin Toys, also needs to access data at Adventure Works. Joe still has an open session on the Adventure Works file server. What must Doris do to retrieve her data?

A. Because Joe is currently using the VPN tunnel, encryption services won't be available to Doris. She could wait for Joe to close his session, at which time encryption services will be available. Alternatively, she could use the existing connection, transmitting his data unsecured.

B. Simply retrieve the data. This type of VPN connection remains active until the preconfigured amount of idle time has elapsed.

C. Doris must wait until Joe's session is closed. Then Doris can create a session, unless the preconfigured amount of idle time has elapsed.

D. When Doris attempts to access the remote resource, an additional VPN connection is established. When Joe's session is closed, the original VPN connection is terminated.

70-220.CS2.008

Which VPN encryption services are available when a remote user dials in to Tailspin Toys' RAS server?

A. 3DES

B. IPSec with AH

C. MPPE

D. IPSec with ESP

70-220.CS2.009

The network administrators for both companies have determined that they want to configure all three VPNs to use the same authentication protocol. Which protocol can they use? (Choose all that apply.)

A. EAP-TLS

B. SPAP

C. PAP

D. MS-CHAP

E. Kerberos

F. EAP-MD5 CHAP

G. CHAP

70-220.CS2.010

What technique should be employed to facilitate secure communications between PRODUCTION and QA?

A. L2TP over IPSec

B. Subnet masking

C. IPSec with AH

D. IPSec with ESP

70-220.CS2.011

How should you administer IPSec policy for PRODUCTION and QA to meet Adventure Works' communication requirements?

A. Create an OU to hold PRODUCTION and QA. Apply the Secure Server (Require Security) IPSec policy at the OU. Apply the Client (Respond Only) IPSec policy at the domain level.

B. Create an OU to hold all of Adventure Works' servers. Apply the Server (Request Security) IPSec policy at the OU. Apply the Secure Server (Require Security) IPSec policy at PRODUCTION and QA. Apply the Client (Respond Only) IPSec policy at the domain level.

C. Apply the Server (Request Security) and the Client (Respond Only) IPSec policies at the domain level.

D. Create an OU to hold PRODUCTION and QA. Apply the Server (Request Security) IPSec policy at the OU. Apply the Client (Respond Only) IPSec policy at the domain level.

70-220.CS2.012

Joe, a developer, joins Adventure Works. Joe is aware of the requirement that the D3 folder on his laptop be secured and confidential. He is also aware that the CA that issues EFS recovery certificates is temporarily offline. What will happen when Joe attempts to encrypt a file?

A. Without a valid certificate, the encryption option won't appear in Windows Explorer. He must wait until the CA comes back online.

B. When Joe attempts encryption, EFS will be unable to locate a certificate for him and will issue its own. When the CA comes back up, Joe's current certificate must be merged into the certificate issued by the CA.

C. When Joe attempts encryption, EFS will be unable to locate a certificate for him and will issue its own. When the CA comes back up, it will issue Joe a basic EFS certificate. Joe will now have two certificates with Encrypting File System listed.

D. When Joe attempts encryption, EFS will be unable to locate a certificate for him, and will issue its own. When the CA comes back up, Joe must decrypt his previously encrypted files. Joe's current certificate must be merged into the certificate issued by the CA. Now Joe may encrypt these files with the new certificate.

70-220.CS2.013

What's the primary security risk for Adventure Works?

A. Unauthorized use of cookies to retrieve personal information from Web customers

B. Unauthorized access to PRODUCTION and QA by Tailspin Toys

C. Unauthorized authentication to the Private folder on WEBSERVER

D. Use of non–Windows 2000 client computers to access EFS-secured file server data

70-220.CS2.014

While creating certificates for Tailspin Toys, the Adventure Works administrator inadvertently requested two-year certificates. What will be the result of this request?

A. A certificate will be issued that expires two years after the issuing certificate's create date.

B. No certificate will be issued.

C. A certificate will be issued that expires on the day after the release date of the project.

D. A certificate will be issued that expires two years after its create date.

70-220.CS2.015

Three members of the Tailspin Toys development team have traveled to Adventure Works to work more closely with their Adventure Works counterparts. They've requested access to the color laser printer. How should the network administrator accommodate the request?

A. Create one domain user account. Set this account to become disabled the day after the release date of the project. Add this account to the color printer domain local security group. Grant the user account the Print permission. Create two copies of this account. Rename and assign one of the new accounts to each of the Tailspin users.

B. Create domain user accounts for the visiting developers. Create a global group called Tailspin Toys Developers. Set this group to become disabled the day after the release date of the project. Add the new accounts to this group. Add the global group to the color printer domain local security group. Grant the group the Manage Printers permission. Instruct the visiting users to use their new domain accounts to log on.

C. Add the Guest account to the color printer domain local security group. Grant the Guest account the Manage Documents permission. Instruct the visiting users to log on as Guest.

D. Instruct the visiting users to log on normally. As members of the Everyone group, they already have the necessary permissions to print.

Case Study 2 Answers

70-220.CS2.001

▶ **Correct Answers: D**

A. **Incorrect:** Enterprise subordinate is an internal CA. This type of CA would be best suited for handling internal authentication and data integrity issues.

B. **Incorrect:** Authenticode 2.0 is client-side software that monitors the attempted download of executable code in order to identify the code's author. Authenticode displays certificate information, such as the name included in the digital signature, an indication of whether it's a commercial or personal certificate, and the date when the certificate expires. This information enables users to make a more informed decision before continuing with the download. The software publisher digitally signs software (including .exe, .dll, .ocx, and .cab files) when it's ready for publication. Software publishers who obtain a code-signing certificate from a CA can use Authenticode signing tools to digitally sign their files for distribution over the Web. Authenticode looks for the signatures (or the lack of signatures) in the files that users attempt to download.

When using Authenticode, you need to make certain decisions regarding software-signing strategy. These include deciding which internal and external groups need the ability to sign software and which strategies will be implemented in order to enroll users as software signers.

C. **Incorrect:** A stand-alone root CA would be used in situations in which Active Directory is not in place. Adventure Works has a single Active Directory tree and is therefore able to use an enterprise root CA. Both the enterprise and stand-alone local CAs are best suited to handle internal authentication and data integrity issues; they would not be used to establish public credibility of the code.

D. **Correct:** Adventure Works must select CAs, both internal and external, that will be the source of their certificates. A local certifying authority, such as the IT department, can handle internal network authentication and data integrity, but it would not be useful for signing externally distributed code such as ActiveX controls. Internet transactions and software signing might require third-party certificates in order to establish public credibility. To encourage public acceptance of Adventure Works custom controls, a third-party CA should be used to sign them.

Domain objective addressed by this question: 4.7.

70-220.CS2.002

▶ **Correct Answers: A and E**

A. **Correct:** For internal authentication and data integrity, Adventure Works has implemented an enterprise root CA. This CA is responsible for certifying two additional CAs, known as subordinate CAs. One subordinate CA issues certificates specifically for developer access needs. The other subordinate CA issues certificates company-wide for many purposes, such as secure e-mail, IPSec, and EFS recovery. This information comes directly from the scenario. The process of issuing and requesting certificates is made easy through the use of certificate templates with enterprise subordinate CAs.

To specify an enterprise root CA, the organization must have implemented Active Directory, which Adventure Works has. Stand-alone CAs, both root and subordinate, are for organizations that haven't implemented Active Directory.

B. **Incorrect:** This is incorrect for the reasons stated in A.

C. **Incorrect:** This is incorrect for the reasons stated in A.

D. **Incorrect:** Enterprise root is an internal CA. The use of an enterprise and subordinate CA structure would be best suited to handling internal authentication and data integrity issues, but the root CA should be stored offline for security. The root CA is used to certify one or more subordinate CAs to handle the issuing of internal company-wide purpose-specific certificates.

E. **Correct:** Although Adventure Works uses a third-party CA for signing in-house ActiveX controls to provide public credibility, it could have elected to use a third-party CA for other needs. These needs might include such things as e-mail and file transfer, as well as Web browsing.

Domain objective addressed by this question: 4.7.

70-220.CS2.003

▶ **Correct Answers: C**

A. **Incorrect:** The user account IUSR_<computername> is created when IIS is installed, and this account, called IUSR_WEBSERVER in our environment, is normally used to provide appropriate access control measures to anonymous users. Using this account for Tailspin Toys developers would have the undesirable side effect of allowing expanded access to the anonymous users as well.

B. **Incorrect:** There's no S/MIME certificate per se. Instead, S/MIME, which allows for e-mail security, is one of the uses for an X.509 certificate.

C. **Correct:** Once you've issued the client certificates to the Tailspin Toys developers, you can map the certificates on a many-to-one basis to a designated user account created specifically for providing Read access to the developer-only area of the site.

You can implement this process from the Active Directory Users And Computers Console. From the View menu, select Advanced Features. Next, right-click a user account, and then click Name Mappings. Click Add to import the certificates when the Security Identity Mapping dialog box appears.

Because all Tailspin Toys developers have identical access needs to Adventure Works' site, only a single user account must be identified. One-to-one mapping would require a separate user account for each Tailspin Toys certificate—an unnecessary expenditure of resources and administrative time and effort.

It's important to remember in this related situation that certificates can be mapped only to individual user accounts. You can't map them to complete security groups.

D. **Incorrect:** It wouldn't be optimal to create separate user accounts for all the Tailspin Toys developers. It would be equally suboptimal to map all these certificates to the IUSR_WEBSERVER account, because it would have the undesirable side effect of allowing expanded access to the anonymous users as well.

Domain objective addressed by this question: 4.7.

70-220.CS2.004

▶ **Correct Answers: A**

A. **Correct:** The Windows operating system is configured to accept only valid users. Because the Internet is anonymous, IIS 5.0 creates the IUSR_<computername> account so that anonymous users can map to an actual user account for access control purposes. With IIS 5.0 you can set up different anonymous accounts for different Web sites, virtual directories, directories, and files. With IIS you can also control user rights and permissions to Web-based resources through mapping user certificates to one or more network user accounts. This provides a great deal of flexibility and fine control by allowing you to assign which accounts will be used where within the site.

B. **Incorrect:** Even though "registered" users provide information about themselves and their preferences, you can still authenticate as anonymous. Remember, our site generates a million hits a day, with most users registering. By using cookies, the responsibility of remembering these bits of data is transferred from Adventure Works to the Web site user. The cookie is stored on the user's computer and is retrieved when the user revisits the site, allowing the browser to display customized information for that user. However, cookies don't affect the authentication process. They simply customize the browser experience.

C. **Incorrect:** Once a visitor becomes a customer, it would be appropriate to use Basic Authentication with SSL to provide security for the transaction. In our site, we aren't generating a user name and password until a visitor becomes a customer. By having users register we are generating information about the customer base, but we can't use Basic Authentication without the user name and password, so general visitors aren't authenticated in this way.

D. **Incorrect:** Using Integrated Windows authentication, the browser attempts to use the current user's credentials from a domain logon. This authentication scheme works especially well in an intranet environment where users have Windows domain accounts. This isn't indicated in our scenario.

E. **Incorrect:** Digest authentication addresses some of the weaknesses of Basic authentication. Currently, Digest authentication is still in the draft phase and hasn't yet become a standard. Like Basic authentication, Digest authentication isn't indicated in this case.

F. **Incorrect:** Issuing client certificates to millions of anonymous users isn't required, although Adventure Works does use client certificates for Tailspin Toys developers to regulate their access to a secured area of the Web site. Because "registered" users are basically anonymous, you gain little by implementing a certificate-based authentication structure for anonymous users.

Domain objective addressed by this question: 4.5.

70-220.CS2.005

▶ **Correct Answers: C**

A. **Incorrect:** Authenticode 2.0 is client-side software that monitors the attempted download of executable code in order to identity the code's author. Authenticode displays certificate information, such as the name included in the digital signature, an indication of whether it's a commercial or personal certificate, and the date when the certificate expires. This information enables users to make a more informed decision before continuing with the download. Authenticode technology doesn't protect financial data during a Web transaction.

B. **Incorrect:** EFS encrypts files on local file systems, but it doesn't provide any encryption services during a data transmission. It also has no means for authenticating users. A combination of EFS and other security techniques provides a strong overall solution, but its use isn't indicated here.

C. **Correct:** By using SSL, communications that contain private data, such as credit card numbers, are encrypted. SSL is the current solution of choice for transmitting confidential financial information across the Internet. With an SSL-enabled client as well as an SSL-enabled server, both machines can correctly establish an encrypted connection. SSL runs above TCP/IP while running below other higher level protocols such as HTTP or IMAP.

Virtually all modern browsers support SSL, making this an effective choice for Internet commerce.

D. **Incorrect:** L2TP is VPN technology that allows for secure, encrypted communications between two end-point computers. L2TP connections are created between two ISPs or directly between a dial-up client and a specialized VPN server connected to the company LAN. This isn't a suitable technology for enabling e-commerce.

Domain objective addressed by this question: 5.2.

70-220.CS2.006

▶ **Correct Answers: D**

A. **Incorrect:** As a baseline for troubleshooting permissions, it's recommended that you set up auditing on your Web server to monitor the activities of the Everyone group for the success and failure of the following events: Traverse folder/Execute file, List folder/Read data, Create files/Write data. If you only audit the Domain Users group, you might miss attempts to gain access to the data.

This lets you see who is accessing and modifying files on your Web server. By monitoring the security log, you can then determine which files and folders are showing signs of possible unauthorized access.

B. **Incorrect:** We're concerned with access. Extending the scope of our audit to deletions isn't indicated by our scenario's conditions. Also, the choice of groupings is inappropriate. The Network group is a system group that automatically contains all users accessing the computer through the network, and the Interactive group automatically contains all users sitting at the keyboard of a particular computer. Furthermore, by only auditing successful access we won't log the failed attempts as someone tries to gain unauthorized access.

C. **Incorrect:** This is incorrect for the reasons stated in B.

D. **Correct:** As a baseline for troubleshooting permissions, it's recommended that you set up auditing on your Web server to monitor the activities of the Everyone group for the success or failure of the following events: Traverse folder/Execute file, List folder/Read data, Create files/Write data, Read permissions. This lets you see who's accessing and modifying files on your Web server. By monitoring the security log, you can then determine which files and folders are showing signs of possible unauthorized access.

Domain objective addressed by this question: 4.1.

70-220.CS2.007

▶ **Correct Answers: B**

A. **Incorrect:** All users of an existing VPN tunnel enjoy all the benefits of the tunnel, including encryption services.

B. **Correct:** Demand-dial routing is the forwarding of packets across a PPP link. The demand-dial interface can be either in a connected state or in a disconnected state. If it's in a disconnected state when the packet is being forwarded, you must change the demand-dial interface to a connected state. Once the connection is established, packets are forwarded across the demand-dial connection. Because the costs of demand-dial connections are typically time sensitive, after a configured amount of idle time the demand-dial link is terminated. Demand-dial connections have the benefit of allowing the user to use cheaper dial-up WAN links and pay for the link only when it's being used. Therefore, once the connection is established, it remains open until it times out. In our scenario, Joe has triggered the connection. Unless it has timed out, Doris can use the established link. If it has timed out, Doris's access attempt will trigger the establishment of a new connection.

C. **Incorrect:** Given the scenario, Doris doesn't need to wait until Joe's session is finished.

D. **Incorrect:** Demand-dial routing isn't the same as remote access. Remote access connects a single user to a network, and demand-dial routing connects networks together. As long as a valid tunnel exists, any authorized user can read and write to the tunnel. The tunnel is the part of the connection in which the data is encapsulated. The data is encrypted in the connection portion of the VPN link. Additional VPN connections aren't established.

Domain objective addressed by this question: 5.3.

70-220.CS2.008

▶ **Correct Answers: C**

A. **Incorrect:** 3DES wouldn't be the correct choice because both DES and 3DES algorithms are used to ensure that the data exchange is confidential, which means that the information gets to its intended receiver.

B. **Incorrect:** IPSec is the future of network security, but it isn't available to Windows NT 4 servers.

The reason for grouping IPSec with AH is that once you decide to utilize IPSec, you have two choices for protocols: ESP and AH. Each can provide security for different purposes.

C. **Correct:** Tailspin Toys' RAS server is running Windows NT 4. This limits the VPN choice to PPTP. As such, the encryption services are provided by MPPE. MPPE provides only link encryption, not end-to-end encryption. End-to-end encryption is data encryption between the client application and the server hosting the resource or service being accessed by the client application.

D. **Incorrect:** ESP is the IPSec configuration you'd choose if you required data encryption. With ESP, the data packet is encrypted before it's transmitted. In an IPSec-enabled environment, you could specify 3DES encryption strength. Standard encryption strength, DES, uses a 56-bit encryption key. 3DES uses three 56-bit encryption keys for higher security.

Domain objective addressed by this question: 5.2.

70-220.CS2.009

▶ **Correct Answers: A and D**

A. **Correct:** The limiting factor for our decision is based on server operating systems. Tailspin Toys uses Windows NT 4. This limits them to PPTP. Either EAP-TLS or MS-CHAP must be used in order for the PPP payloads to be encrypted using MPPE, the encryption services available to PPTP. Although MS-CHAP can be used in this scenario, MS-CHAP v2 can't be used because Tailspin Toys uses Windows NT 4. MS-CHAP v2 becomes available only if both companies are implementing Windows 2000. If Adventure Works wanted to take advantage of the additional capabilities offered by L2TP, L2TP also supports EAP-TLS and MS-CHAP.

B. **Incorrect:** SPAP is a vendor solution for use when connected to Shiva LAN Rover hardware. It's more secure than plaintext but less secure than CHAP.

C. **Incorrect:** Normally, PAP would be used only if the client and the remote access server were unable to negotiate anything better. PAP is normally used for PPP connections and is less secure than CHAP.

D. **Correct:** This is correct for the reasons stated in A.

E. **Incorrect:** Kerberos is the default Windows 2000 authentication mechanism, but its use isn't supported by PPTP. Kerberos isn't backward compatible with any other version of Windows prior to Windows 2000. In this scenario all of the systems are Microsoft clients, so we can use MS-CHAP or EAP-TLS, which are stronger authentication protocols.

F. **Incorrect:** EAP-MD5 CHAP is a required EAP type that uses the same challenge handshake protocol as CHAP, but the challenges and responses are sent as EAP messages. CHAP is an industry-standard authentication protocol used by many non-Microsoft clients.

G. **Incorrect:** CHAP is an industry-standard authentication protocol used by many non-Microsoft clients. It utilizes a three-way handshake to verify the peer's identity.

Domain objective addressed by this question: 4.5.

70-220.CS2.010

▶ **Correct Answers: D**

A. **Incorrect:** PRODUCTION and QA are located on the same network. This rules out a VPN solution such as L2TP, which would normally be used to transport data from network to network through a public network, such as the Internet. This would be indicated if we wanted to securely connect two networks or securely connect a remote user.

B. **Incorrect:** Subnet masking is a technique used in segmenting a TCP/IP network in order to provide greater flexibility. It allows TCP/IP to distinguish the network ID portion of the IP address from the host ID component. Although Adventure Works undoubtedly uses subnet masking in its internal network, this doesn't address the secure communication requirement dictated by our scenario.

C. **Incorrect:** This is incorrect for the reasons stated in D.

D. **Correct:** IPSec provides us with the answer. When providing TCP/IP network communications with security, we must determine if we require encryption in addition to authentication and data integrity functions. Our scenario requires secure, confidential communications, so encryption is required. ESP is the IPSec component that provides this service. The AH protocol provides authentication and data integrity, but not encryption.

ESP provides confidentiality of data through IP packet data encryption. ESP has options for integrity and authenticity, but not the privacy that can be achieved through AH. AH can protect the address information located in the IP header, but ESP can't protect the IP header from being modified.

Domain objective addressed by this question: 6.2.

70-220.CS2.011

▶ **Correct Answers: D**

A. **Incorrect:** Windows 2000 provides a set of predefined IPSec configurations. By default, all predefined policies are designed for computers that are members of a Windows 2000 domain. The predefined policies, filter lists, and filter actions are provided to allow an administrator to establish a security baseline that can be modified to meet specific needs. The three predefined policies are: Client (Respond Only), Server (Request Security), and Secure Server (Require Security).

B. **Incorrect:** A selection of Secure Server (Require Security) is too restrictive.

Placing all of Adventure Works' servers into the same OU would effectively require that all communications be secure, a condition not supported by our scenario. This answer also suggests that the Secure Server (Require Security) policy be applied directly at PRODUCTION and QA. In an Active Directory environment, Group Policy can't be applied below the OU level.

C. **Incorrect:** This is incorrect for the reasons stated in A.

D. **Correct:** Only communications between PRODUCTION and QA need to be secured. In theory, PRODUCTION could communicate with WEBSERVER and not require security. This is why we chose the Server (Request Security) policy. This ensures that PRODUCTION and QA will always communicate securely, but it doesn't require all other communication be secure.

Domain objective addressed by this question: 6.2.

70-220.CS2.012

▶ **Correct Answers: C**

A. **Incorrect:** EFS is integrated into Windows 2000. Assuming an NTFS partition, the appropriate menu options will appear in Windows Explorer, offline CA or not.

B. **Incorrect:** While it's possible for a user to have multiple certificates issued for the same purpose, it isn't possible to merge them into a single certificate.

C. **Correct:** Joe will encounter no difficulties. When he attempts encryption, EFS will be unable to locate a certificate for him and will issue its own. When the CA comes back up, it will issue Joe a certificate. Joe will now have two certificates with Encrypting File System listed. From a management perspective, it might be good to ensure that a centrally managed EFS certificate is available to aid in centralized file recovery.

It's important to remember that EFS is used strictly for file and folder data encryption. For example, if Joe is attempting to encrypt a system file, he won't be able to complete this task under EFS.

D. **Incorrect:** There is no requirement to decrypt files encrypted with one certificate in order to use another certificate.

Domain objective addressed by this question: 4.4.

70-220.CS2.013

▶ **Correct Answers: B**

A. **Incorrect:** Cookies are always controversial. In our scenario only benign preference data is stored in a cookie. Any actual personal information about a user would only become known when the user makes an online purchase. This data, however, isn't stored in a cookie, but in a database file that requires credentials to access.

B. **Correct:** An organization's tolerance for risk will help shape its security policies. Although our scenario has a number of potential risks, the CEO places unauthorized access to the PRODUCTION and QA servers at the top of the list. If proprietary data stored on those machines were available to unauthorized users, the potential is great for Adventure Works to be put at a tremendous competitive disadvantage.

C. **Incorrect:** The Private folder is secured in such a way that Adventure Works developers have Modify access and Tailspin Toys developers have Read access. No one else is granted access to this resource. The concept of *unauthorized authentication* bears research. First, Web visitors would authenticate with IIS, not the Private folder. Assume that an unauthorized user attempts to gain access—by authenticating, IIS has enough information about the user to deny that user access!

D. **Incorrect:** In our scenario the non–Windows 2000 clients aren't on the LAN anyway. Even if they were, EFS encrypted data can be read only by the file's owner or a recovery agent.

Domain objective addressed by this question: 1.3.

70-220.CS2.014

▶ **Correct Answers: C**

A. **Incorrect:** Matching the end date of the certificate with the end date of a different CA isn't correct. Even if the special use CA were subordinate to one of the other subordinate CAs (it isn't), you still can't issue a certificate that's beyond the issuer's end date.

B. **Incorrect:** All else being equal, a certificate will be issued matching the most restrictive guidelines that apply to the given situation.

C. **Correct:** An issuing CA is created at Adventure Works specifically to issue certificates for this joint project. According to the scenario's requirement, all certificates issued by this CA must expire on the day after the release date of the project. No certificate can be issued with a date past the CA's ending date. Even though a two-year certificate was requested, a truncated certificate will be issued. It's important to remember that certificate lifetimes become shorter the deeper the certification hierarchy goes. You should plan certificate life cycles in order to avoid short renewal cycles and overall certificate lifetimes.

D. **Incorrect:** This is incorrect for the reasons stated in C.

Domain objective addressed by this question: 4.7.

70-220.CS2.015

▶ **Correct Answers: A**

A. **Correct:** First, let's look at the permissions required for printing. The Print permission allows you to print and manage your own jobs. Manage Documents allows you to control everyone else's print jobs as well. Manage Printers gives you complete control over the printing environment. You can share, delete, and change permissions on printers. For our scenario, Print is the only permission that's appropriate.

Given the scenario's requirements, the correct thing to do is to create user accounts specifically dedicated to printing. This way, our designated user accounts can only do one thing—print. Our visitors can't use these accounts to roam around inside your domain. Causing the accounts to become disabled as soon as the project is terminated is a nice touch.

B. **Incorrect:** We don't want to grant them the Manage Printers permission. If all they need to do is print, then we should only grant the Print permission to the Tailspin users. You should always grant the lowest permissions possible for any resource.

C. **Incorrect:** In low security networks, it's common to use the Guest account for things like printing. However, the Guest account is disabled and therefore can't be used. Even if we did enable this account, we don't want to grant it the Manage Documents permission.

D. **Incorrect:** By default, the Everyone group has Print permission, and nothing in our scenario indicates this has been removed. However, the visitors are unable to "log on normally" because they don't have accounts in our domain!

Domain objective addressed by this question: 3.2.

Fabrikam, Inc.

Background

Fabrikam, Inc., of Jackson, Mississippi, tracks terrorist attacks worldwide. Its application allows it to manipulate historical data with hypothetical parameters to project probability of attack in a variety of forms. Its customers are corporations that are susceptible to terrorist attacks. They use the Fabrikam model to protect their businesses.

Existing IT Environment

Agents manually encode their information about terrorist attacks while they're in the field. The information is later keyed into the database at headquarters. The data is at least two weeks old before it's available for modeling.

Customers run the TCP/IP-based application and access the results by visiting headquarters in Jackson. They have domain accounts on the Fabrikam Windows NT 4 LAN.

The sales and marketing departments access their resources at headquarters to manage customer accounts. Only the sales department can access the customer data, and each sales representative's accounts are for his or her exclusive use. Sales and marketing personnel currently return to headquarters to use the system's resources.

The entire network uses TCP/IP.

One Windows NT 4 server is running as a Primary Domain Controller (PDC), one as a Backup Domain Controller (BDC), and one as an application server in Jackson. There is also one file and print server. The 10 desktops are all Windows NT 4 workstations.

Envisioned IT Environment

In the sections that follow the CEO and CIO of Fabrikam describe the improvements and changes they want to implement in the company's IT environment.

CEO

The agency hopes to improve the total cost of operations (TCO) by moving to Microsoft Windows 2000. Agents in the field will now be able to enter their own work on secured laptops and upload it on the day the information is captured. Our systems will be protected because the agents will access our network externally with authentication using smart cards. The sales force will also have laptops for their travel requirements. They must be able to carry their current customer accounts with them on the laptops and keep all the data synchronized with their headquarters.

We want to offer our customers better service using the Internet to access our resources.

CIO

We will be able to bill our customers based on their Internet usage by integrating the RADIUS technology into our new Internet resources.

Agents and sales representatives will all have daily access for reference and uploading of their data through VPN technologies. Our customers will have the same benefits and will reduce their travel expenses considerably. We are certain that the added investment in a Web server and RRAS will provide a return on our investment in additional sales and the productivity of our field employees.

Our employees will authenticate with smart cards. Customers will authenticate with certificates. We will use an enterprise policy CA since the PKI is integral to our security configuration.

The one Windows NT domain will become the single Windows 2000 domain with Active Directory directory service. A domain name will have to be selected and registered.

Problem Statement

In the following sections the CIO, sales manager, and marketing manager describe the concerns they have with the transition to their envisioned IT environment.

CIO

We're concerned about security during the move to Windows 2000. The internal risk becomes greater. For this reason, we don't want to use outsourcing. We want to find ways to use our own trusted employees.

The new technical environment will require more servers and they must all be absolutely secure.

We will require automatic mapping of certificates to users and groups. The agency's security configuration plan includes smart cards, IPSec, EFS, certificate templates, mapped certificates, SSL, TLS, and digital signatures. Our users fall into three categories: in-house employees, customers, and field employees.

Sales Manager

Customers want the ability to run our modeling programs from their own offices instead of traveling to Jackson.

Marketing Manager

With customers accessing our modeling engine from their own offices, the potential for new customer growth far outweighs the time and effort involved in moving to Windows 2000.

Case Study 3 Questions

70-220.CS3.001

What business requirement drives the security measures being implemented for Fabrikam's new Windows 2000 network?

A. The need to have data collected in a timely manner

B. The customers' need to access data from their own locations

C. The need to reduce the TCO

D. The need to have customer data available to all sales representatives from dispersed organizational units on the network

70-220.CS3.002

Current costs of operation often result from security measures taken out of necessity without considering technology costs. Which security measures can improve the TCO at Fabrikam? (Choose all that apply.)

A. Existing systems and applications are physically secure at the Jackson headquarters.

B. All technical support is handled by trusted employees.

C. Agents use laptops in the field to capture their data into encrypted files.

D. Sales representatives manage their customer accounts manually.

E. Agents use smart cards to access their laptops.

70-220.CS3.003

Once Fabrikam is using the technologies of Windows 2000 outlined in its plan, what will be its greatest security risk?

A. The network is exposed to the Internet.

B. The agents and sales representatives have data on their laptops.

C. The internal technicians can modify the security configuration.

D. There are many more servers in the new Active Directory network.

70-220.CS3.004

When servers are exposed to the Internet, one security option is to create what is commonly called a perimeter network. After it's in place and network security policies and procedures are defined, what should Fabrikam do to ensure the perimeter network equipment isn't compromised by changes to its security configuration?

A. Apply additional policies and procedures especially for the perimeter network equipment.

B. Physically isolate the perimeter network computers from the other networking servers and equipment.

C. Remove interactive logon privileges from everyone but Enterprise Admins.

D. Place the perimeter network equipment on a separate subnet. Filter the router packets.

70-220.CS3.005

Which templates should you use to establish a secure configuration for the servers, domain controllers, desktops, and laptops? (Choose all that apply.)

A. BASICWK.INF

B. BASICSV.INF

C. BASICWK.INF, BASICDC.INF, BASICSV.INF

D. SECUREWS.INF, SECUREDC.INF

E. COMPATWS.INF, HISECWS.INF, HISECDC.INF

70-220.CS3.006

Because security is a high priority, Fabrikam wants technical support to be tightly controlled. What configurations should you employ for the most secure administration? (Choose all that apply.)

A. Smart card authentication for the administrator account

B. Only one administrator and one backup administrator of the root domain

C. Physical consolidation of all server components

D. Restricted directory access with Group Policy to administrator and backup administrator

E. Restricted use of the Security Log to the administrator and administrator backup

70-220.CS3.007

Lab testing of applications is part of Windows 2000 deployment. All of Fabrikam's corporate applications are required to pass the same level of security as applications approved for the Microsoft Windows 2000 logo. Which criterion must the corporate applications pass in order to be on an equal par with Windows 2000 logo applications? (Choose all that apply.)

A. Run successfully with the Server Gated Cryptography (SGC) protocol

B. Run successfully on unsecured Windows 2000 servers

C. Run successfully across a network connection using the user's Kerberos authentication

D. Run with Microsoft Authenticode technology

E. Run with service accounts

70-220.CS3.008

Only the administrator and backup administrator will manage Automatic Certificate Requests and Encrypted Data Recovery Agents. Where should you place these security policies?

A. In a domain level GPO

B. In an IT OU GPO

C. In a Domain Controllers OU GPO

D. In a site-level GPO

70-220.CS3.009

How should you configure Fabrikam's customer authentication process?

A. Use NTLM authentication

B. Use SSL

C. Use Kerberos-realm authentication

D. Use PKI certificates

70-220.CS3.010

Based on Fabrikam's security requirements, which Certificate Services policy and CA role in the hierarchy should you specify to issue certificates?

A. Enterprise root CA

B. Stand-alone root CA

C. Stand-alone subordinate CA

D. Enterprise subordinate CA

70-220.CS3.011

How should an administrator or technician manage the certificates for Fabrikam's customers when they get new computers?

A. Ask the user to request a certificate on the new computer, map the new certificate to the user's account, and revoke the old certificate.

B. Export the customer's certificate and the corresponding private key from the replaced computer, and import them to the new computer.

C. Revoke the current certificate; have the user request a new certificate on the new computer.

D. Revoke the certificate; shorten the CRL's validity period.

70-220.CS3.012

What must the administrator do so Fabrikam's customers can access resources on the Active Directory network? (Choose all that apply.)

A. Import the customer certificates onto their computers.

B. Export the customer certificates from the CA.

C. Create accounts for the customers in Active Directory by using the Active Directory User And Groups console.

D. Map the customer accounts to the customer certificates.

E. Issue the customers a PKCS#10 file containing their certificate data.

70-220.CS3.013

Which technologies should you employ to protect transmitted data on Fabrikam's LAN? (Choose all that apply.)

A. EFS

B. Certificate-based authentication

C. A third-party security package to protect the core business application

D. IPSec

E. Kerberos V5 authentication

70-220.CS3.014

Which components are necessary to implement security policies for the agents when they're in the field? (Choose all that apply.)

A. Domain-level secure channel communications policy

B. Active Directory stored policies

C. Client (Respond Only) and Server (Request Security) policy

D. Locally defined policies in the registry

E. An Agent OU

70-220.CS3.015

Which automatic security negotiation for integrity and encryption uses the least overhead?

A. IKE, 3DES, MD5, medium(2)

B. IKE, DES, MD5, low(1)

C. IKE, 3DES, SHA1, medium(2)

D. IKE, DES, SHA1, low(1)

Case Study 3 Answers

70-220.CS3.001

► **Correct Answers: A**

A. **Correct:** Fabrikam needs its data collections added to the database faster, but the information must traverse the Internet because the worldwide scope of its field doesn't allow for secure company sites with secure WAN links.

B. **Incorrect:** The customers' preference to use the modeling data from their own offices is secondary to Fabrikam's requirement for timely input of new data.

C. **Incorrect:** Reduction in TCO is an additional benefit of moving to Windows 2000, but Fabrikam is operating a system that's about 50 percent manual before the conversion. Therefore, TCO isn't the reason the security measures are being implemented.

D. **Incorrect:** Even though the sales representatives will greatly benefit from having their customer accounts data accessible on their laptops, this is a secondary gain from the security measures that are being taken to protect the new data collection process.

Domain objective addressed by this question: 1.3.

70-220.CS3.002

▶ **Correct Answers: C and E**

A. **Incorrect:** Physically securing equipment is a security measure, but it doesn't improve the TCO. Costs are reduced by eliminating the length of time or the amount of materials being expended by a company.

B. **Incorrect:** Using trusted employees to make the conversion to Windows 2000 and handle all technical support is an extra measure of security that Fabrikam wants to take, but it isn't necessarily a reduction in costs. Outsourcing is an accepted way to handle technical support cost reduction.

C. **Correct:** Because the data can be stored and transmitted in the field securely, the agents can shorten the process time, which means improved service to the customers.

D. **Incorrect:** Sales representatives managing customer accounts manually isn't cheaper. By keeping the data electronically, the sales representatives can share the data with the corporate office. Data entered once is available for many uses. However, once the data is on a laptop, it must be secured because it's more exposed to the possibility of theft than manually kept records. It's this unsecured data that constitutes a security risk, therefore making this an incorrect choice.

E. **Correct:** Smart cards contribute to the improved TCO in a secondary way. Fabrikam can now use laptops in the field because smart cards allow the data to be stored and transmitted in a safe way. This shortens the process cycle, and a shortened process cycle means a reduction in costs.

Domain objective addressed by this question: 1.3.

70-220.CS3.003

▶ **Correct Answers: A**

A. **Correct:** Exposure of corporate data to the Internet is the greatest risk a company takes. Before the Internet became so prevalent in the business environment, it was the LAN's perimeter that required the most protection. Now company information is outside the perimeter and is much more difficult to protect in the public arena.

Through using such Windows 2000–based technologies as a VPN tunnel encrypted with IPSec, the only information that will be seen across the Internet is the external IP address. The internal address will be protected, thus making it difficult to hack data sent across the VPN tunnel.

B. **Incorrect:** The second biggest risk is having company data on laptops out in the field, where it can be easily stolen.

Depending on the organization's security requirements, EFS can be implemented for encryption of stored data in the event a laptop with secure data is stolen. This is probably the best practice for any one who's part of the company and will travel with sensitive data.

C. **Incorrect:** Employee modification of the security configuration can happen intentionally or through lack of understanding about how the security configuration protects the data. Inadvertent or well-intended changes made by IT staff can sometimes create security risks, but employee modification is not the primary risk because it can be more closely monitored than such risks as those posed by the Internet.

D. **Incorrect:** All the servers will be at headquarters. Having more servers doesn't create more risk, but having servers that interface with the Internet, such as Web servers, does.

Domain objective addressed by this question: 1.6.

70-220.CS3.004

▶ **Correct Answers: A**

A. **Correct:** Because the equipment in the perimeter network is especially vulnerable to attacks from the Internet, the company should take extra measures to ensure that the employees themselves don't modify the security configuration, either intentionally or unintentionally.

The perimeter network also offers the organization the ability to save resources by utilizing the existing infrastructure of the Internet in conjunction with VPNs. This saves the costs of expensive lease communication lines and related wide-area connections.

B. **Incorrect:** It isn't necessary to physically isolate the perimeter network equipment from the company's other networking servers and equipment. On the contrary, a perimeter network usually consists of proxy server groups that the network can utilize for internal Web access, as well as using VPN for remote client secure connections.

C. **Incorrect:** It isn't necessary to remove interactive logon privileges from everyone but Enterprise Admins for servers and domain controllers. It's necessary to limit interactive logon to a few trusted administrators.

D. **Incorrect:** Even though it is a good idea to separate the subnet of your perimeter network from the subnet of your internal network, having the perimeter network on a separate subnet doesn't protect it from changes to its security configuration. Filtering the packets doesn't protect the perimeter network equipment from internal changes, either.

Domain objective addressed by this question: 2.1.

70-220.CS3.005

▶ **Correct Answers: C and D**

A. **Incorrect:** BASICWK.INF alone isn't a complete configuration, nor does it combine with another answer choice to give a correct answer. Basic templates are used to correct configurations by returning them to their baseline settings, thus resetting the security policies to the level of a clean Windows 2000 NTFS installation.

B. **Incorrect:** BASICSV.INF alone isn't a complete configuration. Basic templates are used to correct configurations by returning them to their baseline settings, thus resetting the security policies to the level of a clean Windows 2000 NTFS installation.

C. **Correct:** When the Windows NT 4 computers are upgraded to Windows 2000, they require the basic security templates on NTFS to put them on an equal par with any clean installations of Windows 2000 NTFS computers.

D. **Correct:** After the basic level of security is in place, the secure templates should be applied, which will incrementally add to the security. Fabrikam could also decide to use the highly secure configurations (HISECDC.INF and HISECWS.INF) instead of the secure configuration. Note that file system object permissions aren't affected by using secure template configuration.

E. **Incorrect:** COMPATWS.INF, HISECWS.INF, and HISECDC.INF don't combine to make a valid security configuration. You must use COMPATWS.INF to allow certain applications to be used when the users aren't in the Power Users group. All Windows NT 4 Users become Windows 2000 Power Users by default during the upgrade.

Domain objective addressed by this question: 3.1.

70-220.CS3.006

▶ **Correct Answers: A and B**

A. **Correct:** Using smart cards for authentication makes the administrator's privileges even more inaccessible than they are with account name and password authentication. Smart cards' two-factor authentication process—a physical card plus a PIN number—makes it harder to learn the administrator's authentication factors.

Another example of two-factor authentication would be biometric identification, in which a handprint, voice ID, or another type of identification is used in place of an access card.

B. **Correct:** The administrator of the root domain is also the administrator of the Enterprise Admins group. This group membership should be limited.

C. **Incorrect:** While consolidation of all server components would usually be a recommended practice in this situation, it would also require the physical consolidation of the domain controller consoles. With administrator access privileges, someone can gain access to the server through this console.

D. **Incorrect:** Certain areas and objects of the Active Directory are limited to administrators, but this isn't one of the security measures taken to protect the administrator's privileges. Limited administrator access might be set so that accidents or mistakes caused by administrators will affect only their range of responsibility and no other area.

E. **Incorrect:** Protecting the Security Log from nonadministrators doesn't protect the administrator's privileges.

Domain objective addressed by this question: 2.2.

70-220.CS3.007

▶ **Correct Answers: C and E**

A. **Incorrect:** SGC protocol allows certain types of institutions, such as banks, to get around the restrictions of import and export cryptography laws and still protect their data during transmission. The institutions have to be qualified before they can use SGC. This isn't a correct criterion. SGC protocol uses digital certificates and is used by many existing financial institutions.

B. **Incorrect:** The logo applications can run on secured Windows 2000 servers, but not on ones that are unsecured.

C. **Correct:** Windows 2000 logo applications can run as a network resource using the user's single sign-on, which is Kerberos authentication. Kerberos is the default Windows 2000 network authentication protocol. This is one of the criteria.

D. **Incorrect:** Authenticode is a Microsoft technology that protects code from unwanted modification by attackers. It uses digital signatures to verify that the code is from an authorized source. With Authenticode, developers can use standard X.509 public key certificates to digitally endorse software. This isn't one of the criteria.

E. **Correct:** Service accounts are more secure than a local system account that has full system privileges. This is one of the criteria.

Domain objective addressed by this question: 2.2.

70-220.CS3.008

▶ **Correct Answers: A**

A. **Correct:** The user accounts for administrators don't factor into the placement of the security policies. The security policies themselves are both domain-wide. That means they must be set in a GPO at the domain level. You can implement these changes from the Group Policy snap-in component of MMC if it's installed.

B. **Incorrect:** Because these two security policies are domain-wide they can't be placed in a GPO at any OU level, including one for the IT department or one for Domain Controllers.

C. **Incorrect:** This is incorrect for the reasons stated in B.

D. **Incorrect:** Site level isn't the proper place to put domain-level policies. There is no need for sites in this scenario. Despite that, you can't block inheritance at the site level, because sites don't have any policy to inherit.

There's one central location for headquarters and the network infrastructure equipment. All else is remote access infrastructure. Sites regulate domain controller replication when it goes across WAN links.

Domain objective addressed by this question: 4.3.

70-220.CS3.009

▶ **Correct Answers: D**

A. **Incorrect:** Because the customers will authenticate from remote access when they're in their offices, they won't use NTLM authentication, which is a supported authentication for backward compliance for pre–Windows 2000 operating systems.

B. **Incorrect:** SSL is a protocol that provides secure channels and user authentication for communications on the Web. Fabrikam's customers are allowed to remotely access the company's intranet; the customers aren't using the model on a Web site. TLS is used for this task as well.

C. **Incorrect:** Because the customers will authenticate from remote access when they're in their offices, they won't use Kerberos, which works on the trusted domain framework. The Kerberos-realm authentication usually refers to the UNIX implementation of Kerberos.

D. **Correct:** You'll use certificate-based authentication because the PKI infrastructure is part of the security configuration. Smart cards have been specified for the agents. Smart cards require certificates, and certificates require PKI, so you will have PKI setup for the network. Remote access across the Internet is the primary channel for communications for these agents.

Domain objective addressed by this question: 4.5.

70-220.CS3.010

▶ **Correct Answers: D**

  A. **Incorrect:** The enterprise root CA is an incorrect answer because its role is to issue authority to the subordinate CA. Because the enterprise root CA is the top level, it signs its own CA certificate.

  B. **Incorrect:** Stand-alone policy requires the administrator to manually approve the issuance of a certificate because there's no Active Directory data to rely upon. This is because the stand-alone root CA doesn't require Active Directory or membership in a Windows 2000 domain.

  C. **Incorrect:** Stand-alone subordinate CAs usually issue the certificates from authority given them by the stand-alone root CA. The stand-alone policy can't be used for Fabrikam because of the requirements listed in the scenario. The stand-alone subordinate CA is also capable of issuing certificates directly to users.

  D. **Correct:** Regardless of the complexity of the PKI configuration, if the certificates must be automatically mapped, then the only policy option is the enterprise policy.

Enterprise subordinate CAs usually issue the certificates from authority given them by the enterprise root CA. Because Fabrikam will be using certificates with Active Directory, certificate templates, and smart cards, its certificates will be issued from the enterprise subordinate CA. Another way of looking at it is that like stand-alone subordinate CAs, enterprise subordinate CAs also can issue certificates directly to users. From there, those certificates support services that Fabrikam will be using, such as smart cards.

Domain objective addressed by this question: 4.7.

70-220.CS3.011

▶ **Correct Answers: B**

  A. **Incorrect:** This is incorrect procedure.

  B. **Correct:** Certificates and private keys are correctly transferred using the export and import tools, such as the Certificate Request Wizard and the Automatic Certificate Request Setup Wizard.

  C. **Incorrect:** It's incorrect to revoke the current certificate and have the user request a new one. Revoking a certificate is done, for example, when an employee leaves the company or someone's identity isn't validly mapped to the certificate.

  D. **Incorrect:** It's incorrect to shorten the CRL's validity period, which involves the validity period of other certificates. Overall, your CRL policies specify where CRLs and their publishing schedules will be distributed.

Domain objective addressed by this question: 4.7.

70-220.CS3.012

► **Correct Answers: C and D**

A. **Incorrect:** Importing the customer certificates onto their computers isn't part of the administrator's procedure for mapping a user's certificate to the user account.

B. **Incorrect:** It's incorrect to export the customer certificates from the CA when setting up access to the resources for an external user.

C. **Correct:** The administrator should create accounts for the customers in Active Directory.

D. **Correct:** This is the proper procedure for allowing external users to access resources on the company's intranet. You can create these accounts by using the Active Directory User And Groups console. The result is that authenticated users gain all the rights and permissions for user accounts based on their ownership of the correct valid certificates. These mapped certificates are then used for authentication by means of Kerberos authentication.

E. **Incorrect:** A user can request a certificate from the Web page of a CA using a PKCS#10 request. This isn't a correct way for the administrator to set up certificate mapping, which is required when external users are authenticated with the necessary combination of certificates and user accounts.

Domain objective addressed by this question: 4.7.

70-220.CS3.013

► **Correct Answers: D and E**

A. **Incorrect:** EFS is a stored data protection technology and doesn't provide protection while data is being transmitted. Also, EFS works only on the Windows 2000 NTFS file system. EFS doesn't work on any NTFS partitions from previous versions of Windows NT.

B. **Incorrect:** Certificate-based authentication is required only on the Internet, or with accounts external to the trusted domain, or with non-Kerberos V5 clients.

C. **Incorrect:** The core business application will be protected with IPSec's Layer 3 security, so third-party security packages aren't needed.

D. **Correct:** To protect the LAN's transmitted data where security is critical at every level of the enterprise, you will use strong user authentication and IP packet protection.

IPSec provides packet protection, so it's a correct answer. This packet protection comes from the use of cryptography-based algorithms and keys specific to this protocol.

E. **Correct:** Kerberos authentication is a correct choice because it provides user authentication for domain accounts. The Kerberos authentication protocol is used to provide a singular service of authentication in a distributed network, such as Fabrikam's LAN.

Domain objective addressed by this question: 5.3.

70-220.CS3.014

► **Correct Answers: B and E**

A. **Incorrect:** A domain-level policy for secure channel communications will require security group filtering. You can avoid this by using an Agent OU instead.

B. **Correct:** Use Active Directory stored policies. This makes central administration easier on groups of similar computers. You can use several default group policies to secure communications. You configure these policies using the MMC.

C. **Incorrect:** The Standard security that Client (Respond Only) and Server (Request Security) sets up isn't strong enough. The agents are sending data that requires a High security level.

D. **Incorrect:** Registry-stored policies are appropriate when the computers don't belong to an Active Directory domain. The agents' computers belong to the domain.

E. **Correct:** An Agent OU will allow the administrators to manage Group Policy objects that apply to the agents and their computers. Make certain that the Agent OU doesn't have any special security requirements that require specific Group Policy configuration in order to meet those needs.

Domain objective addressed by this question: 6.2.

70-220.CS3.015

► **Correct Answers: B**

A. **Incorrect:** The keying information is defined by Diffie Hellman (DH) groups 1 and 2. The DH group 1 is low for a 96-bit key; the DH group 2 is medium for a 128-bit key.

B. **Correct:** The IKE service is part of setting up a security association (SA) so information on an insecure link between two computers can be exchanged. The negotiation results in a session agreeable to both computers' policies. With IKE, the negotiation takes place automatically. IKE provides key management services in this context as well.

DES requires less overhead than 3DES, which runs through the encryption algorithm three times. There's also a 56-bit version of DES, which falls between the 40-bit and 3DES versions.

DES having less overhead, and MD5 using a smaller bit key, and low(1) being the smallest of the DH groups, make IKE, DES, MD5, low(1) the correct answer.

C. **Incorrect:** The integrity hash algorithm SHA1 uses a 160-bit key, which is stronger than MD5, which is a 128-bit key.

D. **Incorrect:** This is incorrect for the reasons stated in B and C.

Domain objective addressed by this question: 6.2.

Trey Research

Background

Several lobbyist groups are pooling their resources to form an organization called Trey Research. Currently, each lobbyist group is informally sharing information with the other lobbyist groups that will make up the new organization. The new organization will have a collaborative central administrative office in Virginia, but that office will have minimal influence on the individual lobbyist groups. The new organization's main function will be to provide support to the lobbyist groups through its computer network.

The Organization

The lobbyists in all the groups are mobile users. Their work takes them into various organizations. They're routinely attached to the internal networks of these other organizations for e-mail, Internet connections, printing, and shared folders. At other times they use phone lines in motels and airports. The lobbyist groups' business cycle is determined by the importance of each lobby and the status of pending bills in the U.S. Congress that are associated with that lobby. Some are two years; some are six weeks.

Most of the information required by the lobbyists is in their own SQL Server databases. It's highly confidential information and is at great risk from hackers. Under the new organization's structure, each of the SQL Server databases will be moved to the new location in Virginia where an IT department will handle all network functions and information that will be shared. Each group will determine which part of its database is available to the other groups.

A second type of information is timely documentation gathered and processed by the lobbyists in the form of word-processing documents. At a later time, much of this information will be reorganized into the SQL databases as it becomes more stable in content.

Existing IT Environment

The lobbyist groups have T1 lines from major cities to their offices in Washington, D.C. These small offices have no wire security other than what the private lines afford. Their desktops are running Microsoft Windows 95, Windows 98, and Windows NT 3.5 Workstation. A constantly changing staff manages the domain controllers and SQL Server member servers. Most laptops used by the traveling lobbyists are running Windows 98.

Problems

According to the lobbyist group executives, these small offices have little staff support. The security of the transmitted data is clearly at risk and stored data is being backed up intermittently. Those in the field waste time trying to contact these skeleton offices for help.

The attorneys, who aren't employees of Trey Research, are requesting network access to the Virginia office. They want to use dial-in communications. All their computers run Windows versions earlier than Windows 2000. They have no need for an ISP and have no business plans to use one. Their office is 14 blocks from the new Trey Research office.

Goals and Priorities

Trey Research wants to prevent intruders from accessing its confidential information. The laptops pose a very high risk, especially because lobbyists are frequently at other organizations and in airports.

Trey Research also wants all data from these laptops to be backed up daily and available for another lobbyist if someone must take over someone else's project. Timing is critical in this line of work.

The collaborative venture is new and all groups are concerned about other groups having too much access to their information, especially during the transition period. The shared documents areas must be very closely monitored to be sure there is no misuse of privileges.

Envisioned IT Environment

All laptops will be upgraded to Windows 2000 Professional. Hardware will be replaced as required for the upgrade. Information on all mobile computers will be protected with encryption. Daily backup copies of the lobbyists' documents will be kept on the servers. Each network connection will be a secure channel.

Servers will be upgraded to Windows 2000 Advanced Server to take advantage of new security and communications technologies. The network infrastructure will be built to accommodate the new mobile connections model and the new security model. The infrastructure will be housed completely in the Virginia central office. A new, publicly known Internet name will be established as the Active Directory directory service domain, *treyresearch.com*. All lobbyist groups will fall under this new namespace. The domain will be taken to native mode immediately.

The small central IT staff in Virginia will be running 24 hours a day. The staff members will support the databases and the lobbyists in a consistent manner that isn't possible with the current organizational structure.

The T1 lines will be dropped and all small offices will be closed. Instead, a more dynamic structure supporting the needs of the traveling lobbyists will be the focus. The savings gained by closing the small offices and eliminating the T1 lines can be used for new hardware for the upgraded infrastructure.

The network infrastructure will be centralized in the Virginia office. The new connections' security and flexibility will be achieved with the integrated features of Active Directory. The lobbyist groups will find it much easier to work with each other through the consistency of the Active Directory DNS namespace. The attorneys' request for dial-in services will be granted with a new RRAS server.

Case Study 4 Questions

70-220.CS4.001

Trey Research wants to use the following applications of digital certificates in its new Windows 2000 environment. Which ones will require the planning and implementation of a CA hierarchy before they can be deployed? (Choose all that apply.)

A. Secure e-mail

B. IPSec authentication

C. Local network smart card authentication

D. VPN Remote access authentication

E. EFS recovery agent

70-220.CS4.002

If Trey Research decides to require smart card logons, which users should be included?

A. Users connected to other organizations' LANs

B. Dial-up users only

C. Remote users and dial-up users

D. All users

70-220.CS4.003

You know that the Trey Research staff members will use only e-mail and the Internet, and they work out of the central office in Virginia. You also know the lobbyists will authenticate using remote access to reach the SQL Server databases. Smart cards can be required from everyone who accesses this network. Consider whether Trey Research wants to offer network resources to anonymous persons from a Web site. Also consider whether Trey Research has partners, other than in its own federation, who need access to their network. What mechanism allows management of these various requests for authentication as a means of access to the network's resources?

A. ACLs of shared resources

B. Authentication policy at the client

C. Group Policy in Active Directory

D. Each server's local policy

70-220.CS4.004

Each lobbyist group will have a shared folder that will be administered by a few IT administrators, who are members of the Editors group. The Editors group will be responsible for adding the documents to each lobbyist group's shared folder and subfolders. The Editors group will also manage permissions for all these shared folders. Individuals of a certain lobbyist group will need to see the contents of their shared folder and its subfolders and read the files. They will have no access to the share folders of the other lobbyist groups unless a special request is granted to read a specific file. How should you set up everyone's NTFS permissions?

A. Grant the Editors group Full Control of the shared folder. Grant other members of the lobbyist group Read and Execute folder permission and List Folder Contents folder permission.

B. Grant the Editors group Full Control of the shared folder and delete the Everyone group, grant other members of the lobbyist group Read and Execute folder permission, and grant members of other lobbyist groups Read file permission for a specific file when a special request is made.

C. Grant the Editors group Full Control of the shared folder and delete the Everyone group. Grant other members of the lobbyist group Read, Execute, and List Folder Contents folder permissions. Grant members of other lobbyist groups Read file permission for a specific file when a special request is made and the Traverse Folder/Execute File permission on the shared folder.

D. Delegate administration for each of these shared folders to the Editors group to manage all permissions.

70-220.CS4.005

Several Windows NT domains are in the current network environment. The new Active Directory will have one domain. Assume that the migration details will be managed by another unit of IT administrators and focus only on the resulting organization of objects for your security strategy. What hierarchy for OUs best describes this new organization's model?

A. By location

B. By function

C. By organization

D. By location, and then organization

70-220.CS4.006

What sort of authentication should you provide for the lobbyists when they're working at another organization or business location?

A. Basic authentication with SSL

B. NTLM

C. Basic authentication

D. RADIUS authentication

70-220.CS4.007

You want to monitor the shared documents areas for modification of privileges set on the shared document folders. Which event should you set and where should the policy be associated?

A. Set the Account Management event at the Domain level.

B. Set the Object Access event at the Domain level.

C. Set the Directory Services Access in the policy for Default Domain Controllers container.

D. Set the Privilege Use event at the Default Domain Controllers Container.

70-220.CS4.008

What steps are required to meet the security model for laptop documents that are being transmitted between networks? (Choose all that apply.)

A. The link between the laptop and the server will have to be secured with VPN.

B. No recovery agents would be required.

C. The data will be transmitted to the server in Virginia every 24 hours.

D. The data must be confined to a shared folder.

E. Public Key Infrastructure (PKI) will have to be installed for the new Windows 2000 network.

70-220.CS4.009

One lobbyist group owns a document printer that does digital printing and will be connected to the network. All other lobbyist groups will get access to it and will be charged a usage fee based on the size of their print jobs. The operators and the printer will be in Virginia. Printing from remote access is exactly like printing in-house because of the network connection. Which groups or users will you need to create for those who use the printer? (Choose all that apply.)

A. Individual operator accounts

B. Global group for administrative staff

C. Global group for each lobbyist group

D. A universal group with nested global groups

E. Domain local group

F. Global group for attorneys

70-220.CS4.010

How should you address the use of SNMP for this network design?

A. Provide Read-only access to the management stations and change the community name from Public to something else.

B. Set a filter action on the SNMP-enabled equipment to Permit and let the packets go through in clear text.

C. Implement IPSec on the management stations and SNMP agents and encrypt all data between them.

D. Don't use it; all infrastructure equipment is in a central point.

70-220.CS4.011

Which options can you use on this network to protect it against IP spoofing attacks if IPSec is implemented? (Choose all that apply.)

A. Network address translation (NAT)

B. Private network addressing

C. Perimeter network

D. Stop all unnecessary services on each server

E. Proxy Server

70-220.CS4.012

Trey Research wants to enforce remote access policies. There will be multiple remote access servers to handle the field operations. Auditing of remote access will be standard procedure. How should you manage the remote access for the attorneys?

A. Through remote access policies in Active Directory

B. Through a RADIUS proxy server

C. Through a RADIUS server

D. Through the Connection Manager service profile

70-220.CS4.013

How can you implement a secure channel for the attorneys' file transmissions?

A. Set up a VPN consistent with the setup for lobbyists who must dial-in.

B. Set up the Trey Research servers to require SMB signing using Group Policy. Get the support person at the attorneys' office to configure their clients for SMB signing.

C. Configure the RRAS server to use callback with a specified phone number.

D. Set up the Trey Research servers to request SMB signing using Group Policy. Get the support person at the attorneys' office to configure their clients for SMB signing.

70-220.CS4.014

IPSec is a possibility for the dial-in lobbyists, the attorneys are an external group who could benefit from it, and the staff will only need it for the payroll clerk. What does this line of thinking indicate about IPSec policies?

A. Use Client (Respond Only) as it is and create new server policies using the Server (Request Security) built-in as a model.

B. Use Client (Respond Only) and Server (Request Security) built-ins.

C. Use Client (Respond Only) and Server (Require Security) built-ins.

D. Create new Client (Respond Only) policies at organizational level for each different group of users and Server (Request Security) at domain level.

E. You'll have to look carefully at each group of computers for policy needs before any one policy can fit the needs of these groups.

70-220.CS4.015

Which of the following strategies will best protect the lobbyists' dial-in to the private network?

A. Preshared key / IKE / AH

B. Preshared key / IKE / ESP

C. Kerberos / IKE / AH

D. Kerberos / IKE / ESP

E. Certificates / IKE / AH

F. Certificates / IKE / ESP

Case Study 4 Answers

70-220.CS4.001

▶ **Correct Answers: A and C**

A. **Correct:** The two applications that can produce their own certificates are IPSec and EFS. You can implement these applications in the organization right away. The recovery agent for EFS must be issued a certificate in order to be authorized for this function. If the organization needs any of the other implementations of digital certificates, then the first step will be planning, piloting, and deploying the CA hierarchy. In addition, if you're using smart cards, you must use a trusted enterprise CA, not a third-party CA. An administrator of the organization will enroll the users for logon certificates that are mapped to the user's account. You must plan to spend some time developing and testing your enterprise CA because each company or organization's needs are different and must be piloted before being put into production.

B. **Incorrect:** The two applications that can produce their own certificates are IPSec and EFS. Therefore IPSec authentication isn't a correct option here.

C. **Correct:** If you're using smart cards, you must use a trusted enterprise CA instead of a third-party CA. Therefore, you need to plan and implement the CA hierarchy before you deploy smart card authentication.

D. **Incorrect:** You can't use VPN, because authentication wouldn't be provided in this context.

E. **Incorrect:** This is incorrect for the reasons stated in A.

Domain objective addressed by this question: 1.4.

70-220.CS4.002

▶ **Correct Answers: D**

A. **Incorrect:** The users who connect to other organizations' LANs will require some special planning. Even though it's possible to use a smart card to log on locally without any network connectivity at all, these users might log on to another LAN for printing services and access to certain shared folders. The logon policy, therefore, can be two-pronged: use the smart card when accessing the Trey Research network either locally or through public connections, and don't use the smart card when on-site for another organization. These users can also be protected when on location at other organizations if they're using EFS services on their hard disk drives.

B. **Incorrect:** Dial-up users will definitely want to use smart cards for strong authentication, but they aren't the only ones who should. Local network users should also be using smart cards in this context.

C. **Incorrect:** Remote users going across VPNs and dial-up users, calling from a motel perhaps, will both need smart card logon authentication, but so will all the other users.

D. **Correct:** To protect the network, which is at risk in all aspects because the information is political in nature and highly desirable to opponents, it's necessary to use Active Directory group policy objects to explicitly apply strict policies to the various classes of machines, thus requiring that all users log on with a smart card. If some users are logging on with a password, then the network is only as safe as the one person who is allowed to use a password (shared secret).

Domain objective addressed by this question: 2.1.

70-220.CS4.003

▶ **Correct Answers: C**

A. **Incorrect:** Object-specific ACLs are for each resource using MMC's Active Directory snap-ins. Management of resources isn't the correct mechanism for managing ways of authentication.

B. **Incorrect:** Client settings of authentication policy don't provide a way to centrally control all means of authentication.

C. **Correct:** Group Policy is the means for managing all methods of authentication. This is handled through the use of the various group policy settings available in Windows 2000. When a request comes to the network for authentication, it's always checked through Group Policy's authentication mechanism. The flexibility that Trey Research requires can be managed even though the risk is high and the access types are varied. So, as designer of security for Trey Research, you'll be planning how the users are grouped and placed in the Active Directory. The way in which users access the network helps determine where their user objects are organized in Active Directory.

D. **Incorrect:** Local policy on each server isn't the way to manage authentication for a network. Local policy, however, does address security issues.

Domain objective addressed by this question: 1.3.

70-220.CS4.004

▶ **Correct Answers: B**

A. **Incorrect:** Granting the Editors group Full Control doesn't describe how you should assign permissions to the other users. The question asks how you should set up everyone's NTFS permissions.

B. **Correct:** The Editors group should have Full Control permission to the shared folder so they can manage the shared folder completely. You'll delete the Everyone group, which is a default. The other members of the lobbyist group will need Read and Execute permission to read the documents in their shared folder. They'll also need to see all available files, which they can do because List Folder Contents is part of the Read and Execute permission for folders. If someone from another lobbyist group needs to read a file in this shared folder, that person should be granted the Read file permission. To keep this individual from seeing all documents in this folder and looking through the subfolders, only the Read file permission is applied. To access the file, the individual must be instructed to use the Universal Naming Convention (UNC). The UNC is the naming convention that's used to give a unique name to files on a network. The format is: \\servername\sharename\path\filename.

C. **Incorrect:** It's not necessary to grant the other members of a lobbyist group the List Folder Contents permission if you've also given them Read and Execute permission. So this answer is wrong. It's also wrong because members of other lobbyist groups shouldn't be given the Traverse Folder/Execute File permission on the shared folder. They'd then be able to access subfolders.

D. **Incorrect:** You can delegate administrative authority for an OU to a group such as the Editors, but not to a shared folder.

Domain objective addressed by this question: 2.2.

70-220.CS4.005

▶ **Correct Answers: C**

A. **Incorrect:** The majority of these employees are very mobile. There are no locations other than the central location in Virginia.

B. **Incorrect:** The majority of these employees fall under the same function: traveling lobbyists. The one exception is the staff members in Virginia, who work from desktops instead of the usual laptops.

C. **Correct:** The correct hierarchy is by organization because you'll manage security with the separate lobbyist groups. Besides an OU for each lobbyist group, you'll need one for the staff in Virginia.

D. **Incorrect:** You don't need a hybrid hierarchy because the locations aren't definitive. Locations become the preferred choice when a business has physical plants across the nation or globe, because they don't change. Because your lobbyist groups will probably always want to maintain their separate identities for access control of resources, they're the unchanging element here.

Domain objective addressed by this question: 3.2.

70-220.CS4.006

► **Correct Answers: A**

A. **Correct:** Basic authentication with SSL is the preferred authentication because it provides a more secure connection with a Web browser. Because these users will be in different environments, the Web browser is the preferred way to get their mail.

B. **Incorrect:** NTLM is a challenge/response authentication protocol and is only for trusted domains, not external access.

C. **Incorrect:** Basic authentication without SSL isn't strong enough.

D. **Incorrect:** RADIUS authentication will work if you have a RADIUS server and if the client is using dial-in. The question specifies connections from another environment that might or might not have a modem available.

Domain objective addressed by this question: 4.1.

70-220.CS4.007

► **Correct Answers: C**

A. **Incorrect:** Use the Account Management event to see changes in security principals such as users, groups, or computers. This event can tell you if anyone has modified privileges so that they can now reach the shared folders. It isn't as direct, however, as watching the Directory Services Access. In other words, this event allows you to watch the administrators, not the users.

B. **Incorrect:** You set the Object Access event when you want to monitor files, folders, printers, and so forth. This auditing will notify you that someone's permissions were modified and that they've clandestinely accessed a file or folder. This answer is wrong because we want to catch the change in permissions before anyone actually gets to the shared folders.

C. **Correct:** The permissions for the shared documents areas are very restrictive, as requested by all parties joining the organization. You want to be sure that none get changed by anyone with delegated authority or through access of an administrator's account left unprotected. To audit domain-wide objects of the Active Directory, you correctly audit Directory Services Access for the Default Domain Controllers container. Setting this category, though, doesn't automatically generate the required events. You need to go to the correct Active Directory object property page and set specific user and group auditing parameters.

D. **Incorrect:** The Privilege Use event reveals improper use of system privileges, such as looking at the System log. With the Privilege use event, every privilege a user has gets recorded. This isn't what we want, either, because if you first learn of it in the logs, the security breach has already happened.

Domain objective addressed by this question: 4.4.

70-220.CS4.008

▶ **Correct Answers: A and E**

A. **Correct:** Whenever data is transmitted across network lines, it's unencrypted. The lobbyists will be transmitting the encrypted files on their hard disk drives from remote locations most of the time. A tunneling protocol, such as PPTP or L2TP, is required to create the connection as well as protect the data during transmission.

B. **Incorrect:** The laptop's local administrator will have to be a recovery agent for times when the laptop is remote. Another recovery agent is required for the server copy of the encrypted information in case the job must be turned over to another lobbyist. Therefore, having no recovery agents would make this incorrect.

C. **Incorrect:** Fault tolerance for the timely information is a business requirement, but copying the data to the server every 24 hours isn't a security measure.

D. **Incorrect:** Encrypted files don't have to be in a shared folder on the file server. Access to them will be through a recovery agent. The encrypted files don't have to be in an encrypted folder, either, but that does make maintenance of the files easier.

E. **Correct:** NTFS uses PKI for EFS.

Domain objective addressed by this question: 4.6.

70-220.CS4.009

▶ **Correct Answers: B, C, and E**

A. **Incorrect:** To make administration easier, don't use individual accounts, such as the operators' accounts, for the ACLs. Instead, put the operators in a group, even if you have only one or two.

B. **Correct:** You'll want a global group for administrative staff members because their privileges may be different from the other groups.

C. **Correct:** You'll want a global group for each lobbyist group for organization more than anything else. You can assign the permissions required to global groups in any domain in the forest. The privileges might differ from group to group, but this global group assignment process will allow you to track the print accounts by group.

D. **Incorrect:** When there's only one Active Directory domain, *treyresearch.com*, universal groups aren't used. They're used in native mode domains when more than one domain is in the forest. It's correct that global groups are nested in universal groups.

E. **Correct:** The domain local group, perhaps named DocPrint, automatically documents the group's purpose. The nice option about domain local groups is that members can come either from inside the same domain or outside of it. This is where the ACLs will be configured. In Windows 2000 the domain local group always manages the resource permissions. It's local to a domain, but it can have global and universal groups from other domains nested in it. No other domains are in our question.

F. **Incorrect:** The attorneys don't need a global group; they don't belong to the domain, or even to the organization.

Domain objective addressed by this question: 4.8.

70-220.CS4.010

▶ **Correct Answers: D**

A. **Incorrect:** Giving Read-only access to the management stations and changing the community name from Public are both good security standards if you're running SNMP. However, this network isn't a good candidate for SNMP. The reason is that this network needs to maintain a high degree of flexibility because of the number of mobile users. Using SNMP requires the implementation of a central host and therefore a centrally located infrastructure.

B. **Incorrect:** Setting a filter action on the SNMP-enabled equipment to Permit and letting the packets go through in clear text is necessary when the SNMP parties are unable to run IPSec. This answer is wrong only because all the equipment is local and doesn't need SNMP.

C. **Incorrect:** If your network is running IPSec and you also need to run SNMP, you should encrypt the data between the management stations and the agents.

D. **Correct:** Because all infrastructure equipment is local, you don't really need SNMP, except for the built-in Windows Time Service in Windows 2000.

Domain objective addressed by this question: 5.3.

70-220.CS4.011

▶ **Correct Answers: B and C**

A. **Incorrect:** You can't use NAT with IPSec. IPSec delivers its features by encapsulating and encrypting the entire payload. Only the source and destination IP address aren't encrypted. Therefore, you can't use NAT for IPSec packet forwarding because you can't determine the correct port number.

B. **Correct:** Private networking addressing is a good way to keep the outsider from creating packets that look like they were initiated from the private network. This protects the addressing scheme from the outside world.

C. **Correct:** Using a perimeter network creates two zones: one for the private network hosts and one for the external servers in the perimeter network zone. From that perimeter network, which is exposed to the Internet, all internal transmissions are separate.

D. **Incorrect:** Stopping all unnecessary services on servers is a protection against port scanning, not IP spoofing.

E. **Incorrect:** Using a Proxy Server will prevent the internal addresses from getting to the Internet.

Domain objective addressed by this question: 5.4.

70-220.CS4.012

▶ **Correct Answers: C**

A. **Incorrect:** If the attorneys were the only remote access users, you could manage their activity with Active Directory Policy for the RRAS server. In this case, there will be a RADIUS server in Virginia to handle all the field operations because the question tells us there are going to be multiple remote access servers. A small skeleton staff can't maintain multiple servers individually.

B. **Incorrect:** You use a RADIUS proxy server when multiple organizations are calling and some of the calls are processed on the front end and forwarded to the proper RADIUS server for that organization. In our case all RAS servers will belong to Trey Research. So one RADIUS server should be enough.

C. **Correct:** The local attorneys' office can use the RADIUS server because it will already exist as the authorization mechanism for dial-up users.

D. **Incorrect:** For the large number of new laptops, Trey Research will probably want to set up the remote access client with the Remote Access Connection Manager and Connection Point Services to make its job easier. The attorneys could be included. However, the question is about management, not installation.

Domain objective addressed by this question: 6.1.

70-220.CS4.013

▶ **Correct Answers: D**

A. **Incorrect:** You can't set up a VPN because the attorneys have no plans to get Internet access.

B. **Incorrect:** This solution would work if all the clients were Windows NT 4 SP3 or greater, but that isn't the case here. When the clients are Windows 95, Windows 98, or Windows NT 4 without SP3, you must configure the server to request, but not require, SMB signing. The clients at the attorneys' office must be enabled to use digitally signed communications. If Windows NT 4 clients don't have SP3, then their registry must be configured.

C. **Incorrect:** Using a callback number from the RRAS server is good practice, but it doesn't provide encryption and authentication with an external partner. It doesn't assure a secure channel.

D. **Correct:** When the clients are Windows 95, Windows 98, or Windows NT 4 without SP3, you must configure the server to request, but not require, SMB signing. The clients at the attorneys' office must be enabled to use digitally signed communications. If Windows NT 4 clients don't have SP3, their registry must be configured.

Domain objective addressed by this question: 6.2.

70-220.CS4.014

▶ **Correct Answers: E**

   A. **Incorrect:** You could use the built-in policy for Client (Respond Only) because it applies to the various needs of the user community. The built-in Server (Request Security) policy will require some modifications to meet Trey Research's needs. It will request that clients use the policy and will be in effect for all the lobbyists and staff. It won't be in effect if the attorneys call in because their clients won't be configured for IPSec and therefore they won't respond. Enough information isn't known yet to make a decision about the policies, so this answer is wrong.

   B. **Incorrect:** Generally, you won't use the built-in policies as provided. Trey Research's servers will need their filters, security methods, and so forth, set to the organization's needs. These built-in policies only apply to domain use anyway.

   C. **Incorrect:** Server (Require Security) is so stringent that it'll render some computers unable to reach the servers. With Server (Require Security), even communication within domain controllers is negotiated and secured. It can't be used as it is.

   D. **Incorrect:** Trey Research's servers will need different policies; for example, the SQL Servers of each lobbyist group will probably be different. So you can't put this policy at domain level. The other half of the answer is correct: you could create policies for each type of client and apply the policy on each OU where the computers are grouped by security need.

   E. **Correct:** The policy needs are too vague at this time to decide on an IPSec policy for servers and clients. It's correct that you should group computers by security need and then configure IPSec policies. Again, the built-in policies only apply to domain use.

   Domain objective addressed by this question: 6.2.

70-220.CS4.015

▶ **Correct Answers: F**

A. **Incorrect:** Preshared is the username/password authentication, which is considered the least secure of all authentications in both public and private network traffic. So two answers are eliminated right away. IKE stands for Internet Key Exchange, which is the Internet Engineering Task Force's (IETF) standard way of implementing security association and key exchange resolution. In Microsoft's IP Security Suite of IKE, AH, and ESP, it's IKE that builds the SAs between computers necessary to protect network traffic. AH and ESP are the security protocols.

B. **Incorrect:** This is incorrect for the reasons stated in A.

C. **Incorrect:** Kerberos authentication is limited to trusted domains. The remote access of the lobbyists tells us they aren't on the private network. Kerberos eliminates two answers right away.

D. **Incorrect:** This is incorrect for the reasons stated in C.

E. **Incorrect:** This is incorrect for the reasons stated in F.

F. **Correct:** Certificates are the safest authentication for the dial-up users even though they're employees and have accounts in the domain. Using certificates means Trey Research will also have to use PKI technology. Trey Research has the option of even more security if it chooses to deploy smart cards, which use certificates. IPSec can be configured to use the AH protocol for integrity, or it can use ESP, which can incorporate AH protocol for integrity and, in addition, provide encryption for confidentiality. So certificate-based authentication with ESP for integrity and confidentiality is the best choice.

Domain objective addressed by this question: 5.2.

Contoso, Ltd.

Background

Contoso, Ltd., makes sunglasses for eye protection in specific industries, such as building construction, the snow skiing business, medicine, and manufacturing. Its innovations in eyewear protection are patented and are technical in nature.

The Business

Contoso has recently committed to selling its products on the Internet in addition to using its well-established direct sales channels. The customers from direct sales can choose between Internet orders and continuing with their current arrangements. A 10 percent increase in sales is projected with the addition of e-commerce.

Headquarters is in downtown Chicago, where there are 500 employees. The centrally administered IT department, including the help desk, is located at headquarters.

The research labs, in an outlying district of Chicago, are built on an island to give them additional physical protection. The manufacturing of lenses is also done on the island. The island is the company's most closely guarded facility. Contoso holds many patents for its lens products. There are 1,000 employees on the island.

Contoso's frames are manufactured and the lenses and frames are assembled in Joliet, Illinois. The security requirements for this plant are moderate because no secrets are on location. The employee enrollment is in the range of 300–350.

The plastic raw materials are produced exclusively by a partner in St. Louis and transported to Joliet.

A business cycle is one year.

Goals and Priorities

The new Internet sales effort has the full support of the corporate backers, who want it to be first-class. They want the site ready for the new technologies, which are always introduced in the spring. They also want the strongest network security available to the corporate locations, both internal and external, now that the corporation will be exposed to the Internet. As part of the upgrade in infrastructure technology, they want the St. Louis partner to have remote access for purchasing transactions and shared files.

There's a chance Contoso will get the contract for a major skiing competition in Grenoble one year from now. If so, it will be selling to large businesses in other parts of the world. The Web site will be the point of sale.

Existing IT Environment

The central location in downtown Chicago maintains all SQL servers, Exchange servers, and network infrastructure equipment and supports all users at all locations. The centralized IT function will continue.

There are two T1 connections between the island's research labs/manufacturing plant and the central facility. No security protection, other than authentication, is in use. Bandwidth usage is normally at 25 percent. The Joliet assembly plant has a dial-up connection to headquarters that's used for purchasing and logistics transactions. All contact with the St. Louis partner is through regular postal services and telephone voice requests.

Problems

Even though the IT technologies for Contoso are admittedly out of date, improvements were postponed until the Internet decision could be made. Many workstations and servers will have to be updated and new network technologies will have to be implemented during this change in business practice.

The traditional customers will have to be convinced that the Web transactions are secure, as well as easier to use.

The delivery of plastics is frequently delayed because of communication problems with St. Louis. The mail service is slow, and special delivery services are expensive. Both businesses want a faster alternative to existing communications. The coordination of ordering information between manufacturing and headquarters also causes problems for the St. Louis partner.

Envisioned IT Environment

The Web servers will be isolated from the public networks and from the internal network. A publicly recognized domain name will be purchased and the current Microsoft Windows NT domains will be migrated to Active Directory directory service. The dial-up connection between Joliet and headquarters must be secured. The T1 connection between the island and headquarters must be secured. Contoso will now participate in cooperative online vendor orders with the St. Louis partner using both partners' purchasing and logistics proprietary software.

Case Study 5 Questions

70-220.CS5.001

To improve the delivery of raw materials from the St. Louis partner, new forms of communication will be established. Network links between St. Louis and headquarters and between St. Louis and Joliet will be added. What types of network connections are appropriate between these locations based on Contoso's new network technologies, and secondly, what method of security is necessary?

A. Dedicated connections and Kerberos authentication

B. Internet VPN and PPTP

C. Internet VPN and L2TP over IPSec

D. Dial-up and certificates mapped to user accounts

70-220.CS5.002

Based on Contoso's projected growth in the e-commerce world, what can you suggest to facilitate the customers' authentications when they're using the Web site for placing orders?

A. A RADIUS client

B. A RADIUS server

C. A RADIUS proxy

D. Digital certificates

E. Basic authentication with SSL

70-220.CS5.003

Based on the envisioned environment outlined, the relationship with the supplier in St. Louis, and the Internet sales initiative, which Active Directory design would work best for Contoso?

A. Create a single forest with a tree to contain *contoso.com* and a tree for the St. Louis supplier. Create trusts between the domains for administrative functions, and create operational units to manage resources.

B. Create a single forest with multiple trees to contain each of the business units—headquarters, the island, and Joliet—with operational units to contain resources, separate the e-commerce systems, and manage remote connections with the suppliers.

C. Create a single tree with multiple sites containing each of the business units—headquarters, the island, and Joliet—with operational units to contain resources, separate the e-commerce systems, and manage remote connections with the suppliers.

D. Create a single tree with multiple operational units containing each of the business units—headquarters, the island, and Joliet—and the e-commerce system. Operational units are created within each of the business units to contain the resources.

70-220.CS5.004

How should you secure a Windows 2000 system operating as a router if you decide to enable communications between St. Louis and headquarters and St. Louis and the island with VPN? (Choose all that apply.)

A. Allow UDP 500 with IDs 50 and 51 on the firewall.

B. Configure it as a Terminal Services client with authentication by Active Directory.

C. Use only for dedicated IP routing.

D. Place it in physical isolation.

E. Implement the strongest IKE negotiation settings on the router.

70-220.CS5.005

Consider the major growth and risk possibilities for the next two business cycles. Which of the following areas should be candidates for network load balancing, based on increase in risk for failure, data, users, or peak loads? (Choose all that apply.)

A. Web servers

B. Exchange servers

C. VPN servers

D. SQL servers

E. Network infrastructure equipment: routers, DNS, DHCP

70-220.CS5.006

The human resources department at headquarters must have employee information transmitted from the managers on the island, from Joliet, and at headquarters. What should you use as the means of protecting the data on the wire for this application?

A. IPSec transport mode

B. IPSec tunnel mode

C. VPN using PPTP or L2TP over IPSec

D. SSL

70-220.CS5.007

What authentication methods will Contoso need to use? (Choose all that apply.)

A. Kerberos

B. Certificate-based

C. Smart cards

D. SSL

E. NTLM

F. Digest authentication

70-220.CS5.008

Suppose that Contoso initially uses an off-line stand-alone CA to issue certificates to its St. Louis partner, and the St. Louis partner uses a commercial CA to issue certificates to its customers.

Now suppose that a year later the skiing contract is awarded to Contoso and it decides to use a commercial CA. What new CA arrangement would then be possible for Contoso?

A. Contoso could choose to move its St. Louis partner's list of trusted users to its newly created CA subordinate to the commercial CA.

B. Contoso could use the commercial CA as a failover for its stand-alone to assure continuous service to its users.

C. Contoso could choose the same commercial CA as its St. Louis partner has, and then Contoso and St. Louis will implicitly trust each other.

D. Contoso could configure its stand-alone CA to receive the commercial CA's certificate online.

70-220.CS5.009

If the contract for the skiing competition is granted to Contoso, it will manage sales contracts based on a variety of national rules and regulations. The security technologies of the networked sales transactions will be influenced by these rules and regulations. At contract award time, Contoso will have been using its stand-alone private CA for about one year. What should you plan for CAs to support these new customers?

A. Replace the stand-alone CA with an enterprise CA.

B. Integrate a commercial CA with the stand-alone CA.

C. Manage the global sales with SSL exclusively.

D. Use the enterprise CA for the hosting server of the Web site.

70-220.CS5.010

If you decide to design network security with a perimeter network implemented with two firewalls, how will the DNS servers be configured?

A. The internal firewall will use static address mapping to the internal DNS server.

B. The external firewall has a separate interface directly connected to the DNS server.

C. The internal firewall has a separate interface directly connected to the DNS server.

D. The external firewall will use static address mapping to the external DNS server.

70-220.CS5.011

The St. Louis partners will need an authentication method in order to use the purchasing and logistics software at Contoso's headquarters. What would be the logical choice if the secure channel between them will be a VPN with L2TP over IPSec?

A. Certificates from a stand-alone CA

B. Smart cards

C. Certificates from a commercial CA

D. Preshared key authentication

70-220.CS5.012

What type of authentication should Contoso use to secure the credit card information of established customers who order from the Web site?

A. Digest authentication

B. Basic authentication over SSL

C. Windows authentication

D. Anonymous authentication

70-220.CS5.013

The island research and lens manufacturing plants will be getting new IPSec configurations for all their transactions across the T1 lines that connect them with headquarters. Considering the business security goals, new exposure and vulnerabilities with the Web, and the value of this transmitted data, which means of encryption should you choose?

A. SSL

B. AH

C. ESP incorporating AH

D. VPN router-to-router encryption

70-220.CS5.014

What's the primary means for managing the details of IPSec, which you should therefore include in your management strategy?

A. Use the Security Log errors to learn if IPSec components are malfunctioning.

B. Use the total number of master and session keys displayed in the Security log.

C. Monitor the security association detail lines.

D. Use the Event Viewer's System Log to show policy changes in Active Directory.

Case Study 5 Answers

70-220.CS5.001

▶ **Correct Answers: C**

A. **Incorrect:** The partners don't have Contoso domain user accounts, so any design based on their authentication is premature. Authentication alone isn't adequate security, even on dedicated connections. We do know, however, that the data must be secured through encryption. Dedicated connections aren't a good choice because the new infrastructure allows communications through the public network, which will be less expensive. Each partner can use a local ISP number for Internet connections and then establish the VPN.

B. **Incorrect:** PPTP allows for user authentication but not machine-based certificates, which will be a better choice with a partner business. PPTP does provide encryption with MPPE if either MS-CHAP or EAP authentication is selected.

C. **Correct:** A VPN is cost effective because it allows for the connection to work over a public link, such as the Internet, and therefore eliminates the need for leased lines. L2TP over IPSec offers point-to-point security between two computers (all the way to the application).

D. **Incorrect:** This is incorrect for the reasons stated in A.

Domain objective addressed by this question: 1.3.

70-220.CS5.002

▶ **Correct Answers: D**

A. **Incorrect:** A RADIUS client is another term for a NAS, which receives the dial-up client's request and forwards it to the RADIUS server. All RADIUS answers are incorrect because Contoso's plan is to take orders from a Web site, not receive calls from dial-up customers.

B. **Incorrect:** The RADIUS server centralizes the authentication, authorization, and accounting data for all RAS servers. All RADIUS answers are incorrect because Contoso's plan is to take orders from a Web site, not receive calls from dial-up customers.

C. **Incorrect:** A RADIUS proxy server is a front-end for the RADIUS servers of several organizations. The ISP usually provides the RADIUS proxy service. All RADIUS answers are incorrect because Contoso's plan is to take orders from a Web site, not receive calls from dial-up customers.

D. **Correct:** Digital certificates will identify the regular customers and allow them access to areas unavailable to first-time visitors to the Web site. These certificates will include the public key, which consists of user name, certificate serial number, and a list of the uses for the certificate.

E. **Incorrect:** Basic authentication with SSL will be fine for some Web access, but not for actual customer transactions.

Domain objective addressed by this question: 1.5.

70-220.CS5.003

▶ **Correct Answers: C**

A. **Incorrect:** A multitree forest isn't needed. There are no business requirements to take administrative control of the St. Louis supplier's network. This model doesn't address the needs of the multiple locations within Contoso.

B. **Incorrect:** The additional administrative overhead for the separate trees makes this an incorrect answer. This structure, while good for a decentralized IT environment, wouldn't work well for the central IT group based at headquarters. This group would have to create redundant accounts within each of the trees so that it can manage each unit.

C. **Correct:** This is the best solution for the proposed environment. By creating multiple sites within one tree you can have the central IT management and reduce WAN traffic between sites. By placing the resources within operational units you can delegate some administrative duties to local personnel without giving the local units control over the other sites. You can apply the group policies separately to the different operational units so that you can secure communications with the suppliers and control access through the e-commerce systems.

D. **Incorrect:** While this is a good model for the proposed environment, it would increase the network traffic on the WAN.

Domain objective addressed by this question: 5.2.

70-220.CS5.004

▶ **Correct Answers: C and D**

A. **Incorrect:** Setting the firewall to UDP 500 with IDs 50 and 51 is a method for allowing IPSec packets to pass through.

B. **Incorrect:** You cannot correctly configure the Windows 2000 router as a Terminal Services client because TS is utilized in a thin-client environment, and not one where VPN will be used to enable dial-up communications.

C. **Correct:** If a Windows 2000 computer is being used as a router, no other services should be allowed because they might compromise its security.

D. **Correct:** Routers should always be in a locked closet, physically isolated from intruders.

E. **Incorrect:** IKE negotiations aren't a valid way to protect a router. IKE negotiations establish an SA for two communicating computers that have to agree on how their transmissions are to be protected. IKE becomes involved with routers when the router itself does the negotiations for the target computer (endpoint).

Domain objective addressed by this question: 2.1.

70-220.CS5.005

▶ **Correct Answers: A and D**

A. **Correct:** Web servers will experience an increase in load if e-commerce brings customers who aren't in the forecast. The load will also increase if Contoso wins the skiing competition contract. The way load balancing will work with the Web servers is that each person who logs on to the Web site will connect to the least busy member of a group of servers.

B. **Incorrect:** Exchange servers are for internal employees, and no increase in employees is anticipated.

C. **Incorrect:** VPN servers may need network load balancing for some networks, but for Contoso, VPN is being purchased this year to support the partner's remote access. The VPN servers won't need mission-critical protection during the next two years. The growth areas of e-commerce and the skiing competition contract don't affect the transmissions with the partner in St. Louis.

D. **Correct:** SQL servers are very good candidates for network load balancing. Load-balanced SQL server machines are also called "cluster servers" or "high availability servers." If the corporation gets the skiing competition contract, it will want the SQL servers to be available. The choice to put SQL servers on high availability servers would be to avoid down time, not to increase data capacity.

E. **Incorrect:** The infrastructure equipment isn't an application for network load balancing.

Domain objective addressed by this question: 2.1.

70-220.CS5.006

▶ **Correct Answers: A**

A. **Correct:** IPSec transport mode can protect the data on a private network while it's in transmission. Another option includes the use of L2TP tunneling. Files on the hard disk drive can be protected with NTFS permissions and EFS. Private networks for Contoso include the island-to-headquarters WAN, which is on T1 lines, and the headquarters LAN.

B. **Incorrect:** The IPSec tunnel mode is recommended when the data must go through firewalls and routers or when encryption is required. Contoso's only applications on the wire are private network (island to headquarters) on a WAN, a LAN (headquarters), and dial-up (Joliet to headquarters). There's no application for IPSec tunnel.

C. **Incorrect:** Contoso can use VPN with either PPTP or L2TP over IPSec tunneling protocols, depending on how secure they think employee data should be. This is the choice for Joliet to headquarters, where only dial-up is provided. Joliet will dial its local ISP and then dial the tunnel server at headquarters to create the VPN. Headquarters will do the reverse. Windows 2000 makes L2TP over IPSec possible with VPN connections. Otherwise PPTP would be the only option.

D. **Incorrect:** SSL is for specific applications like Web browsers. It won't cover every type of application that the human resources department might choose to transmit.

Domain objective addressed by this question: 4.2.

70-220.CS5.007

▶ **Correct Answers: A, B, and D**

A. **Correct:** Kerberos will be used on the domain for Joliet frame manufacturing, the island research and lens manufacturing, and headquarters. Its purpose here will be to authenticate Contoso's users into the Windows 2000 network.

B. **Correct:** The St. Louis partner will use certificate-based authentication. Certificate-based authentication is created through the use of the Windows 2000 PKI, which includes Certificate Services.

C. **Incorrect:** Smart cards for authentication aren't specified in the scenario.

D. **Correct:** SSL will be used for Web secure channels.

E. **Incorrect:** NTLM is the default authentication of Windows NT systems. All of Contoso's systems will be Windows 2000 systems.

F. **Incorrect:** Digest authentication, in which two machines share a secret that doesn't cross the network because it employs a hash algorithm, isn't a good choice because not all Web browsers support it.

Domain objective addressed by this question: 4.7.

70-220.CS5.008

▶ **Correct Answers: C**

A. **Incorrect:** It's not possible to move a list of trusted users from one CA to another. If a new CA is created, the users will have to be reenrolled.

B. **Incorrect:** It's not possible to have a fail-safe CA. A CA must be recovered from backup, or all users will lose service.

C. **Correct:** When two CAs trust another CA, they implicitly trust each other.

D. **Incorrect:** The stand-alone CA will have to receive the commercial CA's certificate manually, because the stand-alone is kept offline.

Domain objectives addressed by this question: 1.3, 4.7.

70-220.CS5.009

▶ **Correct Answers: B**

A. **Incorrect:** After the contract is awarded, there won't be time to convert to a new certificate policy. Also, global customers won't know the validity of Contoso's certificates.

B. **Correct:** Contoso's clients will have more confidence in Contoso's Web site if the hosting server uses a commercial CA. Global customers would know the commercial name. Contoso can continue using the stand-alone CA for issuing certificates to its customers. This process is much like applying for a charge-card account with a retail store. After Contoso has the customer's credentials and chooses to do business with that customer, it will manually issue the certificate.

C. **Incorrect:** SSL isn't an option for the scope of this job. Its primary usage is to instigate a secure connection between browser and server. This requires a much larger scope than this option.

D. **Incorrect:** Once the contract is awarded, there won't be time to convert to a new certificate policy. Also, global customers won't know the validity of Contoso's certificates.

Domain objective addressed by this question: 4.8.

70-220.CS5.010

▶ **Correct Answers: D**

   A. **Incorrect:** The internal DNS server and internal firewall don't need protection from the Internet and they won't need static address mapping.

   B. **Incorrect:** The described use of an interface for the DNS server refers to a three-pronged firewall, in which all services exposed to the Internet are in a screened subnet protected by multiple network interface cards. Packets from the Internet are all directed to the interface that connects to the screened subnet. Because there's only one firewall in a three-pronged configuration, this answer is incorrect.

   C. **Incorrect:** This is incorrect for the reasons stated in B.

   D. **Correct:** To protect the DNS with two firewalls, you'll use two separate DNS servers. The Internet firewall will have static address mapping to the external DNS server, which is the screened subnet. The Internet users will never see this DNS server's real address. Another mode of protection would be to use Active Directory–integrated zones instead of the regular zones. Be certain to configure the zones to accept only secure updates.

   Domain objective addressed by this question: 5.2.

70-220.CS5.011

▶ **Correct Answers: A**

   A. **Correct:** The partner is outside the domain user account authentication, so either a stand-alone CA or a commercial CA can issue certificates. Less cost is involved when the certificates are issued internally, rather than by a commercial CA. As the design unfolds, it's not yet clear whether the regular customers who order through the Web site will be using certificates or not. If they do, it will come about slowly, so the administrator can still handle each request individually, which is required of stand-alone CAs. Given this corporation's growth plans and its other domain authentication (Kerberos) for everyone except partners and Web users, a stand-alone CA would be best.

   B. **Incorrect:** Smart cards are especially secure when the users are in exposed situations, such as traveling with laptops or accessing the network from off-site offices, or if the computers are in high-traffic areas where intruders might have opportunities to access a secured session. These partners are in established offices. Smart card expense can't be justified. Smart cards require certificates.

   C. **Incorrect:** Given this corporation's growth and its other domain authentication (Kerberos) for everyone except partners and Web users, it would be safe to specify a stand-alone CA as opposed to a commercial CA.

D. **Incorrect:** Preshared key authentication is supported by IPSec, which will be the security choice for VPN with L2TP over IPSec. However, it's the lowest authentication option of Kerberos, certificate, and preshared key. Preshared key is just another term for password. Many tools available to intruders today can break passwords. The safest way to protect Contoso's most confidential information—its patents—is to secure all entry points, such as partners, with certificates.

Domain objective addressed by this question: 5.3.

70-220.CS5.012

▶ **Correct Answers: B**

A. **Incorrect:** Digest authentication requires a domain user account. It's somewhat like basic authentication, but it doesn't send passwords in clear text.

B. **Correct:** All types of browsers must be supported for customers accessing the Web site, which calls for basic authentication over SSL.

C. **Incorrect:** Not all browsers support integrated Windows authentication. This used to be called the Windows NT Challenge/Response authentication. It works well with intranets in which users have Windows domain accounts. Authentication can be Kerberos or NTLM.

D. **Incorrect:** Anonymous authentication will be used for new customers' inquiries. Actual customers will have better security alternatives, such as SSL.

Domain objective addressed by this question: 6.2.

70-220.CS5.013

▶ **Correct Answers: C**

A. **Incorrect:** Use SSL for applications that understand SSL—for example, Web applications. It has to be configured for each application and only works if that application understands SSL. A better option is to use IPSec, which is configured as part of Group Policy.

B. **Incorrect:** AH that stands alone without the integration of ESP isn't a viable solution.

C. **Correct:** Use the IPSec Protocol AH when you need integrity without encryption. Using these two in tandem will ensure that only the original sender and receiver are sending and receiving packets. Because the corporate secrets travel on these T1 lines, Contoso should use the encryption protocol that incorporates AH, which is ESP.

D. **Incorrect:** If you use IPSec on VPN connections, which are on public lines rather than T1s, it's automatically encrypted between the routers. However, Contoso is using T1 lines between the island and headquarters.

Domain objective addressed by this question: 6.2.

70-220.CS5.014

▶ **Correct Answers: C**

A. **Incorrect:** If you have major problems with IPSec's components—IKE, IPSec policy agent, or IPSec driver—you'll need to reinstall TCP/IP for the computer because IPSec is fully integrated into the stack. This is troubleshooting, not managing the details of IPSec activity.

B. **Incorrect:** Successful SAs create one master key and one session key. Key regenerations are shown as additional session keys. This information can be found using IPSECMON.EXE and is useful for troubleshooting. It's not the primary means of watching the health of the IPSec on the network.

C. **Correct:** The successes and failures of SAs will tell you if there are incompatible security policy settings. The SAs are monitored with the IPSec Monitoring Tool. This tool can be accessed from the Run command by typing *ipsecmon <computername>* and can be used interactively or on a remote computer. For increased security, use dynamic rekeying. Dynamic rekeying is the process of having IPSec automatically generate new keys while the communication is in transit. In this situation a hacker may compromise a solitary key, but the hacker wouldn't be able to obtain the entire communication. This also allows for randomly changing the intervals for default keying.

D. **Incorrect:** The System Log does indeed show any policy changes made by an administrator. Although this is also good to know, it won't show the details of associations, active filter actions, and the filter list of IPSec, for example.

Domain objective addressed by this question: 6.2.

Glossary

A

access control entry (ACE) An entry in an access control list that defines a set of permissions for a group or user.

access control list (ACL) A list containing access control entries. An ACL determines the permissions associated with an object, which can be anything in a Win32 environment.

access controls The list generated by the server to control access to network resources. ACLs illustrate who has permission to an object, as well as what type of permission it is.

Active Directory directory service The hierarchical structure of arranging objects, shared folders, printers, computer information, and other resources in Microsoft Windows 2000.

active window The window with which the user is currently working. Microsoft Windows identifies the active window by highlighting its title bar and border.

agent Software that runs on a client computer for use by administrative software running on a server. Agents are typically used to support administrative actions, such as detecting system information or running services.

AH *See* authentication header.

API *See* application programming interface.

application A computer program designed to do some specific type of work. An application differs from a utility, which performs some type of maintenance (such as formatting a disk).

application programming interface (API) An API is a list of supported functions. Windows 2000 supports the MS-DOS API, Windows API, and Win32 API. If a function is a member of the API, it is said to be a supported or documented function. Functions that make up Windows but are not part of the API are referred to as "undocumented functions."

association The process of assigning a filename extension to a particular application. If an extension has been associated with an application, Windows 2000 will start the application when you choose to open the file from Microsoft Windows Explorer. Associations are critical to the concept of document-centric computing.

auditing The generation of log file entries to record the occurrence of security-related events.

Audit Policy A definition of the type of security-related events that will be recorded by the Event Viewer.

authentication The validation of a user's access to a computer or domain by either the local computer (local validation) or a domain controller for the domain the user is accessing.

authentication header (AH) The modified header portion of an IP packet. Within this portion there are several additional fields of information that can provide the authentication, integrity, and antireplay protection for the packet when using IPSec.

B

Backup *See* Windows 2000 Backup.

backup domain controller (BDC) The Windows NT controller server that performs the validation of user logon requests. The BDC obtains a copy of the master account database for the domain from the primary domain controller (PDC).

Bandwidth Allocation Protocol (BAP) A control protocol utilized by Point-to-Point Protocol (PPP) on a multiprocessing connection that dynamically adds and removes links.

basic input/output system (BIOS) The bootstrap code of a PC. BIOS consists of the low-level routines that support the transfer of information between the various parts of a computer system, such as memory, disks, and the monitor. The BIOS is usually built into the machine's read-only memory (ROM) and can have a significant effect on the computer system's performance.

C

CA *See* certificate authority.

centralized model The model of networking in Windows 2000 that consolidates administrative control of group policies.

central processing unit (CPU) A computer's computational and control unit; the device that interprets and executes instructions. The CPU—or microprocessor, in the case of a microcomputer—has the ability to fetch, decode, and execute instructions, and to transfer information to and from other resources over the computer's main data-transfer path (the bus). The CPU is the chip that functions as the computer's "brain."

certificate authority (CA) A system that creates digital certificates through the use of an available public key.

certificate-based authentication Authentication of users and computers that utilizes digital certificates as the medium for authenticating.

certificate revocation list (CRL) A digitally signed list of certificates that are no longer valid.

CHAP (Challenge Handshake Authentication Protocol) A challenge/response authentication protocol that is defined in RFC 1994. This protocol is utilized by PPP and provides a one-way encryption Message Digest 5 (MD5) hash response when challenged by the remote access server.

character A letter, number, punctuation mark, or control code. Usually expressed in either the ANSI or ASCII character set.

client A computer that accesses shared network resources provided by another computer called a server. *See also* server.

Client Service for NetWare (CSNW) A Windows 2000 Professional service that provides connections to multiple versions of NetWare server software.

communications protocol The rules that govern a conversation between two computers that are communicating through an asynchronous connection. The use of a communications protocol ensures error-free delivery of the data being communicated.

compressed Reduced in size for the purpose of using a lower amount of disk space. In Windows 2000, files on NTFS can be compressed.

Computer Browser Service An executive service that identifies the Windows NT or Windows 2000 machines that have resources available for use within a workgroup or domain.

computer local groups Security groups that are defined on a single Windows NT or Windows 2000 computer.

computer name A unique name that identifies a particular computer on the network. Microsoft networking uses NetBIOS names, which can have up to 15 characters but can't contain spaces.

Configuration Manager One of three central components of a Plug and Play system (one for each of the three phases of configuration management). The configuration managers drive the process of locating devices, setting up the hardware tree, and allocating resources.

controller *See* domain controller.

Control Panel One of the primary Windows 2000 configuration folders. Each option that you can change is represented by an icon in the Control Panel window.

conventional memory The first 640 KB of memory in a computer; used to run real-mode MS-DOS applications.

cooperative multitasking The method by which Windows 2000 requires a running application to check the processor message queue periodically and to relinquish system control to other applications.

crash A serious failure of software.

CRL *See* certificate revocation list.

cryptography The discipline of creating and decoding encrypted or encoded messages.

D

data frame The structured packets into which data is placed by the data link layer of the TCP/IP stack.

datagram A packet of information and delivery data that's routed on a network.

decentralized model The model of networking in Windows 2000 that delegates the handling of administrative tasks down to a lower level.

default An operation or value that the system assumes unless the user makes an explicit choice.

denial of service attacks An attack from an outside source that floods the target machine with data, therefore overloading it and causing it to fail.

desktop The background of the screen on which windows, icons, and dialog boxes appear.

destination directory The directory to which a user intends to create, copy, or move one or more files.

device A generic term for a computer component, such as a printer, serial port, or disk drive. A device

frequently requires its own controlling software, called a "device driver."

device driver A piece of software that translates requests from one form into another. Most commonly, drivers are used to provide a device-independent way to access hardware.

DFS *See* Distributed File System.

DHCP *See* Dynamic Host Configuration Protocol.

dialog box The type of window that's displayed when user input is needed. A dialog box usually contains one or more buttons, edit controls, option buttons, and drop-down lists.

dial-up networking Formerly known as Remote Access Service (RAS), it provides remote access to networks. Dial-up networking allows a remote user to access the network. Once the user is connected, it's as if the remote computer is logically on the network. Users can do anything they could do when physically connected to the network.

digital signature The message digest that's attached to a document and used to identify the sender, as well as to indicate that the document has not been tampered with while in transit.

Digital Signature Algorithm (DSA) A public-key algorithm that generates a hash value.

directory Part of a structure for organizing files on a disk. A directory can contain files and other directories (called subdirectories).

Directory Replication Service A service that provides a means of copying a directory and file structure from a source Windows NT server to a target Windows NT server or workstation. *See also* File Replication Service (FRS).

Distributed File System (DFS) The method of centralizing the organization of shared resources on a Windows 2000 Server network.

DLL *See* dynamic link library.

DMA channel A channel for direct memory access transfers that occur between a device and memory without involving the CPU.

DNS *See* Domain Name System.

DNS name servers The servers that hold the DNS name database and supply the IP address that matches a DNS name in response to a request from a DNS client. *See also* Domain Name System (DNS).

domain A collection of connected area components.

domain controller The Windows 2000 or Windows NT Server computer that authenticates domain logons and maintains a copy of the security database for the domain.

domain local groups Security groups that are defined on a Windows 2000 native mode domain. These groups can contain members from throughout the active directory forest, but they can only control access to resources within the domain in which the group exists.

Domain Name System (DNS) A static, hierarchical name service for TCP/IP hosts.

domain naming master The domain controller that oversees the addition or removal of domains within the forest.

DOS Protected Mode Interface (DPMI) A technique used to allow DOS-based applications to access extended memory.

DRAM *See* Dynamic Random Access Memory.

DSA *See* Digital Signature Algorithm.

Dynamic Data Exchange (DDE) A form of inter-process communication (IPC) implemented in the Microsoft Windows family of operating systems.

DDE uses shared memory to exchange data. Most DDE functions have been superseded by OLE.

Dynamic Host Configuration Protocol (DHCP) A protocol for automatic TCP/IP configuration that provides static and dynamic address allocation and management.

dynamic link library (DLL) Functions compiled, linked, and saved separately from the processes that use them. Functions in DLLs can be used by more than one running process. The operating system maps the DLLs into the process' address space when the process is starting up or while it is running. Dynamic link libraries are stored in files with the .dll extension.

Dynamic Random Access Memory (DRAM) A computer's main memory.

E

EAP *See* Extensible Authentication Protocol.

EAP-MD5 CHAP *See* Extensible Authentication Protocol–Message Digest 5 Challenge Handshake Authentication Protocol.

EAP-TLS *See* Extensible Authentication Protocol–Transport Layer Security.

EFS *See* Encrypting File System.

Encapsulating Security Payload (ESP) The mechanism whereby a packet is encrypted and signed when using IPSec.

Encrypting File System (EFS) A file format new to Windows 2000 wherein the contents are encrypted for security purposes.

encryption The process of changing data so that it is unreadable by anyone other than the intended recipient. This process usually employs mathematical algorithms and can be of various strengths.

EPS file A file containing code written in the Encapsulated PostScript printer programming language. Often used to represent graphics for use by desktop publishing applications.

ESP *See* Encapsulating Security Payload. .

expanded memory Memory that complies with the Lotus-Intel-Microsoft Expanded Memory specification. Used by DOS-based spreadsheet applications.

Extended Industry Standard Architecture (EISA) An enhancement to the bus architecture used on the IBM PC/AT, which allows the use of 32-bit devices in the same type of expansion slot used by an ISA adapter card. EISA slots and adapters were formerly common in server computers but have been mostly replaced with PCI slots.

Extensible Authentication Protocol (EAP) An extension to PPP that allows for arbitrary authentication mechanisms to be employed for the validation of a PPP connection.

Extensible Authentication Protocol–Message Digest 5 Challenge Handshake Authentication Protocol (EAP-MD5 CHAP) A mechanism that allows for the use of EAP to encrypt the MD5 CHAP challenge/response process when authenticating a PPP connection.

Extensible Authentication Protocol–Transport Layer Security (EAP-TLS) A mechanism based on SSL that allows for the encryption and integrity validation of PPP authentication and communications.

external authenticated users Users connected to a network who have been authenticated by a remote access server such as RADIUS.

F

family name The name of a given font family. Windows employs five family names: Decorative, Modern, Roman, Script, and Swiss. A sixth family

name, Dontcare, specifies the default font. *See also* font family.

FAT file system A file system based on a file allocation table. Windows 2000 uses a 32-bit implementation called VFAT. *See also* file allocation table (FAT); virtual file allocation table.

FAT32 file system A file system based on enhancements to FAT. First released with Windows 95 OSR2, it was included with Windows 98 and is now supported in Windows 2000.

file A collection of information that's stored on a disk and is accessible using a name.

file allocation table (FAT) A table or list maintained by some operating systems to keep track of the status of various segments of disk space used for file storage. *See also* virtual file allocation table.

File and Print Service for NetWare A Windows 2000 service that makes a Windows server look like a NetWare server. This allows NetWare clients to attach to and use the printers and file resources on the Windows server.

File Replication Service (FRS) The service that enables DFS to offer automatic replication. *See also* Directory Replication Service.

file system In an operating system, the overall structure in which files are named, stored, and organized.

File Transfer Program (FTP) A utility, defined by the TCP/IP protocol suite, that's used to transfer files between dissimilar systems.

File Transfer Protocol (FTP) The standard method of transferring files using TCP/IP. FTP allows the user to transfer files between dissimilar computers with preservation of binary data and optional translation of text file formats.

firewall   A software or hardware device that isolates one network from another. Often used to isolate an internal network from the Internet.

font family   A group of fonts having common stroke width and serif characteristics.

G

gateway   A computer connected to multiple networks. It is capable of moving data between networks using different transport protocols.

Gateway Service for NetWare (GSNW)   The subcomponent that allows access for Microsoft clients on Novell systems.

global groups   A Windows 2000 security group that can be granted rights and permissions within a single domain. These groups can become members of local groups, but they can only contain user accounts from within their domain.

GPOs   *See* Group Policy objects.

Graphical Device Interface (GDI)   The subsystem that implements graphical drawing functions.

graphical user interface (GUI)   A computer system design in which the user interacts with the system using graphical symbols, tools, and events, rather than text-based displays and commands. The normal Windows user interface is a GUI.

Group Policy   An efficient method of placing security and system administration on all (or a large number of) users through a single file. In Windows 2000, Group Policy replaces the System Policy that existed in Windows NT.

Group Policy objects (GPOs)   The area in which group policies are stored before being applied to either the site, domain, or OU level.

GSNW   *See* Gateway Service for NetWare.

H

hierarchical namespace   An object naming system in which the full object name identifies the object and its relation to the network in which it resides. A common example is DNS, in which there are several top-level domains (TLD) such as com, net, and org, which are combined with the private domain, and then resource or host names within the private domain, to get a fully qualified name such as *www.microsoft.com.*

HKEY_CLASSES_ROOT   The Registry tree that contains data relating to OLE. This key is a symbolic link to a subkey of HKEY_LOCAL_MACHINE\ SOFTWARE.

HKEY_CURRENT_USER   The Registry tree that contains the currently logged-on user's preferences, including desktop settings, application settings, and network connections. This key maps to a subkey of HKEY_USERS.

HKEY_LOCAL_MACHINE   The Registry tree that contains configuration settings that apply to the hardware and software on the computer.

HKEY_USERS   The Registry tree on a computer that contains the preferences for every user that ever logged on to that computer.

host   Any device that's attached to the internetwork and uses TCP/IP.

host ID   The portion of the IP address that identifies a computer within a particular network ID.

host name   The name of an Internet host, which may or may not be the same as the computer name. In order for a client to access resources by host name, the host name must appear in the client's HOSTS file or be resolvable by a DNS server.

HOSTS file   A local text file in the same format as the 4.3 Berkeley Software Distribution (BSD)

UNIX /etc/hosts file. This file maps host names to IP addresses.

host table The HOSTS and LMHOSTS files, which contain cross references of known IP addresses mapped to host names.

I

IAS *See* Internet Authentication Service.

ICMP *See* Internet Control Message Protocol.

ICS *See* Internet Connection Sharing.

IKE *See* Internet Key Exchange.

INF file A file, usually provided by the manufacturer of a device, that provides the information that Setup routines need in order to set up a device. INF files usually include a list of valid logical configurations for the device, the names of driver files associated with the device, and other information.

Infrared Data Association (IrDA) The governing body overseeing infrared specifications.

Integrated Services Digital Network (ISDN) A digital communications method that permits connections of up to 128 kilobits per second (Kbps). ISDN requires a special adapter for a computer. An ISDN connection is available in most countries or regions for a reasonable cost.

internal command Commands that are built into the COMMAND.COM file.

Internet The worldwide interconnected wide-area network, based on the TCP/IP protocol suite.

Internet Authentication Service (IAS) A service that enables authentication, authorization, and account of VPN and dial-up users. IAS is supported by RADIUS.

Internet Connection Sharing (ICS) Windows 2000 technology that's utilized for address translation when connecting a few computers on a smaller LAN.

Internet Control Message Protocol (ICMP) A required protocol in the TCP/IP protocol suite. It allows two nodes on an IP network to share IP status and error information. ICMP is used by the ping utility.

Internet Engineering Task Force (IETF) A consortium that introduces procedures for new technology on the Internet. IETF specifications are released in documents called Requests for Comments (RFCs).

Internet group names A name known by a DNS server that includes a list of the specific addresses of systems that have registered the name.

Internet Key Exchange (IKE) The protocol that establishes the security association as well as the two keys needed when engaging in data transfer by IPSec.

Internet Printing Protocol (IPP) The protocol used for Web printing in Windows 2000.

Internet protocol (IP) The network layer protocol of TCP/IP that's responsible for addressing and sending TCP packets over the network.

Internet Service Provider (ISP) A company or organization that allows users to connect to the Internet through their network.

I/O address A single location within the input/output address space of a computer that is assigned to a device such as a printer or modem.

IP address A network numerical identifier assigned to a host and comprised of four numbers ranging from zero to 255 separated by periods (for example, 192.168.001.001). Used to identify a node on a network and to specify routing information on an internetwork. Each node on the internetwork must be assigned a unique IP address, which is made up of the network ID plus a unique host ID assigned by the network administrator. The subnet mask is used to separate an IP address into the host ID and network ID. In Windows 2000, you can assign an IP address either manually or automatically using DHCP.

IPP *See* Internet Printing Protocol.

IP packet filtering A method employed by network devices, usually firewalls and routers, to restrict TCP/IP traffic by packet source or type.

IPSec (IP Security) A new feature in Microsoft Windows 2000 that provides data encryption as information travels from computer to computer.

IPX/SPX Internetworking Packet Exchange/ Sequenced Packet Exchange. Transport protocols used in Novell NetWare networks. Windows 2000 includes the Microsoft IPX/SPX compatible transport protocol (NWLINK).

ISDN *See* Integrated Services Digital Network.

ISO Development Environment (ISODE) A research tool developed to study the upper layer of OSI. Academic and some commercial ISO products are based on this framework.

ISP *See* Internet Service Provider.

K

Kerberos The default authentication protocol for Windows 2000.

kernel The Windows 2000 core component responsible for implementing the basic operating system functions, including virtual memory management, thread scheduling, and file I/O services.

L

L2TP *See* Layer Two Tunneling Protocol.

LAN *See* local area network.

Layer Two Tunneling Protocol (L2TP) A protocol used in the creation of VPNs by using IPSec. L2TP provides tunneling services over IPSec.

legacy application An application that was designed for use on a previous version or type of operating system.

link A connection at the LLC layer that's uniquely defined by the adapter's address and the destination service access point (DSAP). Also, a connection between two objects or a reference to an object that's linked to another.

LLC *See* logical link control.

local area network (LAN) A computer network confined to a single building or campus.

localization The process of adapting software for different countries, languages, or cultures.

logical drive A division of an extended partition on a hard disk that is accessed using a drive letter.

logical link control (LLC) One of the two sublayers of the data link layer of the OSI reference model, as defined by the IEEE 802 standards.

logon The process by which a user is identified to the computer in a Microsoft network.

logon script In Microsoft networking, a batch file that runs automatically when a user logs into a Windows 2000 or Windows NT Server. Novell networking also uses logon scripts, but they're not batch files.

M

MAC address The address for a device as it is identified at the media access control layer in the network architecture. MAC addresses are usually stored in ROM on the network adapter card and are unique.

mandatory user profile   A user environment profile that can't be changed by the user. If the profile is unavailable, the user won't be able to log on to the Windows NT domain.

message   A structure or set of parameters used for communicating information or a request. Every event that happens in the system causes a message to be sent. Messages can be passed between the operating system and an application, different applications, threads within an application, and windows within an application.

Microsoft Challenge Handshake Authentication Protocol (MS-CHAP)   The Microsoft implementation of CHAP, which uses Message Digest 4 rather than Message Digest 5 to hash the challenge and response messages.

Microsoft Challenge Handshake Authentication Protocol version 2 (MS-CHAP v2)   The new version of the Microsoft implementation of CHAP. This version uses stronger data encryption and utilizes separate keys for sending and receiving encrypted data. This version also supports mutual authentication.

Microsoft Point-to-Point Encryption (MPPE)   A 128/40-bit encryption package that provides for packet security between the client and the tunnel server.

MS-CHAP   *See* Microsoft Challenge Handshake Authentication Protocol.

MS-CHAP v2   *See* Microsoft Challenge Handshake Authentication Protocol version 2.

multitasking   The process by which an operating system creates the illusion that many tasks are executing simultaneously on a single processor. *See also* cooperative multitasking and preemptive multitasking.

multithreading   The ability of a process to have multiple simultaneous paths of execution (threads).

N

named pipe   A one-way or two-way channel used for communication between a server process and one or more client processes. A server process specifies a name when it creates one or more instances of a named pipe. Each instance of the pipe can be connected to a client. Microsoft SQL Server clients use named pipes to communicate with the SQL Server.

name registration   The way a computer registers its unique name with a name server on the network, such as a WINS server.

name resolution   The process used on the network to determine a computer's address by using its name.

NAS   *See* Network Access Server.

NAT   *See* network address translation.

native mode   The mode on a Windows 2000 network that establishes all domain controllers as Windows 2000 domain controllers.

NBF transport protocol   NetBEUI frame protocol. A descendant of the NetBEUI protocol, which is a transport layer protocol, not the programming interface NetBIOS.

NetBEUI transport   NetBIOS (network basic input/output system) Extended User Interface. A transport protocol designed for use on small subnets. It's not routable, but it's fast.

NetBIOS interface   The method an application can use to communicate with applications on another computer through NetBIOS. It has been superseded by NetBEUI.

NetBIOS over TCP/IP   The networking module that provides the functionality to support NetBIOS name registration and resolution across a TCP/IP network.

Network Access Server (NAS) The device that accepts PPP connections and authenticates clients for the network that the NAS serves. Common types of NAS are RADIUS and RAS servers.

network address translation (NAT) The translation parameter that offers internal users access to external resources without jeopardizing the security of the internal framework.

network basic input/output system (NetBIOS) A software interface for network communication. *See also* NetBIOS interface.

Network File System (NFS) A service for distributed computing systems that provides a distributed file system, eliminating the need for keeping multiple copies of files on separate computers. Usually used in connection with UNIX computers.

network ID The portion of the IP address that identifies a group of computers and devices located on the same logical network. It's separated from the host ID using the subnet mask.

Network Information Service (NIS) A service for distributed computing systems that provides a distributed database system for common configuration files.

network interface card (NIC) An adapter card that connects a computer to a network.

network-interface printers Printers with built-in network cards, such as Hewlett-Packard laser printers equipped with JetDirect cards. The advantage of network-interface printers is that they can be located anywhere on the network.

Network Load Balancing The idea of disbursing network traffic across a team of computers to in turn generate better performance.

network operating system (NOS) The operating system used on network servers, such as Windows 2000 Server or Novell NetWare.

network provider The component that allows the operating system to communicate with the network. Windows 2000 includes providers for Microsoft networks and for Novell NetWare networks. Other network vendors may supply providers for their networks.

network transport This can be either a particular layer of the OSI Reference Model between the network layer and the session layer or the protocol used between this layer on two different computers on a network.

New Technology file system (NTFS) *See* Windows NT file system.

NFS *See* Network File System.

NIC *See* network interface card.

NIS *See* Network Information Service.

NOS *See* network operating system.

NTFS *See* Windows NT file system.

O

object A particular instance of a class. Most of the internal data structures in Windows 2000 are objects.

organizational chart A logical description of the structure of a business that's organized by group, divisions, and individuals.

OU (organizational unit) Object in a Windows 2000 hierarchy that's a container for other objects such as users, groups, or other OUs.

OU (organizational unit) level The abstract level of the Active Directory structure that the OU containers occupy. The OU level is between the domain level and the object level.

output filter One of the two types of packet filters that can be configured.

P

packet A transmission unit of fixed maximum size that consists of binary information representing both data, addressing information, and error-correction information, created by the data link layer.

PAP *See* Password Authentication Protocol.

partition A portion of a physical disk that functions as though it were a physically separate unit. *See also* system partition.

partition table A table that contains entries showing the start and end point of each of the primary partitions on the disk. The partition table can hold four entries.

password A security measure used to restrict access to computer systems. A password is a unique string of characters that must be provided before a logon or an access is authorized.

Password Authentication Protocol (PAP) An authentication method used over a Point-to-Point Protocol connection. It is less secure than CHAP.

path The location of a file or directory. The path describes the location in relation to either the root directory or the current directory (for example, C:\WINNT\System32). Also, a graphic object that represents one or more shapes.

PDC *See* primary domain controller.

Peer Web Services (PWS) A subset of Internet Information Server (IIS) that can be installed on a Windows client machine. Also referred to as Personal Web Server.

performance monitoring The process of determining the system resources that an application uses, such as processor time and memory.

PKI *See* Public Key Infrastructure.

Point-to-Point Protocol (PPP) The industry standard that's implemented in Dial-up networking. PPP is a line protocol used to connect to remote networking services, including Internet service providers. Prior to the introduction of PPP, another line protocol (SLIP) was used.

Point-to-Point Tunneling Protocol (PPTP) An enhancement to PPP, wherein TCP/IP is used to tunnel other protocols across the Internet. Commonly used in the creation of virtual private networks (VPNs).

port The socket to which you connect the cable for a peripheral device. *See also* I/O address.

port ID The method that TCP and UDP use to specify which application running on the system is sending or receiving the data.

PPP *See* Point-to-Point Protocol.

preemptive multitasking A multitasking technique that breaks time up into time slices, during which the operating system allows a particular program thread to run. The operating system can interrupt any running thread at any time. Preemptive multitasking usually results in the best use of CPU time and overall better perceived throughput. *See also* cooperative multitasking.

primary domain controller (PDC) A domain controller that emulates a Windows NT PDC in the domain, processing password changes and replication information to the BDC.

private key The key used to decrypt a public key.

program file A file that starts an application or program. A program file has an .exe, .pif, .com, or .bat file name extension.

program information file (PIF) A file in which Windows 2000 stores information about how to configure the VM for running MS-DOS applications.

Properties   The dialog boxes that are used to configure a particular object in Windows 2000.

protocol   A set of rules and conventions by which two computers pass messages across a network. Protocols are used between instances of a particular layer on each computer. Windows 2000 includes NetBEUI, TCP/IP, and IPX/SPX-compatible protocols. *See also* communications protocol.

provider   The component that allows Windows 2000 to communicate with the network. Windows 2000 includes providers for Microsoft and Novell networks.

proxy server   A server used as a doorway to an external system or network.

public key   A digital code that's used to encrypt information. Public keys are decrypted by a private key.

Public Key Infrastructure (PKI)   A system comprised of digital certificates, certification authorities, and other registration authorities that verifies and authenticates each party involved in an electronic transaction.

PWS   *See* Peer Web Services.

R

RADIUS (Remote Authentication Dial-In User Service)   The protocol used to authenticate dial-in clients that allows for centralized authentication.

Registry   The Windows 2000 and Windows NT binary system configuration database.

Registry Editor (REGEDT32.EXE or REGEDIT.EXE)   A utility supplied with Windows 2000 that allows the user to view and edit Registry keys and values.

Registry key   A Registry entry that can contain other Registry entries.

relay attack   A type of network attack in which an unauthorized sender uses an unsecured SMTP server to propagate an SMTP message so that the message appears to originate from the compromised server.

Remote Access Service (RAS)   A Windows NT executive service that provides remote networking access to the Windows NT Enterprise for telecommuters, remote users system administrators, and home users. *See also* dial-up networking.

remote administration   The process of administrating one computer from another computer across a network.

Remote Installation Services (RIS)   A service that allows unattended installations of Windows 2000 Professional from a Windows 2000 Server.

remote procedure call (RPC)   An industry-standard method of interprocess communication across a network. Used by many administration tools.

replay attack   A type of attack in which the hacker records the information being sent and then plays it back to the receiver at a different time from when it was sent.

Requests for Comments (RFCs)   The official documents of the Internet Engineering Task Force that specify the details for protocols included in the TCP/IP family.

RIP   *See* Routing Information Protocol.

RIS   *See* Remote Installation Services.

risk tolerance   The amount of security risk an organization can incur until it begins to cause a disruption in network services and processes.

roaming user   Any dial-up or remote user who accesses the network from a removed location, or a local network user who uses different machines to access the network.

router A computer with two or more network adapters, each attached to a different subnet. The router forwards packets on a subnet to the subnet they are addressed to.

routing The process of forwarding packets until they reach their destination.

Routing and Remote Access Service (RRAS) The remote access component of Windows 2000 that combines such aspects as packet filtering and support into one subsystem.

Routing Information Protocol (RIP) A protocol that supports dynamic routing. Used between routers.

routing protocols Any protocol that's used to route data or authentication information through a network.

RRAS *See* Routing and Remote Access Service.

S

Secure Sockets Layer (SSL) A socket-level security protocol used to secure both the client and server side of Web site traffic.

security baseline The current or base level of network security.

Serial Line Internet Protocol (SLIP) The predecessor to PPP, SLIP is a line protocol supporting TCP/IP over a modem connection. SLIP support is provided for Windows NT 4. *See also* Point-to-Point Protocol (PPP).

server A computer or application that provides shared resources to clients across a network. Resources include files and directories, printers, fax modems, and network database services. *See also* client.

server message block (SMB) A block of data that contains a work request from a workstation to a server or that contains the response from the server to the workstation. SMBs are used for all network communications in a Microsoft network.

Server Service An executive service that makes resources available to the workgroup or domain for file, print, and other RPC services.

service A process that performs a specific system function and often provides an application programming interface (API) for other processes to call.

session layer A layer of the OSI reference model that performs name recognition and the functions needed to allow two applications to communicate over the network. Also, a communication channel established by the session layer.

shell The part of an operating system with which the user interacts. The Windows 2000 shell is Windows Explorer.

Shiva Password Authentication Protocol (SPAP) The encrypted authentication protocol utilized by Shiva remote access servers. This protocol is also supported in Windows 2000.

Simple Mail Transfer Protocol (SMTP) The application layer protocol that supports messaging functions over the Internet.

Simple Network Management Protocol (SNMP) A standard protocol for the management of network components.

SLIP *See* Serial Line Internet Protocol.

smart card A device that resembles a credit card, contains a digital certificate, and is used with a PIN number to authenticate clients.

SMB *See* server message block.

SMS *See* Systems Management Server.

SMTP *See* Simple Mail Transfer Protocol.

SNMP *See* Simple Network Management Protocol.

social engineering   The idea of breaking into a network simply by getting someone to reveal his or her password to an unauthorized user.

SPAP   *See* Shiva Password Authentication Protocol.

SSL   *See* Secure Sockets Layer.

string   A sequence of characters representing human-readable text.

subdirectory   A directory within a directory.

subnet   On the Internet, any lower network that's part of the logical network identified by the network ID.

subnet mask   A 32-bit value that's used to distinguish the network ID portion of the IP address from the host ID.

subtree   An Active Directory tree that resides within another tree.

swap file   A special file on a hard disk that's used to hold memory pages that are swapped out of RAM. This is also called a paging file.

symmetric key encryption   An encryption algorithm that requires the same key for both encryption and decryption.

system directory   The directory that contains the Windows DLLs and drivers. Usually \windows\system on the C drive.

system disk   A disk that contains the files necessary to start an operating system.

system partition   The volume that contains the hardware-specific files needed to load Windows 2000.

Systems Management Server (SMS)   A Windows NT subsystem that's used to monitor network usage as well as other network functions.

T

TAPI   *See* Telephony Application Programming Interface.

TCO   *See* total cost of operations.

TCP   *See* Transmission Control Protocol.

TCP/IP   *See* Transmission Control Protocol/Internet Protocol.

TDI   *See* transport driver interface.

Telephony Application Programming Interface (TAPI)   A subset of functions in the Win32 API that let a computer communicate directly with telephone systems.

Terminal Services   A Windows 2000 service that allows client applications to be run on a server in a multisession environment so that client computers can function as terminals or thin clients rather than independent systems.

TLS   *See* Transport Layer Security.

total cost of operations (TCO)   The total amount of revenue required to sustain an organization. Includes both revealed and hidden costs.

Transmission Control Protocol (TCP)   A connection-based protocol that's responsible for breaking data into packets that the IP protocol sends over the network. TCP provides a reliable, sequenced communication stream for internetwork communication.

Transmission Control Protocol/Internet Protocol (TCP/IP)   The primary wide area network used on the worldwide Internet, which is a worldwide internetwork of universities, research laboratories, military installations, organizations, and corporations. TCP/IP includes standards for how computers communicate and conventions for connecting networks and routing traffic, as well as specifications for utilities.

transport driver interface (TDI)   The interface between the session layer and the network layer; used by network redirectors and servers to send network-bound requests to network transport drivers.

Transport Layer Security (TLS)   A standard protocol that provides for secure Web traffic to and from the server. Clients can use TLS for server authentication, or it can be used to have servers authenticate clients.

traveling users   Users who are not at a stationary location and are accessing network resources either through a dial-up or Web-based link.

trust relationship   A security relationship between two domains in which the resource domain "trusts" the user of a trusted account domain to use its resources. Users and groups from a trusted domain can be given access permissions to resources in a trusting domain.

U

UNC   *See* Universal Naming Convention.

Unimodem   The universal modem driver used by TAPI to communicate with modems. It uses modem description files to control its interaction with VCOMM.

universal groups   Windows 2000 security groups that can exist in multiple domain tree Active Directory structures. These groups have access to every domain in the forest.

Universal Naming Convention (UNC)   Naming convention, including a server name and share name, used to give a unique name to files on a network. The format is as follows: *servername\ sharename\path\filename*.

UPS service   A software component that monitors an uninterruptible power supply and shuts the computer down gracefully when line power has failed and the UPS battery is running down.

V

value entry   A parameter under a key or subkey in the Registry. A value entry has three components: name, type, and value. The value component can be a string, binary data, or a DWORD.

VCOMM   A device drive within TAPI, which virtualizes the physical communication ports to the operating system.

virtual file allocation table   A file access system that uses protected-mode code to write to the disk. Used in FAT32 implementations.

virtual machine (VM)   An environment created by the operating system in memory. By using virtual machines, the application developer can write programs that behave as though they own the entire computer.

virtual memory   The technique by which Windows 2000 uses hard disk space to increase the amount of memory available for running programs.

virtual private networking (VPN)   Creates secure networks over the Internet by tunneling other network protocols through TCP/IP. In the Microsoft world this is implemented through PPTP (Point-to-Point Tunneling Protocol).

VPN   *See* virtual private networking.

VxD   Virtual device driver. The x represents the type of device. For example, a virtual device driver for a display is a VDD, and a virtual device driver for a printer is a VPD.

W

Win32 API   The 32-bit application programming interface used to write 32-bit Windows-based applications. It provides access to operating systems and other functions.

window name   A text string that identifies a window for the user.

Windows 2000 Backup   The built-in file backup and restore utility that is supplied with Windows 2000. Also called Microsoft Windows Backup.

Windows Internet Name Service (WINS)   A name resolution service that resolves Windows networking computer names to IP addresses in a routed environment. A WINS server handles name registrations, queries, and releases.

Windows NT file system (NTFS)   The native file system used by Windows 2000 and Windows NT. Windows 2000 can use NTFS version 5, FAT32, or FAT. It can detect, but not use, other partitions (such as HPFS).

WINS   *See* Windows Internet Name Service.

wizard   A tool that asks the user questions and performs a system action according to the user's answers. For example, use the Add Printer Wizard to add new printer drivers or connect to an existing network printer.

workgroup   A collection of computers that are grouped for viewing purposes, but don't share security information. Each workgroup is identified by a unique name. *See also* domain.

X

X.25   A connection-oriented network facility.

Index

A

access. *See also* secure access between networks
by external users to private networks, 130, 139–42
facilitating with multiple-tree forest, 16, 18
forest structure limiting, 15, 17
locking out remote access accounts, 26, 29
outsourcing remote, 140, 141
between private networks, 130, 133–37, 143–46
security required for Internet, 71
to shared folders, 176, 183, 186–87
troubleshooting Local Group Policy object, 66, 69
access controls
defined, 71
enabling with IPSec, 163
Account Locked Out checkbox, 26, 29
Active Directory
centralizing administration with stored policies, 216, 225
delegating administrative control, 14, 16
designing single tree with multiple sites, 248–49, 254
enterprise CAs and, 122
facilitating resource access with multiple-tree forest, 16, 18
forest structure designs for expansion, 10–11
limiting access with forest structure design, 15, 17
Active Directory Domains and Trusts snap-in, 162
administrative models, 2, 31–35
centralized and decentralized, 31, 32–33, 34–35
scenarios for centralized, 172, 179
supplemental readings, 4
tested skills and practices for analyzing, 2
Administrators group, 56, 58
Adventure Works, case study, 189–208
problem statement, 191–92
Q & A, 193–208
scenario, 189–91
Agent OU, 216, 225
AH (Authentication Header) protocol
authentication required, 8, 11
ESP incorporating, 259
with IPSec, 235, 244
lacking encryption, 179
Always Call Back To option, 28
anonymous user account, 194, 201
Audit Object Access category, 87, 181
audit policies, 78, 83–87
adding process tracking, 84, 86, 174, 176, 181, 188
auditing system log for viruses, 84, 86, 188

audit policies, *continued*
designing, 83
enabling auditing, 87, 181
halting computer when security log fills up, 84, 85
monitoring changes to permissions, 232, 238–39
setting auditing options, 84–85, 87
setting for personnel folders, 176, 188
suggested reading, 79–80
tested skills and practices, 78
for Web server to monitor Everyone group, 194, 202–3
authentication. *See also* Kerberos; smart cards
browser support for Windows, 259
certificate-based, 20–21, 22–23
configuring multiple VPNs with same, 195, 204–5
designing strategy, 79, 109–12
for dial-up connections, 235, 244
EAP-TLS, 149, 151, 175, 180–81, 185
with IAS, 10, 110–11
for Internet printing, 74
with Kerberos, 40, 214, 221, 250, 256
Kerberos-realm, 222
for LAN connections using Kerberos, 176, 187
managing remote user, 38, 40
managing with Group Policy, 230, 236
of previously registered Web visitors, 194, 201
required with AH protocol, 8, 11
selecting methods for VPNs, 110–11, 112
for sending encrypted PPP packets, 148, 149
SMB and mutual, 157
Authentication Header protocol. *See* AH protocol
Authenticode 2.0, 198, 202, 214, 221

B

background refreshes of Group Policy, 49, 53
backing up CD-RW drive, 27
bandwidth capacities and restrictions, 46
Basic authentication
for previously registered Web visitors, 194, 201
with SSL, 232, 238–39, 252, 259
Basic template, 160, 161, 162
Blue Yonder Airlines, case study, 167–88
problem statement, 171
Q & A, 172–88
scenario, 167–70
branch-office business model, 5
browser support with Basic authentication over SSL, 259
business models, 1, 5–11
designing domains and OUs for system migration, 6, 9
designing security for confidential data, 8, 11

business models, *continued*
    OU hierarchy in Windows 2000, 7, 10, 11
    overview, 5
    tested skills and practices, 1
business requirements for security, 1–42
    administrative models, 2, 31–35
    analyzing end user security requirements, 2, 25–30
    designing security after, 212, 217
    factors influencing company strategies, 2, 19–23
    identifying current security risks, 2, 37–42, 197, 207, 212, 218–19
    organizational structures, 2, 13–18
    reviewing business models, 1, 5–11
    supplemental readings, 3–4
    tested skills and practices, 1–2

C

CA (certificate authority) servers, 143
callback settings
    configuring RRAS, 20, 22, 26, 28, 234, 242
    for remote access users, 148, 150
CAs (certificate authorities), 119
    certificate-based authentication, 20–21, 22–23
    certificate trust lists, 122
    choosing commercial, 251, 257
    encryption for users when temporarily offline, 196, 206
    enterprise, 120, 121, 122, 193, 199
    enterprise subordinate, 215, 223
    hierarchy, 230, 235
    with implicit trust for each other, 250, 257
    issuing, 120, 121, 197, 207
    managing certificates for users with new computers, 215, 223
    stand-alone, 121, 122, 199, 257
    using third-party, 199
CD-RW drive, 27
centralized administrative model
    with Active Directory stored policies, 216, 225
    decentralized vs., 32–33, 34–35
    defined, 31
    recognizing, 32, 34
    scenarios, 172, 179
certificate authorities. *See* CAs
certificates. *See also* CAs
    certificate-based authentication, 20–21, 22–23
    client Read-only access, 193, 200
    digital, 119, 230, 235
    exporting to customers' new computers, 215, 223
    issued by EFS, 197, 206

certificates, *continued*
    mapping accounts to customer, 215, 224
    for regular e-commerce customers, 248, 254
    smart card, 214, 222
certificate trust lists, 122
Challenge/Response, 72, 74
CHAP, 151, 204, 205
charting organization structure, 2
child domains
    limiting access for project group with, 15, 17
    with shared resource access for business partners, 16, 18
CIFS (Common Internet File System). *See* SMB signing
Client (Respond Only) policy, 184, 185, 206
clients
    certificates providing Read-only access, 193, 200
    choosing templates to enable signing, 158, 161
    configuring for secure communications, 99, 101
    ensuring communications digitally signed, 158, 160
    permitting unsecured traffic with IPSec to accommodate older, 164, 165
cluster servers, 249, 255
commercial CAs, 251, 257
Common Internet File System (CIFS). *See* SMB signing
communication channels, 153–66
    designing IPSec solution for secure, 154, 163–66
    designing SMB-signing solution for secure, 154, 157–62, 234, 242
    subnet masking and secure, 196, 205
    supplemental reading, 154–55
    tested skills and practices, 154
Compatible template, 160, 161
computer local group, 113
Contoso, Ltd., case study, 245–60
    Q & A, 248–60
    scenario, 245–47
cookies, 194, 197, 201, 207
creating
    logical network diagram, 45–46
    physical network diagram, 45–46
    secure tunnel to company's server, 27, 30
    server clusters, 23
customers. *See also* e-commerce
    exporting certificates to new computers, 215, 223
    mapping accounts to customer certificates, 215, 224
    securing credit card information for established, 252, 259

D

data
    designing security for confidential, 8, 11
    IPSec transport mode protection, 250, 256

data, *continued*
  limiting access, 15, 17
  protecting on disks with EFS, 20, 22, 105, 107
  providing security for laptop real-time access, 27, 30
  retrieving with demand-dial connections, 195, 203
  securing LAN's transmitted, 216, 224
decentralized administrative model
  centralized vs., 32, 34
  decentralizing operations by delegating authority, 91, 94
  defined, 31
  recognizing, 32–33, 34–35
delegating authority, 78, 89–95
  in Active Directory, 14, 16
  to decentralize operations, 91, 94
  overview, 89
  with security groups, 56–57, 58–59, 72, 74–75
  with specific OUs, 92, 95
  tested skills and practices, 78
  to two security groups for project resources, 90, 93
demand-dial connections
  retrieving shared data, 195, 203
  for VPNs, 10
denial of service attacks, 39, 42
DES (Data Encryption Standard), 216, 225
designing
  analyzing business requirements before, 212, 217
  audit policies, 83
  authentication strategies, 79, 109–12
  baseline security for laptop computers, 67, 70
  domains, 6, 7, 9, 10–11
  EFS strategy, 78, 103–7
  forest structure, 10–11, 15, 17
  groups and users for printers, 232–33, 240
  IPSec solution for secure communications, 154, 163–66
  network services security, 79
  PKI, 79, 119–22
  remote access security, 131, 147–51
  security for confidential data, 8, 11
  security group strategies, 79, 113–17
  shared resource access for business partners, 16, 18
  single tree with multiple sites, 248–49, 254
  SMB-signing solution for secure communications, 154, 157–62, 234, 242
  technical environment to include security, 44, 55–59
  Windows 2000 security, 78–79
DHCP servers, 124–25, 126–27
dial-up connections
  certificate authentication, 235, 244
  configuring callback to specified number, 26, 28
  demand-dial, 10, 195, 203

dial-up connections, *continued*
  encrypted PPP connections for external users, 141, 142
  secure VPN, 27, 30
  transfer of confidential data, 11
dictionary attacks, 26
Digest authentication, 194, 201, 252, 259
digital certificates. *See* certificates
Directory Services Access, auditing modified permissions in, 232, 238–39
Distributed File System (DFS), 20, 22
DNS (Domain Name Service)
  accommodating DNS names, 35
  DNS round-robin distribution, 21, 23
  dynamic updates, 48, 52, 124, 126
  firewall protection for servers, 251, 258
  providing interoperability with UNIX servers, 14, 16
DNSProxyUpdate group, 124–25, 126–27
domain controllers
  requiring digital signature for traffic, 159, 162
  where to add, 49, 53
domain local groups
  assigning specific resources, 114, 116
  best uses, 176, 186
  defined, 113
  using for printer access, 232–33, 240
domains
  child, 15, 16, 17, 18
  delegating authority, 93
  designing, 6, 7, 9, 10–11
  master/resource model in Windows 2000, 7, 11
  placement and inheritance of security policies, 97
  placing security policies in GPO, 214, 222
dynamic rekeying, 260

E

EAP-MD5 CHAP, 112, 151, 205
EAP-TLS
  authenticating with smart cards, 149, 151, 175, 180–81, 185
  with Windows NT 4, 195, 204
e-commerce
  digital certificates for regular customers, 248, 254
  encryption, 194, 202
  securing customer credit card information, 252, 259
  using commercial CAs, 251, 257
EFS (Encrypting File System)
  confidentiality for sensitive data on laptops, 38, 41
  configuring laptop systems, 20, 22, 67, 70
  copying encrypted files to another drive, 104, 106

EFS (Encrypting File System), *continued*
   designing strategy, 78, 103–7
   encrypting IPSec traffic with ESP, 104, 107, 196, 205
   issuing certificate to user, 197, 206
   local security for laptop files and folders, 172, 178
   PKI implementation, 119
   protecting sensitive data on disks, 105, 107
   tested skills and practices, 78
   Windows support, 27, 30
e-mail, company-wide, 7, 10–11
Encapsulated Security Payload. *See* ESP
Encrypting File System. *See* EFS
encryption. *See also* EFS
   of confidential materials, 38, 40
   laws and regulations affecting, 19
   3DES, 180, 204
end users. *See* users
enterprise CAs, 120, 121, 122, 193, 199
enterprise subordinate CAs, 215, 223
ESP (Encapsulated Security Payload), 8, 11
   certificate-based authentication, 235, 244
   encrypting IPSec traffic, 104, 107, 196, 205
   gaining integrity and encryption, 252, 259
Everyone group, 183, 194, 202–3
external authenticated user, 25
external user access to private networks, 130, 139–42
   evaluating need for encrypted PPP dial-up connections,
      141, 142
   outsourcing remote access, 140, 141
   RAS and VPN solutions, 139
   RRAS with RADIUS authentication, 140, 142

F

Fabrikam, Inc., case study, 209–25
   problem statement, 210–11
   Q & A, 212–25
   scenario, 209–10
factors influencing company strategies, 2, 19–23
   handling rapid growth of Web server traffic, 21, 23
   overview, 19
   protecting unauthorized database access, 20–21, 22–23
   supplemental readings, 3
   tested skills and practices for analyzing, 2
FAT permissions, 73, 75
files
   copying encrypted files to another drive, 104, 106
   monitoring Everyone group for unauthorized access, 194,
      202–3
   providing EFS security, 172, 178

files, *continued*
   recovering protected EFS, 107
file systems. *See also* EFS
   DFS, 20, 22
   NTFS, 104, 106
   securing as network resource, 72, 74–75
   setting NTFS and FAT permissions for shared folder
      access, 73, 75
firewalls
   assessing current use, 55
   packet filtering to allow VPN traffic, 27, 30, 135, 137
   protecting DNS servers, 251, 258
folders
   monitoring Everyone group for unauthorized access, 194,
      202–3
   providing EFS security, 172, 178
   restricting access to shared, 176, 183, 186–87
   setting audit policies for sensitive data, 176, 188
forests
   designing for expansion, 10–11
   Kerberos adaptability, 47, 51
   multiple-tree, 15, 16, 17, 18, 248–49, 254
   structuring to limited access, 15, 17
Full Control access rights, 57, 58–59, 183, 231, 237

G

Gateway Service for NetWare, 110, 112
global groups
   defined, 113
   regulating access, 176, 186–87
   strategies, 116–17
   using for printer access, 232–33, 240
Group Policy
   background refreshes, 49, 53
   enabling audit policies, 181
   exempting members from Group Policy object, 115, 117
   inheritance, 98, 100, 173, 180–81
   managing authentication, 230, 236
   slow link detection setting, 49, 53
   Windows 2000, 26, 29, 117
Group Policy object, 115, 117

H

halting computer when security log full, 84, 85
hiding objects with OUs, 98, 100–1
High Secure template, 160, 161, 162
"Honeywell Europe S.A." (Microsoft), 3
HTTPS (Hypertext Transfer Protocol Secure), 70

I

IAS (Internet Authentication Services), 10, 110–11
ICS (Internet Connection Sharing), 129
identifying security risks, 37–42
    Internet connections and, 212, 218–19
    for laptop computers, 38, 40–41, 212, 218
    for network resources, 62, 71–75
    overview, 37
    providing data integrity and confidentiality with VPNs, 38, 41
    reviewing business models for risks, 1, 5–11
    supplemental readings, 4
    tested skills and practices, 2
    viruses and malicious code, 39, 42, 188
IIS (Internet Information Server)
    controlling Web-based resources with different anonymous accounts, 194, 201
    security for print servers, 74
IKE (Internet Key Exchange), 216, 225, 244, 255
implicit trust relationships, 250, 257
inheritance of group policies, 98, 100, 173, 180–81
integrated zones, 258
Internet
    as corporate security risk, 212, 218–19
    identifying security required for access, 71
    pass-through connections between intranet and, 134, 136
    preventing internal addresses from reaching, 233, 241
    protecting interface with VPN from unauthorized users, 48, 52
Internet Authentication Services (IAS), 10, 110–11
Internet Connection Sharing (ICS), 129
Internet Key Exchange (IKE), 216, 225, 244, 255
Internet printing, 74
Internet Protocol Security. *See* IPSec
Internet user, 25
intranets
    Internet connections, 134, 136
    securing connections between subnets, 144, 145
IP address filtering, 26, 28
IPSec (Internet Protocol Security). *See also* ESP
    data security between servers on same network, 173, 179
    designing secure communications, 153, 154, 163–66
    dynamic rekeying and, 260
    enabling packet filtering, 164, 165
    encrypting traffic with ESP, 104, 107, 196, 205, 252, 259
    implementing secure client communications, 99, 101
    IP spoofing protection, 233, 241
    not operable with UNIX, 17
    permitting unsecured traffic for older clients, 164, 165
    predefined security settings, 206

IPSec (Internet Protocol Security), *continued*
    protecting transmitted data on LAN, 216, 224
    providing encryption services, 184
    secure Internet connections with L2TP over, 163, 248, 253
    Secure Server (Require Security) policy, 101, 175, 184–85
    setting policies for diverse needs, 144, 146, 234, 243
    SNMP message protection, 125, 127
    testing policies, 66, 68
    transferring confidential information, 8, 11
    transport mode, 250, 256
    Windows 98 SE computers unaware, 164, 166
IPSec Monitoring Tool, 260
IP spoofing, 233, 241
issuing CAs, 120, 121, 197, 207

K

Kerberos
    adaptability to forest structures, 47, 51
    authentication, 40
    as default Windows 2000 network authentication protocol, 214, 221
    protecting transmitted data on LAN, 216, 224
    selecting, 250, 256
    unsupported by PPTP, 205
    using with LAN connections, 176, 187
    on Windows NT and Windows 2000, 14, 16
Kerberos-realm authentication, 222

L

L2TP (Layer Two Tunneling Protocol), 8, 11
    e-commerce inappropriate, 194, 202
    mutual computer authentication, 145
    for secure Internet connections, 163, 248, 253
    security advantages, 48, 52
LANs (local area networks)
    IPSec policy for users with different needs, 144, 146
    Kerberos authentication for connections, 176, 187
    protecting transmitted data, 216, 224
laptop computers
    authenticating users with RADIUS, 38, 40
    designing security baseline, 67, 70
    providing EFS security for files and folders, 105, 107, 172, 178
    providing secure real-time database access, 27, 30
    securing link to server with VPN, 232, 239
    security risks of, 38, 40–41, 212, 218
Layer Two Tunneling Protocol. *See* L2TP

legacy applications, 50, 54, 56, 58
local area networks. *See* LANs
Local Group Policy object, 66, 69
logical network diagram, 45–46
logon with smart card, 230, 236

M

macro viruses, 39, 42
malicious code, 39, 42
mapping customer accounts to customer certificates, 215, 224
master domains in Windows 2000, 7, 11
master/resource domain model, 7, 9, 11, 17, 33, 35
*MCSE Training Kit: Designing Microsoft Windows 2000
    Network Security*, 3, 4
*Microsoft Windows 2000 Server Deployment Planning
    Guide*, 3
*Microsoft Windows 2000 Server TCP/IP Core Networking
    Guide*, 4
migrating to Windows 2000
    designing domains and OUs, 6, 9
    reviewing business models before, 1, 5–11
    troubleshooting application problems after, 57, 59
mission statements, 2
MPPE (Microsoft Point-to-Point Encryption), 70, 195, 204
MS-CHAP v.2, 112, 150
multiple-domain single-tree structure, 33, 35
multiple-tree forest, 15, 17
    evaluating need, 248–49, 254
    facilitating resource access, 16, 18
multiprocessor scaling, 21, 23
mutual computer authentication with L2TP, 145

N

NAT (network address translation), 233, 241
national model of businesses, 5
nesting groups, 116
network load balancing, 23, 249, 255
networks. *See also* private networks; secure access between
        networks; VPNs
    designing shared resources for business partners, 16, 18
    domain design for expanding infrastructure, 7, 10–11
    evaluating TCO, 19, 212, 218
    identifying security required, 62, 71–75
    providing acceptable security and performance, 49, 53
    public, 130, 133–37
    secure connections between private and public, 130,
        133–37
network security. *See* requirements for network security;
        security

network services security, 79, 123–27
    adding DHCP servers to DNSProxyUpdate group, 124–25,
        126–27
    designing for Windows 2000, 79
    DNS dynamic updates not accepted, 124, 126
    maintaining NetWare file and print services, 110, 112
    overview, 123
    with SNMP service, 125, 127
Novell NetWare file and print services, 110, 112
NTFS file system, 104, 106
NTFS permissions, 73, 75, 231, 237
NTLM (Windows NT LAN Manager), 17

O

organizational structures, 2, 13–18
    developing company's organization chart, 13
    facilitating resource access with multiple-tree forest,
        16, 18
    incorporating Active Directory, DNS dynamic update, and
        Kerberos, 14, 16–17
    limiting access to with forest structure design, 15, 17
    supplemental readings about analyzing, 3
    tested skills and practices, 2
OU hierarchy
    determining, 231, 237
    limiting access for projects, 15, 17
    in Windows 2000, 7, 10, 11
OUs (organizational units)
    delegating authority with specific, 92, 95
    delegating control, 89
    determining hierarchy, 231, 237
    hiding objects, 98, 100–1
    hierarchical structure, 7, 10, 11
    placement and inheritance of security policies, 97, 173,
        180–81
    placing servers for secure communications in own, 177
    structuring for information flow requirements, 6, 9
outsourcing
    IT management, 31
    remote access, 140, 141

P

packet filtering
    for IPSec traffic on Internet interface, 164, 165
    perimeter networks and, 219
    PPTP, 144, 145
    of VPN traffic through firewalls, 27, 30, 135, 137
PAP authentication, 151

pass-through VPN connections, 134, 136
Peer Web Services (PWS), 74
performance
    effect of SMB on CPU, 157
    providing acceptable network security and, 49, 53
perimeter networks, 213, 219, 233, 241
permissions
    auditing changes, 232, 238–39
    designating two security groups to administer, 93
    Full Control access rights, 57, 58–59, 183, 231, 237
    granting for security groups, 174, 182
    running legacy applications from Power Users group, 50, 54, 56, 58
    setting temporary access to printers, 198, 208
physical consolidation of servers, 213, 221
physical network diagram, 45
PKI (public key infrastructure). *See also* CAs
    designing, 79, 119–22
    importance, 46
    in securing links between laptops and servers, 232, 239
    setting up certificate-based authentication, 20–21, 22–23, 250, 256
    smart card certificates and, 214, 222
placement of security policies, 78, 97–101
Point-to-Point Encryption (MPPE), 70, 195, 204
Point-to-Point Protocol. *See* PPP
Point-to-Point Tunneling Protocol. *See* PPTP
Power Users group
    delegating administrative control, 72, 74–75
    running legacy applications, 50, 54, 56, 58, 59
PPP (Point-to-Point Protocol)
    about, 70
    choosing authentication protocol to send encrypted packets, 148, 149
    encrypted dial-up connections for external users, 141, 142
PPTP (Point-to-Point Tunneling Protocol)
    encryption for VPNs using Windows NT 4 operating system, 195, 204
    Kerberos unsupported by, 205
    packet filtering, 144, 145
preshared key authentication, 259
printers
    designing groups and users, 232–33, 240
    granting temporary access, 198, 208
    identifying required security for network, 71
printing, Internet, 72, 74
private network addressing, 233, 241
private networks, 130, 133–37, 143–46. *See also* external user access to private networks; VPNs
    configuring PPTP packet filtering, 144, 145

private networks, *continued*
    external user access, 130, 139–42
    IPSec policy for users on same LAN with different needs, 144, 146
    with secure connections to public networks, 130, 133–37
    securing connections between subnets on same network, 144, 145
Privilege Use event, 239
process tracking, 84, 86, 174, 176, 181, 188
protocols. *See also* specific protocols
    authentication by IAS, 111
    selecting for secure network communications, 175, 184
proxy servers
    about, 133
    preventing internal addresses from reaching Internet, 233, 241
    security provided by, 26, 28
public key infrastructure. *See* PKI
public networks, 130, 133–37
PWS (Peer Web Services), 74

R

RADIUS (Remote Authentication Dial-In User Service)
    authenticating laptop users, 38, 40
    managing remote access users with RADIUS server, 234, 242
    RRAS, 140, 142
RAS (Remote Access Service)
    using VPNs and, 139
    VPN encryption services for remote users, 195, 204
recovering protected EFS files, 107
regional offices, 5
remote access. *See also* remote access users
    demand-dial routing vs., 195, 203
    enabling account lockouts, 26, 29
    outsourcing, 140, 141
Remote Access Service. *See* RAS
remote access users, 131, 147–51. *See also* dial-up connections
    in Blue Yonder Airlines scenario, 172, 178
    choosing authentication protocol to send encrypted PPP packets, 148, 149
    configuring callback settings, 148, 150
    EAP-TLS authentication with smart cards, 149, 151, 180–81
    managing with RADIUS server, 234, 242
    testing objectives, 147
Remote Authentication Dial-In User Service. *See* RADIUS

replication latency, 26, 29
requirements for network security, 61–75
    assigning folder permissions for FAT and NTFS volumes,
        73, 75
    designing security baseline, 61–62, 65–70
    identifying appropriate security for network resources, 62,
        71–75
    overview, 61
    supplemental reading, 63
    tested skills and practices, 61–62
RIS (Remote Installation Services), 123
risk management, 38–39, 41
roaming user, 25
root domain, 213, 220
router, operating Windows 2000 system as, 249, 255
router-to-router VPN connections, 134, 136–37
routing protocols, binding to Internet interface, 48, 52
RRAS (Routing and Remote Access Service)
    configuring callback security, 20, 22, 26, 28, 234, 242
    with RADIUS authentication, 140, 142
    setting input and output permit filters, 48, 52
    unlocking user accounts, 26, 29

S

SAs (security associations), 252, 260
secure access between networks, 129–51
    designing Windows 2000 for remote access users, 131,
        147–51
    from private to public network, 130, 133–37
    providing external users with access to private networks,
        130, 139–42
    securing access between private networks, 130, 143–46
    services used, 129–30
    skills and practices, 130–31
    supplemental readings, 131–32
secure communications
    configuring client computers, 99, 101
    ensuring laptop communication security with VPNs, 67, 70
    providing SSL, 20–21, 23
    between servers, 47, 51
Secure Server (Require Security) policy, 101, 175, 184–85
Secure template, 160, 161, 162
Secure Web transactions, 47, 51
security. *See also* secure access between networks; security
        baseline
    analyzing requirements for network, 61–75
    assessing risk-management plans, 38–39, 41
    business requirements and security design, 212, 217
    delegating administrative control, 56–57, 58–59
    evaluating company's tolerance for breaches, 19

security, *continued*
    evaluating technical environment, 43, 45–54
    identifying risks, 2, 37–42, 197, 207
    impact of design on technical environment, 44, 55–59
    information flow and, 2, 13–18
    for laptop access of real-time database, 27, 30
    for malicious code, 39, 42
    maximizing for deployed sales force, 20, 22
    preventing unauthorized database access, 20–21, 22–23
    protecting confidential data, 8, 11
    reviewing business models for risks, 1, 5–11
    for routers, 25, 249
    secure communications between servers, 47, 51
    types of templates, 160, 161, 162
    vulnerability of DNS and multiple-tree structures, 35
security associations (SAs), 252, 260
security baseline, 61–62, 65–70
    overview, 65
    for remote users' laptop computers, 67, 70
    testing IPSec policies, 66, 68
    troubleshooting administrator access problems, 66, 69
Security Configuration Manager, 58
security groups
    Administrators, 56, 58
    delegating administrative control, 56–57, 58–59
    delegating authority for project resources to two, 90, 93
    designing strategies, 79, 113–17
    exempting members from Group Policy object, 115, 117
    function, 101
    granting permissions, 174, 182
    inheritance of group policies, 98, 100
    moving from universal to global groups, 114, 116
    nesting, 116
    placement of, 47, 51, 78, 97–101
    regulating access to shared folders, 176, 186–87
    running legacy applications from Power Users, 50, 54,
        56, 58
security policies, 78, 97–101
    components necessary to implement for field agents,
        216, 225
    configuring client computers for secure communications,
        99, 101
    in GPO at domain level, 214, 222
    hiding objects with OUs, 98, 100–1
    inheritance, 98, 100, 173, 180–81
    overview, 97
    tested skills and practices, 78
security templates
    choosing for Windows NT 4 computers, 213, 220
    choosing to enable client and server signing, 158, 161

security templates, *continued*
  types, 160, 161, 162
Security Templates snap-in, 160
server clusters, 23
Server Gated Cryptography (SGC) protocol, 214, 221
server message block signing. *See* SMB signing
Server (Request Security) policy, 206
servers
  certificate authority, 143
  choosing security templates to enable signing, 158, 161
  data security between same-network, 173, 179
  ensuring all communications digitally signed, 158, 160
  forests and effect on secure communications between, 47, 51
  handling growing traffic on Web server, 21, 23
  physical consolidation, 213, 221
  placing in own OU, 177
  securing link to laptop with VPN, 232, 239
  types of certificate server roles, 119
Set By Caller option, 29
SGC (Server Gated Cryptography) protocol, 214, 221
Simple Network Management Protocol. *See* SNMP
single domain structures
  administering for limited access projects, 15, 17
  evaluating for decentralized models, 33, 35
single tree with multiple sites, 248–49, 254
sites
  placement and inheritance of security policies, 97
  placement of domain-level policies, 222
  single tree with multiple, 248–49, 254
smart cards
  authentication, 149, 151, 175, 180–81, 185, 213, 220
  expense, 251, 258
  implementing CA hierarchy before authenticating, 230, 235
  requirements for certificates and PKI infrastructure, 214, 222
  requiring user logon, 230, 236
SMB (server message block) signing, 153, 154, 157–62
  about, 153
  effect of on CPU performance, 157
  enabling client and server signing, 158, 161
  ensuring all communications digitally signed, 158, 160
  requesting (not requiring), 234, 242
  requiring domain controller traffic to be digitally signed, 159, 162
SMS (Systems Management Server), 45
SNMP (Simple Network Management Protocol)
  network services security, 125, 127
  unnecessary with centralized equipment, 233, 240–41
SPAP, 151, 204

SQL servers, 249, 255
SSL (Secure Sockets Layer)
  basic authentication, 232, 238–39, 252, 259
  encrypting private data, 194, 202
  implementing, 70
  providing confidential communications, 20–21, 23
  for Web secure channels, 250, 256
stand-alone CAs
  about, 121, 122, 199
  issuing certificates for secure VPN channel, 251, 258
  receiving commercial CA's certificate offline, 257
static routing, 48, 52
subnet masking, 196, 205
subtrees, 89
supplemental readings
  for analyzing business requirements, 3–4
  for communication channels, 154–55
  on designing secure access between networks, 131–32
  for network security requirements, 63
  for technical requirements of network security, 44
  for Windows 2000 security solutions, 79–82
Systems Management Server (SMS), 45

T

TCO (total cost of operations)
  impact on security, 212, 217
  for networks, 19, 212, 218
technical environment, 43, 45–54
  diagraming logical and physical network, 45–46
  including security in design, 44, 55–59
technical requirements of network security, 43–59
  analyzing security design on technical environment, 44, 55–59
  application problems after migrating to Windows 2000, 57, 59
  delegating administrative control, 56–57, 58–59
  evaluating technical environment, 43, 45–54
  forest planning and, 47, 51
  maintaining legacy applications, 50, 54, 56, 58
  network performance, 49, 53
  overview, 43
  supplemental readings, 44
  tested skills and practices, 43–44
templates. *See* security templates
Terminal Services, 123, 129
tested skills
  for analyzing business requirements, 1–2
  for designing security for communication channels, 154
  for designing Windows 2000 security, 78–79

tested skills, *continued*
   for secure access between networks, 130–31
   for technical requirements of network security, 43–44
   for Windows 2000 network security requirements, 61–62
testing
   audit strategies, 83
   IPSec policies, 66, 68
   of Windows 2000 logo applications, 214, 221
third-party CAs, 199
3DES encryption, 180, 204
TLS (Transport Level Security) with smart cards, 149, 151, 175, 180–81, 185
total cost of operations. *See* TCO
tracking. *See* audit policies
traveling user, defined, 25
tree design. *See also* multiple-tree forest
   security requirements and, 177
   single tree with multiple sites, 248–49, 254
   subtrees, 89
Trey Research, case study, 227–44
   Q & A, 230–44
   scenario, 227–29
Trojan horse, 39, 42, 188
troubleshooting
   access problems with Local Group Policy object, 66, 69
   application problems after migrating to Windows 2000, 57, 59
trusts, 117

U

unauthorized authentication, 207
UNC (Universal Naming Convention), 237
universal groups
   defined, 113
   regulating access, 114, 116–17, 176, 187
Universal Naming Convention (UNC), 237
UNIX servers, interoperability with, 14, 16
user accounts
   anonymous, 194, 201
   lockout for remote, 26
   placement in forest, 47, 51
   unlocking, 26, 29
users, 2, 25–30
   categories, 2, 25
   configuring callback to specified number, 26, 28
   enabling remote access account lockouts, 26, 29
   exempting from Group Policy object, 115, 117
   granting permissions to through security groups, 174, 182
   laptop access to real-time database, 27, 30
   logging on with smart card, 230, 236

users, *continued*
   managing authentication of remote, 38, 40
   running legacy applications from Power Users group, 50, 54, 56, 58
   supplemental readings on security analysis, 4
   tested skills and practices for analyzing security, 2

V

vendors, 2
virtual private networks. *See* VPNs
virus detection software, 55
viruses
   auditing system log, 84, 86, 188
   as security risk, 39, 42
VPNs (virtual private networks)
   allowing through firewalls, 27, 30, 135, 137
   authentication methods, 110–11, 112
   components of connections, 133
   configuring multiple, 195, 204–5
   connecting subnets on same network, 144, 145
   creating secure tunnel to company's server, 27, 30
   data integrity and confidentiality, 38, 41
   demand-dial connections, 10
   ensuring laptop communication security, 67, 70, 232, 239
   L2TP over IPSec security, 248, 253
   locking out remote access account, 26, 29
   pass-through connections, 134, 136
   protecting Internet interface from unauthorized users, 48, 52
   router-to-router connections, 134, 136–37
   secure data transfers, 11
   using RAS and, 139

W

Web secure channels, 250, 256
Web servers. *See also* e-commerce
   handling rapid growth of traffic, 21, 23
   monitoring unauthorized access to files and folders, 194, 202–3
   network load balancing, 249, 255
Web sites
   anonymous user accounts, 194, 201
   authenticating Web secure channels, 250, 256
Windows 98 SE, 164, 166
Windows NT 4
   delegation of authority, 93
   PPTP encryption for VPNs, 195, 204
   redesigning domain model for Windows 2000 domains, 9

Windows NT 4, *continued*
   security templates, 213, 220
Windows NT LAN Manager (NTLM), 17
Windows 2000, 77–127
   audit policies, 78, 83–87
   authentication strategies, 79, 109–12
   delegating authority, 78, 89–95
   designing for remote access users, 131, 147–51
   domain design, 6, 9
   EFS strategies, 78, 103–7
   enabling auditing, 87
   Group Policy, 26, 29, 117
   Internet printing, 74
   NetWare file and print services, 110, 112
   network services security, 79, 123–27
   operating system as router, 249, 255
   overview, 77–78
   PKI, 79, 119–22
   placing security policies, 78, 97–101

Windows 2000, *continued*
   retrofitting security to Windows NT 4, 56, 58
   reviewing business models before migrating to, 1, 5–11
   security group strategies, 79, 113–17
   security templates, 160, 161
   supplemental reading for network solutions, 79–82
   tested skills and practices for network solutions, 78–79
   troubleshooting application problems after migrating, 57, 59
Windows 2000 Advanced Server, 21, 23
Windows 2000 Professional, 27, 30
Windows 2000 Server Clustering, 21, 23
Windows 2000 Server Resource Kit, 3
Windows 2000 System Administrator's Black Book, 4

Z

zones, 258

Readiness Reviews
Test your readiness
for the MCSE exams

For the skills you need on the job.
And on the MCP exam.

Learn by doing—learn for the job—with official MCSE TRAINING KITS. Whether you choose a book-and-CD Training Kit or the all-multimedia learning experience of an Online Training Kit, you'll gain hands-on experience building essential systems support skills—as you prepare for the corresponding MCP exam. It's official Microsoft self-paced training—how, when, and where you study best.

Windows 2000 Track

MCSE Training Kit, Microsoft® Windows® 2000 Core Requirements
ISBN 0-7356-1130-0

MCSE Training Kit, Microsoft Windows 2000 Server
ISBN 1-57231-903-8

MCSE Online Training Kit, Microsoft Windows 2000 Server
ISBN 0-7356-0954-3
COMING SOON

MCSE Training Kit, Microsoft Windows 2000 Professional
ISBN 1-57231-901-1

MCSE Online Training Kit, Microsoft Windows 2000 Professional
ISBN 0-7356-0953-5
COMING SOON

MCSE Training Kit, Microsoft Windows 2000 Active Directory™ Services
ISBN 0-7356-0999-3

MCSE Training Kit, Microsoft Windows 2000 Network Infrastructure Administration
ISBN 1-57231-904-6

Upgrading to Microsoft Windows 2000 Training Kit
ISBN 0-7356-0940-3

Microsoft SQL Server™ 7.0 System Administration Online Training Kit
ISBN 0-7356-0678-1

Windows NT® 4.0 Track

Microsoft Certified Systems Engineer Core Requirements Training Kit
ISBN 1-57231-905-4

MCSE Training Kit, Networking Essentials Plus, Third Edition
ISBN 1-57231-902-X

MCSE Online Training Kit, Networking Essentials Plus
ISBN 0-7356-0880-6

Electives

Microsoft SQL Server 7.0 Database Implementation Training Kit
ISBN 1-57231-826-0

Microsoft SQL Server 7.0 Database Implementation Online Training Kit
ISBN 0-7356-0679-X

Microsoft SQL Server 7.0 System Administration Training Kit
ISBN 1-57231-827-9

Microsoft®
mspress.microsoft.com

The practical *guide* to
Windows 2000 Server
planning, deployment, and maintenance—
straight from the **experts!**

Microsoft

Microsoft
Windows 2000 Server Administrator's Companion

The expert guide to planning, deployment, and maintenance

Charlie Russel
Sharon Crawford

IT Professional

U.S.A.	**$69.99**
U.K.	£45.99 [V.A.T. included]
Canada	$107.99
ISBN: 1-57231-819-8	

Microsoft® Windows® 2000 Server provides landmark advances in network management, hardware support, Internet access, directory services, and more. Get up to speed fast on this operating system with the MICROSOFT WINDOWS 2000 SERVER ADMINISTRATOR'S COMPANION. It's the essential everyday resource for IT professionals who need to install, configure, and maintain Windows 2000 Server in their organizations. Appendixes provide quick guides to interface changes and optional components in Windows 2000 Server, and an enclosed CD-ROM gives you more than 20 practical, timesaving utilities, plus an electronic copy of the book. You'll learn all about how to:

- Prepare for installation
- Install and configure
- Use support services and features
- Use Internet services
- Tune, maintain, and repair

Microsoft®
mspress.microsoft.com

MICROSOFT LICENSE AGREEMENT

Book Companion CD

IMPORTANT—READ CAREFULLY: This Microsoft End-User License Agreement ("EULA") is a legal agreement between you (either an individual or an entity) and Microsoft Corporation for the Microsoft product identified above, which includes computer software and may include associated media, printed materials, and "online" or electronic documentation ("SOFTWARE PRODUCT"). Any component included within the SOFTWARE PRODUCT that is accompanied by a separate End-User License Agreement shall be governed by such agreement and not the terms set forth below. By installing, copying, or otherwise using the SOFTWARE PRODUCT, you agree to be bound by the terms of this EULA. If you do not agree to the terms of this EULA, you are not authorized to install, copy, or otherwise use the SOFTWARE PRODUCT; you may, however, return the SOFTWARE PRODUCT, along with all printed materials and other items that form a part of the Microsoft product that includes the SOFTWARE PRODUCT, to the place you obtained them for a full refund.

SOFTWARE PRODUCT LICENSE

The SOFTWARE PRODUCT is protected by United States copyright laws and international copyright treaties, as well as other intellectual property laws and treaties. The SOFTWARE PRODUCT is licensed, not sold.

1. **GRANT OF LICENSE.** This EULA grants you the following rights:

    a. **Software Product.** You may install and use one copy of the SOFTWARE PRODUCT on a single computer. The primary user of the computer on which the SOFTWARE PRODUCT is installed may make a second copy for his or her exclusive use on a portable computer.

    b. **Storage/Network Use.** You may also store or install a copy of the SOFTWARE PRODUCT on a storage device, such as a network server, used only to install or run the SOFTWARE PRODUCT on your other computers over an internal network; however, you must acquire and dedicate a license for each separate computer on which the SOFTWARE PRODUCT is installed or run from the storage device. A license for the SOFTWARE PRODUCT may not be shared or used concurrently on different computers.

    c. **License Pak.** If you have acquired this EULA in a Microsoft License Pak, you may make the number of additional copies of the computer software portion of the SOFTWARE PRODUCT authorized on the printed copy of this EULA, and you may use each copy in the manner specified above. You are also entitled to make a corresponding number of secondary copies for portable computer use as specified above.

    d. **Sample Code.** Solely with respect to portions, if any, of the SOFTWARE PRODUCT that are identified within the SOFTWARE PRODUCT as sample code (the "SAMPLE CODE"):

    i. **Use and Modification.** Microsoft grants you the right to use and modify the source code version of the SAMPLE CODE, *provided* you comply with subsection (d)(iii) below. You may not distribute the SAMPLE CODE, or any modified version of the SAMPLE CODE, in source code form.

    ii. **Redistributable Files.** Provided you comply with subsection (d)(iii) below, Microsoft grants you a nonexclusive, royalty-free right to reproduce and distribute the object code version of the SAMPLE CODE and of any modified SAMPLE CODE, other than SAMPLE CODE, or any modified version thereof, designated as not redistributable in the Readme file that forms a part of the SOFTWARE PRODUCT (the "Non-Redistributable Sample Code"). All SAMPLE CODE other than the Non-Redistributable Sample Code is collectively referred to as the "REDISTRIBUTABLES."

    iii. **Redistribution Requirements.** If you redistribute the REDISTRIBUTABLES, you agree to: (i) distribute the REDISTRIBUTABLES in object code form only in conjunction with and as a part of your software application product; (ii) not use Microsoft's name, logo, or trademarks to market your software application product; (iii) include a valid copyright notice on your software application product; (iv) indemnify, hold harmless, and defend Microsoft from and against any claims or lawsuits, including attorney's fees, that arise or result from the use or distribution of your software application product; and (v) not permit further distribution of the REDISTRIBUTABLES by your end user. Contact Microsoft for the applicable royalties due and other licensing terms for all other uses and/or distribution of the REDISTRIBUTABLES.

2. **DESCRIPTION OF OTHER RIGHTS AND LIMITATIONS.**

    - **Limitations on Reverse Engineering, Decompilation, and Disassembly.** You may not reverse engineer, decompile, or disassemble the SOFTWARE PRODUCT, except and only to the extent that such activity is expressly permitted by applicable law notwithstanding this limitation.

    - **Separation of Components.** The SOFTWARE PRODUCT is licensed as a single product. Its component parts may not be separated for use on more than one computer.

    - **Rental.** You may not rent, lease, or lend the SOFTWARE PRODUCT.

- **Support Services.** Microsoft may, but is not obligated to, provide you with support services related to the SOFTWARE PRODUCT ("Support Services"). Use of Support Services is governed by the Microsoft policies and programs described in the user manual, in "online" documentation, and/or in other Microsoft-provided materials. Any supplemental software code provided to you as part of the Support Services shall be considered part of the SOFTWARE PRODUCT and subject to the terms and conditions of this EULA. With respect to technical information you provide to Microsoft as part of the Support Services, Microsoft may use such information for its business purposes, including for product support and development. Microsoft will not utilize such technical information in a form that personally identifies you.

- **Software Transfer.** You may permanently transfer all of your rights under this EULA, provided you retain no copies, you transfer all of the SOFTWARE PRODUCT (including all component parts, the media and printed materials, any upgrades, this EULA, and, if applicable, the Certificate of Authenticity), **and** the recipient agrees to the terms of this EULA.

- **Termination.** Without prejudice to any other rights, Microsoft may terminate this EULA if you fail to comply with the terms and conditions of this EULA. In such event, you must destroy all copies of the SOFTWARE PRODUCT and all of its component parts.

3. **COPYRIGHT.** All title and copyrights in and to the SOFTWARE PRODUCT (including but not limited to any images, photographs, animations, video, audio, music, text, SAMPLE CODE, REDISTRIBUTABLES, and "applets" incorporated into the SOFTWARE PRODUCT) and any copies of the SOFTWARE PRODUCT are owned by Microsoft or its suppliers. The SOFT-WARE PRODUCT is protected by copyright laws and international treaty provisions. Therefore, you must treat the SOFTWARE PRODUCT like any other copyrighted material **except** that you may install the SOFTWARE PRODUCT on a single computer provided you keep the original solely for backup or archival purposes. You may not copy the printed materials accompanying the SOFTWARE PRODUCT.

4. **U.S. GOVERNMENT RESTRICTED RIGHTS.** The SOFTWARE PRODUCT and documentation are provided with RESTRICTED RIGHTS. Use, duplication, or disclosure by the Government is subject to restrictions as set forth in subparagraph (c)(1)(ii) of the Rights in Technical Data and Computer Software clause at DFARS 252.227-7013 or subparagraphs (c)(1) and (2) of the Commercial Computer Software—Restricted Rights at 48 CFR 52.227-19, as applicable. Manufacturer is Microsoft Corporation/One Microsoft Way/Redmond, WA 98052-6399.

5. **EXPORT RESTRICTIONS.** You agree that you will not export or re-export the SOFTWARE PRODUCT, any part thereof, or any process or service that is the direct product of the SOFTWARE PRODUCT (the foregoing collectively referred to as the "Restricted Components"), to any country, person, entity, or end user subject to U.S. export restrictions. You specifically agree not to export or re-export any of the Restricted Components (i) to any country to which the U.S. has embargoed or restricted the export of goods or services, which currently include, but are not necessarily limited to, Cuba, Iran, Iraq, Libya, North Korea, Sudan, and Syria, or to any national of any such country, wherever located, who intends to transmit or transport the Restricted Components back to such country; (ii) to any end user who you know or have reason to know will utilize the Restricted Components in the design, development, or production of nuclear, chemical, or biological weapons; or (iii) to any end user who has been prohibited from participating in U.S. export transactions by any federal agency of the U.S. government. You warrant and represent that neither the BXA nor any other U.S. federal agency has suspended, revoked, or denied your export privileges.

DISCLAIMER OF WARRANTY

NO WARRANTIES OR CONDITIONS. MICROSOFT EXPRESSLY DISCLAIMS ANY WARRANTY OR CONDITION FOR THE SOFTWARE PRODUCT. THE SOFTWARE PRODUCT AND ANY RELATED DOCUMENTATION ARE PROVIDED "AS IS" WITHOUT WARRANTY OR CONDITION OF ANY KIND, EITHER EXPRESS OR IMPLIED, INCLUDING, WITHOUT LIMITA-TION, THE IMPLIED WARRANTIES OF MERCHANTABILITY, FITNESS FOR A PARTICULAR PURPOSE, OR NONINFRINGEMENT. THE ENTIRE RISK ARISING OUT OF USE OR PERFORMANCE OF THE SOFTWARE PRODUCT REMAINS WITH YOU.

LIMITATION OF LIABILITY. TO THE MAXIMUM EXTENT PERMITTED BY APPLICABLE LAW, IN NO EVENT SHALL MICROSOFT OR ITS SUPPLIERS BE LIABLE FOR ANY SPECIAL, INCIDENTAL, INDIRECT, OR CONSEQUENTIAL DAM-AGES WHATSOEVER (INCLUDING, WITHOUT LIMITATION, DAMAGES FOR LOSS OF BUSINESS PROFITS, BUSINESS INTERRUPTION, LOSS OF BUSINESS INFORMATION, OR ANY OTHER PECUNIARY LOSS) ARISING OUT OF THE USE OF OR INABILITY TO USE THE SOFTWARE PRODUCT OR THE PROVISION OF OR FAILURE TO PROVIDE SUPPORT SERVICES, EVEN IF MICROSOFT HAS BEEN ADVISED OF THE POSSIBILITY OF SUCH DAMAGES. IN ANY CASE, MICROSOFT'S ENTIRE LIABILITY UNDER ANY PROVISION OF THIS EULA SHALL BE LIMITED TO THE GREATER OF THE AMOUNT ACTUALLY PAID BY YOU FOR THE SOFTWARE PRODUCT OR US$5.00; PROVIDED, HOWEVER, IF YOU HAVE ENTERED INTO A MICROSOFT SUPPORT SERVICES AGREEMENT, MICROSOFT'S ENTIRE LIABILITY REGARDING SUPPORT SERVICES SHALL BE GOVERNED BY THE TERMS OF THAT AGREEMENT. BECAUSE SOME STATES AND JURISDICTIONS DO NOT ALLOW THE EXCLUSION OR LIMITATION OF LIABILITY, THE ABOVE LIMITATION MAY NOT APPLY TO YOU.

MISCELLANEOUS

This EULA is governed by the laws of the State of Washington USA, except and only to the extent that applicable law mandates governing law of a different jurisdiction.

Should you have any questions concerning this EULA, or if you desire to contact Microsoft for any reason, please contact the Microsoft subsidiary serving your country, or write: Microsoft Sales Information Center/One Microsoft Way/Redmond, WA 98052-6399.

PN 097-0002296

Get a **Free**
e-mail newsletter, updates,
special offers, links to related books,
and more when you

register on line!

Register your Microsoft Press® title on our Web site and you'll get a FREE subscription to our e-mail newsletter, *Microsoft Press Book Connections.* You'll find out about newly released and upcoming books and learning tools, online events, software downloads, special offers and coupons for Microsoft Press customers, and information about major Microsoft® product releases. You can also read useful additional information about all the titles we publish, such as detailed book descriptions, tables of contents and indexes, sample chapters, links to related books and book series, author biographies, and reviews by other customers.

Registration is easy. Just visit this Web page and fill in your information:

http://mspress.microsoft.com/register

Microsoft

System Requirements

To use this book's Readiness Review compact disc, you need a computer equipped with the following minimum configuration:

- Microsoft Windows 95 or Microsoft Windows NT 4 with Service Pack 3 or later, or Microsoft Windows 98, Microsoft Windows Me, or Microsoft Windows 2000

- Multimedia PC with a 75-MHz Pentium or higher processor

- 16 MB RAM for Windows 95 or Windows 98, or

- 32 MB RAM for Windows Me or Windows NT, or

- 64 MB RAM for Windows 2000

- Microsoft Internet Explorer 5.01 or 5.5

- 17 MB of available hard drive space for installation (additional 70 MB minimum of hard disk space to install Internet Explorer 5.5 from this CD-ROM)

- A double-speed CD-ROM drive or better

- Super VGA display with at least 256 colors

- Microsoft Mouse or compatible pointing device